christian family
guide to

Managing People

Series Editor: James S. Bell Jr.

by Arthur R. Pell, Ph.D. with Craig Bubeck

ALPHA

A Pearson Education Company

International Standard Book Number: 0-02-864454-9
Library of Congress Catalog Card Number: 2002115296

04   03   02   8   7   6   5   4   3   2   1

Interpretation of the printing code: The rightmost number of the first series of numbers is the year of the book's printing; the rightmost number of the second series of numbers is the number of the book's printing. For example, a printing code of 02-1 shows that the first printing occurred in 2002.

Printed in the United States of America

For marketing and publicity, please call 317-581-3722.

The publisher offers discounts on this book when ordered in quantity for bulk purchases and special sales.

Outside the United States, please contact International Sales, 317-581-3793 or international@pearsontechgroup.com.

Contents

Introduction

"Of making many books there is no end, and much study wearies the body." (Ecclesiastes 12:12) So laments the preacher, and for good reason. There are so many books today available to Christians on just about any topic. What does this one have to offer? Why won't this be just one more wearisome book that will end up on your shelf?

The truth is, there are many excellent resources available to you on how to be a better Christian leader (check out some of our own references and recommendations in the appendix, for a start), but while their theoretical and principle-oriented subjects are important for leaders, such books often fall short when it comes to the practical. That's where the *Christian Family Guide to Managing People* steps in as an invaluable resource and complement to your library. With its powerful, experienced insights into management by Dr. Pell, framed in the context of relevant biblical perspectives and a Chris-tian worldview, you will have the information you need to be a great Christian manager, whether you're working in a Christian or secular organization.

Of course, beyond the practical, the *Christian Family Guide to Managing People* does offer important advice on principles of leadership, too. However, we will not only de-scribe concepts, but provide suggestions and examples of how you can apply them with godly integrity in the day-to-day situations you face on the job.

Part 1, "What's the Fun in Being a Boss If You Can't Boss Anybody Around?" explores how the team concept enables you to take advantage of the skills, brains, and creativity of every person on your team. This part looks at the myths and mis-conceptions that have often dictated management style. Then it gets right into the pragmatic approaches to setting goals and developing channels of communication so that you can make sure that your ideas and instructions are understood and accepted by your team members. You'll also learn equally important techniques to encourage team members to contribute ideas and suggestions about every aspect of the work they do.

Part 2, "The Supervisor as Coach," tells you how to develop your team for optimum performance. You'll learn about not only the techniques of training and development, but also how to get the most from your training buck.

The ramifications of the equal employment opportunity (EEO) laws are discussed in **Part 3, "Understanding and Complying with Equal Employment Laws."** This part presents a list of pre-employment questions that you can and cannot ask. This part of the book pays special attention to the latest developments in this area, including the Americans with Disabilities Act, how to avoid sexual harassment complaints, and the role of the team leader in affirmative action.

Part 4, "Choosing Team Members," discusses the important issue of choosing team members who can not only do the job, but also fit in as part of your team. Also covered is writing realistic job specs, pricing the job, and locating hard-to-find personnel.

Part 5, "Motivating Your Team for Peak Performance," is on methods for motivating your team members. Some of the issues covered in this part are money (does it really motivate?), incentive pay programs, recognition programs that work, how to motivate people when they have the opportunity for advancement, and what "empowerment" is all about.

Part 6, "Dealing With Employee Problems on the Job," covers the day-to-day problems that leaders face on the job, including dealing with poor performance, stress and burnout, overly sensitive people, and alcohol and drug addiction. You'll learn how to counsel employees and when and how to refer them to professionals for help. This part also discusses how to manage people who don't work on-site, such as telecommuters and subcontractors, and how to work with self-directed teams.

Part 7, "Doling Out Discipline," explores traditional and nontraditional methods of discipline, up to and including termination. This part also explores voluntary quits and ways of reducing turnover. This part pays special attention to layoffs and downsizing, including a discussion of the WARN law and the concept of "employment at will."

How to Make This Book Work for You

Reading a book like this one can be interesting, enlightening, and amusing. We hope that this book will be all these things to you. But more importantly, it will provide you with sound advice on how to be a strong witness to Christ, not only because of your integrity, but also because of your strengths and effectiveness.

But God's Word warns, "faith by itself, if it is not accompanied by action, is dead." There are many faith concepts addressed in this book that will sound nice in theory, but will be useless and a waste if you aren't willing to put them into practice. The same goes for the pragmatic principles. If you don't take the words you read and put them into effect in the way you perform your day-to-day managerial functions, the powerful voice of experience will become muted and (worse) irrelevant.

Following these five steps should ensure that this book isn't just a reading exercise, but also a plan of action for you:

1. At the end of the first chapter is a section that explains how to create an action plan to implement what you've learned. Create this type of action plan after you read each chapter. Indicate what action you will take, with whom you will take the action, and when you will begin.

2. Share your plan of action with your associates. Get them involved.

3. Set a follow-up date to check whether you did what you planned to do.

4. If not, reread the chapter, rethink what you did or didn't do, and make a new plan of action.

5. Do it, review it, renew it.

Extras

To aid in understanding and to enhance the material in the main text of the book, five series of boxes have been added throughout the book to highlight specific items.

Interpret and Apply

You may have a good idea of what most of these new expressions mean, but you don't have to guess about their meanings and implications. These definitions will put you in the know, so you won't have to bluff your way through when your boss throws these terms at you.

Power Principles

These tips and techniques will help you implement some of the ideas you pick up in the book. Some of them come from the writings of management gurus, and others come from the experience of managers like you, who are happy to share them.

Avoiding Stumbling Blocks

Learn from these common mistakes made by managers, and save yourself time, money, energy, and embarrassment.

That's the Spirit

Biblical insight and wisdom to help you be both a godly example and a powerful leader.

Wise Counsel

These provide you with practical instructions for enhancing your management expertise.

Part 1

What's the Fun in Being a Boss If You Can't Boss Anybody Around?

In many regards, the new approaches to management are more compatible with a Christian worldview. The old legalistic approach of "my way or the highway" has been supplanted by something more akin to discipleship: the leader who develops and coordinates an intelligent, motivated team to get things done.

You can learn to mold a team and help your team members become creative, contributing, collaborative colleagues. To do this, stop thinking like a legalist and think more in terms of grace—working with favor toward your associates, regardless of what they may or may not deserve. Bosses resemble Old Testament kings, making decisions and giving orders. Today's managers in many regards resemble Jesus' model of a "master" or "teacher" working with disciples. Jesus said in Matthew 20:26, "Whoever wants to be a leader among you must be your servant."

Managing Ain't What It Used to Be

The Bible states that "Jesus Christ remains the same—yesterday, today, and forever." (Hebrews 13:8) So even though we and everything else around us changes, we can trust in him to manage change—in our own lives and the lives we lead. Management, like all other aspects of life, is *always* in a state of flux. Nothing stays the same. Then why is the changing of management so important now?

For one thing, mastering these changes is key to your walking with integrity as a Christian. Sound like a stretch? Consider this: Doing your work with excellence is as much a witness in the modern work culture as is doing your work with moral integrity. Indeed, excellence in utilizing professional skills is a part of being a person of integrity.

This chapter looks at some of these practical changes that have taken place in the management of people and how they've affected the way leaders lead and the way people follow. You'll see how these changes affect you and how you can integrate them into your own management style.

That's the Spirit

Every person who has ever made it to the top, every person who has achieved anything for God, every person who has been effective has learned to stretch.

—John Maxwell

Sound like a stretch? On the one hand, it really isn't. I've done it, I've helped my clients do it, and during the past few years, progressive managers in many companies have done it. But on the other hand, maybe a little stretching to meet the challenges of change is exactly what's called for.

The first thing you have to do is examine your current management style (the quiz in this chapter will help you). Then by utilizing your gifts and following through with the step-by-step methods I'll present, I firmly believe that God will enable you to excite and motivate your team more effectively.

Am I Ready to Face the Twenty-First Century?

The world of work has changed radically during the past decade. Now managers have immediate and continuous access to new information, revolutionizing their decision making. Gone is the old hierarchical structure. It used to be that top management made all the decisions and filtered them down through a series of layers to the rank-and-file workers. Today people at all levels are expected to contribute to every aspect of their organization's activities.

Many of those intermediate organizational layers—or middle management—have also been eliminated. More and more, the responsibility to get things done is assumed by team members who plan, implement, and control the work together.

Hey! What's All This Change About?

Companies are rapidly replacing old philosophies with approaches that take advantage of new technologies and modern managerial thinking. I've outlined some of these approaches here:

- **Flatten the organizational structure.** Eliminating superfluous layers of management unclogs the channels through which orders and information flow.
- **Encourage participatory decision making.** Employees at all levels now collaborate to plan the work and get it done.

Interpret and Apply

A **team** is a group of people who collaborate and interact synergistically to reach a common goal—a concept familiar to members of Christ's body, who use their spiritual gifts to fulfill his goals for the Kingdom of God.

- **Use teams to get the work done.** The team leader has replaced the "boss." The team is a collaborative group, not just people taking orders and carrying them out.
- **Implement total project management.** Managers supervise entire projects, coordinating with departments other than their own.
- **Outsource rather than employ.** To save money, a company subcontracts various phases of a job to other firms (sometimes coordinating with several).
- **Adopt just-in-time delivery.** Rather than store large inventories, companies have them delivered as needed. Managers coordinate with suppliers to ensure deliveries.
- **Re-engineer.** When a company re-engineers, its managers have to radically rethink every aspect of their jobs in order to incorporate the changes.

That's the Spirit

The first management consultant in recorded biblical history was Jethro, the father-in-law of Moses. When Jethro saw how overworked Moses was, he advised him to establish a management hierarchy—to choose leaders "to be rulers of thousands, and rulers of hundreds, rulers of fifties and rulers of tens." (Exodus: 18:21)

How Do These Organizational Changes Affect Me?

Whether you have management responsibilities or are preparing for a promotion, now is the time to examine how you'd like to be a better manager. You must stretch your skills, learning what effective managers are doing to become even more productive.

As you read this book, you'll learn how to better deal with the day-to-day problems of managing people, and you'll learn that *you can't do it alone.* You must rely upon God's guidance through his spirit and his word. Likewise, you must learn to utilize the talents of others. But the humility of dependence on God and others is a perfect place to start—not only if you're going to be a godly leader, but also if you want to be an effective one.

Taking an Eagle-Eye Look at Management Style

You've been managing people for years, and you think you've got your department running like a well-oiled piece of machinery when your boss says you aren't meeting the company's goals. Or you've just been promoted to your first supervisory job—with no training and no advice. Or maybe the people who report directly to you are giving you a hard time.

So it's time to do some soul searching. Use the quiz later in this chapter to take inventory of how you manage now. Then take a look at how your approach to management compares to what management experts consider the "right way."

Don't Dictate—Facilitate

First, admit it: People don't respond well to authoritative styles. Most people work best with a manager who treats them as adults—who encourages suggestions and listens to ideas that may even conflict with the manager's own. Truly successful managers are those who obtain the willing cooperation of all involved.

Team Members—Your Not-So-Secret Treasure

How do you get people to cooperate willingly? Use the team approach. A team is a group of people working together by combining their energies to achieve a common goal. People working together collaboratively (with each team member benefiting from the knowledge, work, and support of the others) are much more productive than a mass of isolated individual efforts.

Consider the analogy of a rocket ship. In order for the ship to function, each of its stages, or components, must be in tip-top condition. But even if all the components are in A-1 shape, the rocket won't get off the launching pad until every component works together by sharing and combining, and benefiting from the others.

That's the Spirit

Two people effectively working together as a team can accomplish much more than two individuals working alone. This principle is clearly expressed in Ecclesiastes 4:9 (TLB): "Two can accomplish more than twice as much as one, for the results can be much better."
—Myron Rush

If you want your project to lift off and reach success, you must ensure that your team members work at optimum capacity individually—and then that they all work together with the whole being greater than the sum of its parts.

Molding Your Ragtag Group into a Team

Teams don't happen by magic. Building your team requires careful planning. Start by clearly explaining the following factors to your team members:

* How they are expected to work
* How this new method of operation differs from what they are used to
* Where they can go for help
* How the new team approach works

Power Principles

Start delegating as many tasks as you can. Help your team members develop their skills; then give them the ball and let them run with it.

You've met Christians who talk about God but don't really walk with God. In the same way, be wary of giving mere lip service to the team approach. You must "walk the talk." For example, encourage your team members to come up with their own solutions. You should guide and facilitate—not direct—the work of your team. The participation of all team members is the key to success (see Chapter 14).

When the Company Downsizes

Over the past several years, downsizing—reducing the work force—has become a way of life for many large organizations. More so, it is reported that two thirds of firms that cut jobs in a given year will do it again the next year.

This poses a big problem for managers who have to maintain the morale and productivity of the survivors.

How do these survivors feel?

Lucky that they still have a job? Sure, for the moment.

Guilty because their co-workers were cut and they weren't? Quite often.

Loyal to the company? Not a chance. Downsizing erodes any sense of loyalty.

Downsizing is usually accompanied by salary freezes for the survivors (the company figures they're lucky enough to still have their jobs). Many people who survive the downsizing are forced to accept pay freezes or even lower-ranking positions. And for those who get to keep their positions, their opportunity for advancement is stifled.

And that's just the beginning. After the downsizing, employees have to work harder and pick up the slack for those who were laid off. Not only that, but the colleagues who once facilitated their work are no longer there to help. Worse, teams can fall apart, with some of the key team members gone.

Challenges to Managers

What can you do as a manager when your company downsizes your department?

> **Wise Counsel**
>
> Companies that downsize through buyouts and attrition—that help the workers get new jobs—have a better chance of retaining the loyalty of the surviving workers.
>
> —Robert Reich

1. Once the downsized people have left the company, bring the rest of your team together and have an open discussion about the situation. You may not be able to assure them that the worst is over, but point out that everyone must work together to make the most of the situation.

2. Elicit ideas on how to restructure the work most effectively, and have the team create a plan to re-delegate duties.

3. Meet with team members individually to deal with personal concerns.

4. Determine what additional training is needed to cover the work once done by the laid-off members. Arrange for such training.

5. Encourage team members to learn skills that might be needed in the future (computer skills, foreign languages, and so forth).

6. Once the dust has settled, boost morale by attending to each person's concerns, rebuilding team spirit, and recognizing accomplishments.

> **That's the Spirit**
>
> The story of the leader Gideon in Judges chapters 6–9 is an example of effective downsizing. He reduced the army of the Israelites from 32,000 to 300! They won the battle against the Midianites by supernatural means. If it's God's will, then he will give you the grace to succeed with fewer staff.

Working with Generation X'ers

The culture of the so-called Generation X is a new challenge for the contemporary manager. These young people see the world differently than their parents, their school teachers, and, of course, their bosses.

Sure, many may jump from one interest to another, but there's an upside to this phenomenon. These young people have trained their minds to operate on many tracks at once. It's a worthy skill on the job when, for instance, a young banker handles multiple phone conversations with clients while responding to e-mail. Managers should embrace the Gen X'ers, drawing upon their valuable assets.

> **Power Principles**
>
> Thanks in part to computer games and MTV, Gen X'ers process information far more quickly than their predecessors did. Take advantage of their agile minds when assigning them work.

Test Your Managerial Skills

Okay, you agree that the role of the manager has changed. "Enough of this theory," you say. You want to learn the actual techniques that will help you meet your goals and the goals of your team. That's what this book is about. But before we get down to the tools of the trade, you'll have to take stock of your current style of management.

The following inventory will help you assess your managerial style. Read each statement, decide whether you agree or disagree with it, and check the appropriate box on the right. Then compare your responses to the answers that follow.

Agree	Disagree		
❏	❏	1.	It's unnecessary for a manager to discuss long-range goals with team-member subordinates. As long as team members are aware of the immediate objective, they can do their work effectively.
❏	❏	2.	The best way to make a reprimand effective is to do it in front of co-workers.
❏	❏	3.	Managers risk losing respect if they answer a question with, "I don't know, but I'll find out and let you know."
❏	❏	4.	It pays for managers to spend a great deal of time with a new employee to ensure that training has been effective.
❏	❏	5.	Managers should ask their associates for ideas about work methods.
❏	❏	6.	When disciplining is required, managers should avoid saying or doing anything that may cause resentment.
❏	❏	7.	People work best for tough managers.
❏	❏	8.	It's more important for a team to be composed of members who like their jobs than of people who do their jobs well.
❏	❏	9.	Work gets done most efficiently if managers lay out plans in great detail.
❏	❏	10.	To lead an effective team, managers should keep in mind the feelings, attitudes, and ideas of the team's members.

Okay, you've answered all the questions. Now look at the responses based on the advice of successful managers:

1. Disagree. People who know where they're going—who can see the big picture—are more committed and will work harder to reach those objectives than people who are aware only of immediate goals.

2. Disagree. Flaying a person doesn't solve the problem—it only makes the person feel small in front of co-workers. A good reprimand shouldn't be humiliating. It's best to reprimand in private—*never* in front of others.

3. Disagree. It's better to admit ignorance of a matter than to try to bluff. People respect leaders who accept that they don't know everything.

4. Agree. The most important step in developing the full capabilities of associates is good training on the part of managers.

5. Agree. People directly involved with the job can often contribute good ideas toward solving problems.

6. Agree. Resentment creates low morale and often leads to conscious or subconscious sabotage.

7. Disagree. Toughness is not as important as fairness or an inspiring attitude.

8. Disagree. The happiness and satisfaction of team members are important, but they are secondary to getting the job done.

9. Disagree. Psychologists have shown that most people work better when they are given broad project guidelines and can work out the details themselves. But some people work better when tasks are given to them in detail. Good managers recognize the styles in which people work and then adapt to them.

> **Power Principles**
>
> A leader expresses the most profound inspiration when he believes in his people—when they feel and know that he thinks they are the best and his total confidence is in them.
>
> —John Maxwell

10. Agree. Communication is a two-way street. To manage effectively, it's important to know what team members are thinking and how they feel about their jobs.

You may not agree with all the experts' answers, but do pay them some heed. Most of these issues will be discussed in detail later in this book.

Creating Your Own Plans of Action

Based on what you learn in each of the following chapters, decide what new actions you will take. By the time you've finished reading this book, you should be able to identify two or three new techniques to incorporate into your managerial style. For each technique, spell out these details on paper:

1. Action (What will you do?)
2. Collaborators (With whom will you do it?)
3. Time (When will you start?)

Periodically review your progress toward completing these plans of action. More important, begin to pray regularly about these steps. Perhaps you could start a spiritual journal recording your thoughts and the wisdom God is giving to you as your plan takes shape.

Do It, Review It, Renew It

As you begin to implement the ideas outlined later, use the phrase "Do it, review it, renew it" to help you remember the key steps in planning a task:

Do it. After you've decided what to do, coordinate with your team members and set a time for it to be done.

Review it. Doing it is only the first step. Next, you must review what you've accomplished. What did you and your team learn from this action?

Renew it. Fine-tune new approaches and add them to the repertoire of methods and techniques that your team will use in facing similar situations later.

Chapter

2

"Everything I Know I Learned from My Old Boss—And Boy, Was He Wrong!"

Chapter 1 explored the changing practice of management and the importance of team leaders adapting to these new approaches. But managers' efforts to change are often frustrated by old-style bosses, colleagues, and associates who resist anything new.

Much as believers can find themselves enslaved to legalisms that have no real basis in God's truth, businesses also have their myths and misconceptions that have governed people's thinking for years, though they have no basis in truth.

But as a manager, you must move beyond rules for the sake of tradition if you want to be effective and relevant. This chapter examines some common myths, tells you how they impede progress, and explains how you can put them in perspective.

Managing Like a Professional

Some people are reluctant to take on leadership roles, insisting that they must first have certain God-given leadership traits—traits that they're certain they do not have.

It's true that some of the world's greatest leaders have unique gifts—they have that special charm, which enraptures the public. But as is the case with any gift, they had to develop skills through work, too. In truth, leaders are basically ordinary people who have worked hard to get where they are. Essentially, leadership is an *acquired* skill.

That's the Spirit

When called by God to be a leader of his people, Moses protested that he wasn't eloquent or clever enough—he was certain he didn't have the *charisma* it takes to lead. (Exodus 4:10) But God responded (a little angrily) by shifting attention to the source of all skill: "Who gave man his mouth? ... Is it not I, the Lord?" (v. 11) If you're called to lead, God will give you the mouth. But that's not all: God tells the leader-to-be, "Now go!" God made Moses a great leader over time, but Moses had to get going.

Unlike professionals in other industries who are required to complete advanced study and pass exams for certification, managers learn primarily on the job. Some managers may have special education, but *most are promoted from the ranks and have little or no training in management.* More successful managers are making an effort to acquire skills through structured courses of study, but most still pick up their techniques and philosophies by observing their bosses.

Debunking Myths and Misconceptions

Some of the following ideas may have been valid in the past but are no longer; others were never true. Let's look at some of these myths and misconceptions about management.

Management = Common Sense

One manager said, "When I was promoted to my first management job, I asked a long-time manager for some tips about how to deal with people who report to me. He told me, 'Just use common sense, and you'll have no trouble.'"

Power Principles

Keep up with your field:

- Attend seminars and read current books about management.
- Read trade and professional journals.
- Take an active role in business associations.
- Network with other managers.
- Benchmark the best companies in your field. (Benchmarking is explained later.)

That sounds good, but what is "common sense," exactly? What appears sensible to one person may be nonsense to another. Truth be told, we tend to use our own experiences to develop our particular brands of common sense. The problem is, a person's individual experience provides only limited perspective. And more so, we know that our own human reason isn't sufficient—we need God's wisdom as well.

To be a real leader, you must look beyond common sense. Books written by management experts abound. Make a practice of reading those books (see the recommended resources at the back of this book), subscribing to periodicals, and learning from the experiences of those who have been successful leaders in your trade. There is a whole new field of Christian management books that can teach you to apply your faith at work.

Interpret and Apply

One of the fastest-growing phenomena of the past decade is **total-quality management.** In this system, a company focuses entirely on producing high-quality products or services. It involves statistical processes, training in all aspects of quality management, and a commitment from every employee to work continuously toward improvement.

Managers Know Everything

Only God is omniscient, so accept that you don't have all the answers. But know that you need the skills to get the answers. Get to know people in other companies who have faced similar situations, and you can learn a great deal. This *networking* process gives you access to valuable assistance in solving problems.

Seeking organizations that have been successful in certain areas and learning their techniques is called *benchmarking*. Companies that participate in competitions such as the Malcolm Baldridge Awards (an annual recognition by the U.S. Department of Commerce of firms that demonstrate high quality in their work) must agree to share their techniques with any organization that requests this information. Benchmarking is one of the peripheral benefits of *total-quality management*, explained later.

"It's My Way or the Highway!"

Management by fear is still a common practice. And it works—sometimes. People will work if they fear that they might lose their jobs, but how much work will they do? Just enough to keep from getting fired. That's why this technique isn't considered effective management. Successful management involves getting the *willing* cooperation of your associates.

> **Avoiding Stumbling Blocks**
>
> Praise *can* be overdone. If people are repeatedly praised for every trivial accomplishment, its value is diminished. As Proverbs warns, "A flattering mouth works ruin." (26:28)

Moreover, it's not that easy to fire people. As we'll see later, firing people may, in fact, cause more problems than keeping employees with whom you're not satisfied.

You can't keep good workers for long when you manage by fear. When jobs are scarce in your community or industry, workers might tolerate high-handed arbitrary bosses. But when the job market opens up, the best people will leave for companies with more pleasant working environments. Employee turnover can be expensive and often devastating.

Recently, I was retained by a company to help staff an entire office facility. As we reviewed the incoming resumes, we noticed loads of applications from one particular firm. My immediate assumption was that this other company was shaky and that its employees were seeking more stable employment. But the company was in excellent shape. Applicant after applicant told us that the company's arbitrary management style made their working environment unpleasant. Despite good pay and benefits, they wanted out.

The moral of this story is that you should use positive rather than negative techniques to motivate people (see Part 5).

"Give Them Some Praise and They'll Ask for a Raise"

People need to be praised. Everyone wants to know that his or her good work is appreciated. Yet many managers are reluctant to praise their employees.

Why? Some managers fear that if they praise a team member's work, that person will become complacent and stop trying to improve. Certainly, some people do react this way. The key is to phrase your praise in a way that encourages the team member to continue the good work (see Chapter 16).

> ### Avoiding Stumbling Blocks
>
> Don't promise employees raises or bonuses based on the accomplishment of a specific task. Financial reward should be based on overall performance over time. Promise a raise only if it's part of a compensation or management-by-objective plan that has been formally approved by those who have the authority to approve compensation changes.

Other managers are concerned that if team members are praised for good work, they will expect pay raises or bonuses. And some folks might. But that's no reason to withhold praise when it's warranted. Employees should already know how financial rewards are determined, and they should be assured that the good work for which they are praised will be considered in the evaluation.

Some managers simply don't believe in praise. One department head told me, "If I have to speak to them, they know they're in trouble." Offering no feedback other than reprimands isn't effective, either. Use positive reinforcement.

"The Best Way to Get People to Work Is a Swift Kick"

Sure, some managers still give their employees a swift kick—not literally, but verbally. Every year, James Miller, management consultant and author of *The Corporate Coach,* holds a contest for Best and Worst Boss of the Year. The employees do the nominating. Miller reports that nominations for worst boss always outnumber those for best boss. One of the chief reasons employees dislike their bosses, Miller found, is that the bosses use verbal kicks—continually finding fault with subordinates, expressing sarcasm, gloating over failures, and frequently screaming at employees.

We all raise our voices occasionally, especially when we're under stress. Sometimes it takes great self-discipline not to yell. Effective leaders, however, control this tendency. An occasional lapse is okay—God himself can get angry when those he's leading won't be led. (In Exodus 4:14, it's clear that it wasn't only the bush that was burning: God's anger "burned" against Moses' continual resistance, and his words reveal his righteous frustration.)

But when yelling becomes your normal manner of communication, you're admitting your failure to be a real leader. You cannot get the willing cooperation of your associates by screaming at them.

The Golden Rule? Yes, but All That Glitters Is Not Gold!

When you manage people, Christ's words "Do to others what you would have them do to you" (Matthew 7:12) are truer than most want to realize. The problem is, we are all too inclined to think, "Well, if I were him, this is what I'd want," and we "do to others" accordingly.

But Christ was calling us to be empathetic in our dealings with others—and empathy is putting yourself in another's shoes, not forcing him or her into yours. The ethic of empathy in the Golden Rule calls for sensitivity to and respect for another's concerns—far from the imposition of what you think he or she needs. (That's merely fool's gold.)

For example, Linda prefers to be given broad objectives so she can work out the details of her job on her own. But her assistant, Jason, is not comfortable receiving an assignment unless all the details are spelled out for him. So when Linda delegates work to Jason the way she prefers to have work assigned to her, she is far from being golden. If Linda expects Jason to operate as she operates, she is ignoring his needs and imposing her own.

> **Power Principles**
>
> When you practice the Golden Rule, remember the ethic of empathy: It's not about you. It's about them—making the effort to figure out their needs.

To be an effective manager, you must know each member of your team and tailor your method of management to each. When following the golden rule, remember that empathy is truly golden. Try thinking of it this way: "Do unto others as they would have you do unto them."

Of course, in some situations work must be done in a manner that may not be ideal for some people. But by knowing ahead of time what needs to be accomplished, you can anticipate problems and prepare team members to accept their tasks.

Production, Performance, and Profit: The Manager's Job

Production, performance, and profit are important aspects of your job as a manager, but are these all you have to consider? Certainly, if a business is to survive, it must produce results. Equally important, however, is the development of its employees' potential. If you ignore people's potential, you limit your team's ability to achieve results. Instead, you reap short-term benefits at the expense of long-term success … and even survival.

Managers must keep track of their P & Ls (profits and losses), but they also must balance their team's *P-factor* (potential of people) and *R-factor* (results desired). If you put too much emphasis on the R, you may attain short-range goals, but long-term goals will suffer. But if you tilt the scale too heavily in favor of the P (for example, overemphasizing training), your company may not be able to continue to stay in business. The P/R balance is shown in the accompanying figure.

Wise Counsel

Surveys indicate that people think companies make 20 to 30 percent profits. Truth be told, most companies make closer to a 5 percent profit.

The P/R Balance

P   R

P = Potential of people

Development of current job skills
Preparation for future job opportunities
Encouragement of creativity
Opportunity for growth
Improvement of interpersonal relations
Self-development

R = Results desired

Improved performance
Attention to quality
Concern for customer satisfaction
Collaborative team activity
Contribution to bottom line

The comparison between people's potential and desired results. List potential factors on the left and results factors on the right to see whether they are in balance.

That's the Spirit

Work hard and become a leader; be lazy and become a slave. (Proverbs 12:24)

To obtain superior performance from the entire team, you must keep the P and R factors balanced. When people are given the opportunity to hone their skills, develop their own careers, and branch out in their fields, they are stimulated to work harder and achieve greater results.

You Gotta Know Where You're Going and How to Get There

Now that you've cleared away the management myths that have been holding you back, you're ready to take the first steps toward becoming a modern manager. This process begins when you set goals. Like a wise builder, you determine how and when you want to reach those goals.

But first consider this: Does the setting of goals indicate a lack of faith? To the thinking of some Christians, setting goals is contrary to God's will. They reason that they don't want to be like the power-planner whom Jesus portrayed in his parable of the rich fool (Luke 12:13-21)—rather than building barns, we should simply trust.

Obviously, there is a danger for Christians in leadership to think they are the gods of their own destiny. Despite the common wisdom, the aphorism "God helps those who help themselves" is unbiblical.

Even so, Jesus' parable was not about the folly of making plans. What made the man a fool was his being bankrupt when it came to his relationship with God (v. 21). In and of themselves, his plans for bigger barns were rather wise—his folly was in making God irrelevant to them.

Wise Counsel

The Living Bible nicely paraphrases God's perspective on the wisdom of setting goals: "Any enterprise is built by wise planning, becomes strong through common sense, and profits wonderfully by keeping abreast of the facts." (Proverbs 24:3–4) But, of course, the starting point for all of our plans must be "the fear [awe-inspired trust] of the Lord" (Proverbs 1:7), since that is the beginning of all wisdom.

This chapter's purpose is to help you begin the practical process of setting short- and long-term goals, and planning how to reach them. And as we do, we must always keep ourselves honest by acknowledging who is in control: "Many are the plans in a man's heart, but it is the Lord's purpose that prevails." (Proverbs 19:21)

Planting Your Goal Posts

Unless you know exactly what you want to achieve, there's no way to measure how close you are to achieving it. Specific goals give you a standard against which to measure your progress.

The goals that you set for your team must be in line with the larger goals your company sets for you. If you don't coordinate the objectives of your job, department, or team with the objectives of your organization, you'll waste your time and energy.

Goals Are More Than Hopes

The process of setting goals takes time, energy, and effort. Goals aren't something you scribble on a napkin during your coffee break. You must plan what you truly want to accomplish, establish timetables, determine who will be responsible for which aspect of the job, and then anticipate and plan a resolution for any obstacle. The same goes for spiritual growth: though not as quantifiable, it, too, requires concrete steps such as setting aside time for prayer and time in the Word.

The suggestions in this section provide a systematic approach to setting goals.

Pipe Dreams or Goals?

Are you ready to set your goals? To prevent your goals from ending up mere pipe dreams, make sure they meet the following three conditions:

- **Clear and specific.** It's not enough to state that your goal is "to improve market share of our product." Make it specific and measurable: "Market share of our product will increase from its current 12 percent to 20 percent in five years."
- **Attainable.** Pie-in-the-sky goals are self-defeating. If you can see your progress in reaching your goals, you'll have more incentive to continue working than if your goals seem completely unattainable.
- **Flexible.** Sometimes you just can't reach a goal. Circumstances may change: What once seemed viable may no longer be. Don't be frustrated—God remains sovereign.

Changing Goals with Changing Circumstances

All of us set goals based on certain circumstances that we anticipate during the life of our project. Circumstances do change, however, and original goals may have to be adjusted. To that end, many companies use a goal-setting program that involves three levels:

A main, or standard goal: What you plan to accomplish if everything goes well.

Alternative 1: A slightly lower goal. If circumstances change and it becomes obvious that your main goal cannot be achieved, you can shift to this alternative instead of starting from scratch in redefining your goal.

Alternative 2: A higher-level goal. If you're making greater progress than you had originally thought you could, shift to this alternative and accomplish even more, instead of being complacent about being ahead of target.

Take, for example, CSC, a company in the metropolitan Philadelphia area that services and repairs computers. Its sales goal for a year was to open 10 new accounts. But when a national competitor opened a similar service in the same community, all of CSC's energies had to be redirected toward saving its current accounts. The goal for attracting new clients then had to be reduced.

Getting the Team to Buy into the Process

At a recent goal-setting seminar, one participant complained, "I have trouble getting people to buy into the big-picture concept. They're so absorbed in their individual jobs that they can't see beyond their own problems."

Here's how you can overcome this type of situation:

- Bring everyone in your department or team into the early stages of the planning process.
- Discuss the major points of the overall plan.
- Ask each person to describe how he or she will fit into the big picture plan.
- Give each person a chance to comment on each stage of the project.

Breaking a long-term goal into bite-size pieces can help people see how their part in a project fits together with the others. It can also help them set overall team or project goals for the long run.

Sopping Up SOPs

Your company may have a set of standard operating procedures (SOPs) or SPs (standard practices) that detail company plans and policies. Progressive companies usually restrict their SOPs to such matters as personnel policies, safety measures, and related matters. Many companies, however, incorporate specific job methods and procedures into "instruction manuals." Because SOPs set standards that everyone must follow, they ensure consistent employee behavior in dealing with particular situations.

If you have to develop SOPs, keep them simple. Too often, managers draw up complicated SOPs in hopes of covering every possible contingency. *It can't be done.* Managers frequently must make decisions based on unforeseeable factors. SOPs should cover common issues in detail, but leave room for managers (or nonmanagerial people, where appropriate) to make spontaneous decisions when circumstances warrant them.

SOPs shouldn't be perceived as absolute laws, such as the Ten Commandments, where there's no possibility of change. SOPs should be flexible. Don't make SOPs so rigid that they can't be changed with changing circumstances. Plans may become obsolete because of new technologies, competition, government regulations, or the development of more efficient methods. Build into SOPs a policy for periodic review and adjustment.

Power Principles

To ensure that standard operating procedures are effective, follow these guidelines:

- Clearly state any expected actions.
- Provide guidelines for acceptable deviation from procedure.
- Be specific about areas in which no deviation may occur.
- Before setting any method as an SOP, test it on the job to ensure that it's the one best way.

Planning, Planning, Who'll Do the Planning?

Standard operating procedures are just one phase of planning. SOPs should cover only broad policy matters so that specific plans can be designed for each new project. Your entire team should be involved in developing the team's plans. As team leader, you should coordinate and lead the process: Delegate particular aspects of the planning to the team members who know the most about them.

Because planning is so important, many organizations have planning specialists work with the managers in the development and coordination of this function. The people who are closest to the work should also be directly involved. Planning experts can help facilitate the process, but only the people who will carry out the project's duties can create a realistic and workable plan.

Hands-On: How to Plan

To illustrate how planning works, let's look at how Louise, the owner and manager of Featherdusters (a janitorial service company in Rock Hill, South Carolina), developed a plan to clean a five-story office building. The following list shows you the steps Louise deemed necessary to implement her plan:

Step 1: List what needs to be done. After consulting with her client, Louise made the following list:

Must be done daily	**Must be done weekly**
Empty wastebaskets into dumpsters	Sanitize telephones
Carry dumpsters to pick-up location	Polish brass railings
Dust furniture	Wax tile floors
Mop tile floors	**Must be done monthly**
Vacuum carpeted floors	Wash windows
Clean restrooms	Wash glass partitions
Clean lounges	

Step 2: Determine staffing. Louise hired two teams of three people. Each team was responsible for cleaning six floors. Each team was comprised of a trained floor waxer, a window washer, and a supervisor. The owner/manager oversaw the entire operation.

Step 3: Acquire supplies and equipment. Louise then acquired these supplies:

- Vacuum cleaners
- Dust cloths
- Sponges
- A waxing machine
- Floor wax
- Disinfectant
- Window-washing solvent

Step 4: Estimate timing. Louise calculated that the cleaning job would take five hours (from 5 P.M. to 10 P.M.) five days a week to complete. The following list serves as a guide to Louise and the supervisors to ensure that scheduled tasks get done at the scheduled time:

Daily tasks: All tasks are performed daily.

Weekly tasks: The supervisor assigns one floor every day to one or more workers to complete each of the weekly tasks.

Monthly tasks: The owner/manager and window washer schedule these tasks every month. The schedule must be flexible enough to account for weather conditions.

Step 5: Specify methods. All work will be performed according to the company's SOP for cleaning methods. Supervisors are responsible for quality of work, and the owner/manager will inspect work on an ad hoc basis.

Step 6: Budget. Specific figures should be included to cover the cost of materials, equipment amortization, labor, transportation to and from the site, and miscellaneous costs.

Step 7: Set contingencies. Unforeseen circumstances can develop that impede the completion of scheduled tasks. Louise anticipated the types of contingencies most likely to be encountered:

Truck or van breakdown: Make arrangements for renting replacement vehicles.

Equipment breakdown: Additional waxing machines are stored in a warehouse.

Personnel: The owner/manager and supervisors have lists of substitutes available on short notice.

Step 8: Follow up. The owner/manager makes periodic visits to the site to inspect the work and meets at least once per quarter with the client to ensure satisfaction with the work.

The following planning worksheet will enable you to plan and schedule your projects. Feel free to photocopy it or adapt it to meet your special needs.

Converting Plans into Action

Plans similar to that of the Featherdusters are virtually self-starting. Implementing an already developed and tested plan with a new client is relatively easy. The introduction of a brand new product, however, requires a much more complex plan, which may involve several phases spread out over several months or even years.

Planning Worksheet

Objective: _____

Specified actions to be taken: _____

_____

Staffing: _____

_____

Equipment and supplies: _____

Timing (include deadlines, where required): _____

_____

Methods and techniques to be used: _____

_____

Budget: _____

_____

Contingencies: _____

_____

Follow-up: _____

_____

The Daily Grind: Planning for Daily Activities

You've set your goals, and now you must apply them to your day-to-day work schedule. You'll achieve your goals only if you break down, day by day, how you plan to reach them.

Unless your work is primarily routine and already standardized in the SOPs, the next step for you and your team members is to determine when and what task each member will undertake.

The $25,000 Suggestion

In the early 1900s, Ivy Lee, a pioneer in management consulting, paid a visit to Charles Schwab, the president of U.S. Steel. Lee told Schwab that he could help U.S. Steel become more effective. When Schwab expressed skepticism, Lee said, "I'll give you one suggestion today, and I want you to put it into effect for one month. At the end of that time, we will meet again, and you can pay me whatever you think that idea was worth to you. If it was of no value, you owe me nothing."

Schwab accepted the challenge and implemented Lee's suggestion. When they met again, Schwab handed Lee a check for $25,000 and said, "That was the best advice I ever had. It worked so well for me that I passed it on to all my subordinate managers."

So, what was Lee's advice? Prioritize.

Every morning when you get to work (or every night before you go to bed), make a list of all the things you want to accomplish that day and put them in order of priority. Then work on the first item, and don't move on to the next one until you have done all you can. You'll be interrupted, of course—no job is free from interruption—so just handle the interruption and then return to what you were working on. Don't let any interruption make you forget what you were doing.

At the end of the day, add the remaining tasks to the new ones that have developed, and compile another prioritized list for the next day. At the end of the month, you might notice that certain items remain on your list day after day. That's a sign that they weren't important enough to do. You should either delegate them to someone else or perhaps not do them at all.

What Do I Do First?

In his book *The Seven Habits of Highly Effective People,* Steven Covey cautions that many managers confuse what is urgent with what is truly important. Urgent matters must be attended to immediately or else serious consequences might ensue, but if you spend all your time putting out fires, your truly important goals won't be met.

That's the Spirit

"Be very careful, then, how you live—not as unwise but as wise, making the most of every opportunity, because the days are evil." (Ephesians 5:15–16) The wise leader knows that time is his or her most valuable commodity; likewise, the squandering of that commodity is bitter folly.

Scheduling Team Projects

After your team has planned the actions it will take to complete a project, you must develop a schedule. Lay out what will be done, who will do it, and when each task should be started and completed. Your schedule can be as simple as notes on a wall calendar or as complex as specially designed planning charts and computer-based schedules (see Chapter 6).

The daily planning organizer here breaks down activities into categories. Feel free to reproduce it. When you use this type of planner, identify priorities in each category by number or color coding.

Daily Planning Organizer

Date: _____

Priorities	Things to Do	Phone Calls
Correspondence	Appointments	Miscellaneous

A planning organizer helps your team schedule daily activities and achieve its goals.

Enough of This Preparation— Let's Get It Done!

The first step in setting plans to action is assembling the necessary resources—obtaining and allocating funds, accumulating equipment and materials, and acquiring pertinent information. The major tasks of choosing, training, and assigning personnel to the project are discussed later in this book.

That's the Spirit

Satan always tries to convince the Christian leader or manager there are not enough resources to accomplish the job. People involved in resource planning should keep in mind that if the plans are in accordance with God's will for the individual and/or organization, he will provide the resources to accomplish the activities.

—Myron Rush

Where's the Dough?

Inadequate funding will doom any project to failure. The most common reason that start-up companies fold is lack of capital. Even large, well-established organizations must determine how much money they should spend to get a project started and to keep it going until it pays off.

Avoiding Stumbling Blocks

If you're not sure how much money is necessary for a project, err on the high side. You'll look much better if you come in under budget than if you have to plead for more funds. Here's a safe rule: Underpromise and overdeliver!

When figuring out the budget for a project, be careful not to underestimate costs just to make the numbers impressive. You don't want to be like Mike: Mike wanted to impress his boss, Sheila. When Mike was assigned a new project, he cut corners and came up with an impossibly tight budget. Sheila praised him for his business acumen and gave his project the go-ahead. But Mike's lowball figures proved to be inadequate. shamefaced, he had to ask Sheila for additional funds. This mistake stalled not only the project but also Mike's career.

You may have no control over determining budgets for your department or team. If so, carefully study the budget you are given before starting a project. If the budget seems unrealistically small, discuss it with your manager. Whoever allotted the money for your work may not have been aware of certain factors. By presenting your case, you may persuade the company to provide a more realistic budget.

> **That's the Spirit**
>
> Speaking of priorities, remember the big ones with the most important order for your life—God first, family second, then business third.

Sometimes you'll have to work with a less than ideal budget. That's when you have to sharpen your pencil and calculate how you can save money with minimal loss of productivity. Can some of the work you're farming out be done more cheaply in-house, or vice versa? Can some of the work be re-engineered so that fewer costly hours are spent on it? Can deadlines be delayed to eliminate the need for overtime or additional temporary workers? Saving small amounts of money in several areas can add up to your meeting the budget.

Everything in Its Place: Lining Up Your Tools

Do you need any special equipment for the job? Most departments have easy access to the company's machinery, computers, and other hardware, but sometimes access is limited.

Information: The Golden Key to Accomplishment

The nineteenth century brought us the Industrial Revolution; the twentieth century gave us the Information Revolution. Knowledge is now the key to accomplishment.

> **Interpret and Apply**
>
> **Real time** refers to the actual time in which a process occurs (what's going on in the here and now).

Having an accurate, balanced, and unbiased picture of what is happening in your company, in your industry, and in the economy is essential to sound decision making. Today, *real time* is the magic formula for success.

Reports tell you what happened yesterday, last week, and last month. They're helpful, of course, because it's useful to review the past; but to be an effective manager today, you have to know what's going on now.

You need better and faster information—a report is a snapshot, a still picture of how things were at the time it was taken. Instead, you need a telecast—information that's reported as it happens. The tools are in place, but are you taking advantage of them? Take a look at what they can do for you:

If you're a sales manager, you can get up-to-the-minute sales information from field salespeople. Have them send the results of each sales call from their laptops directly to your home office.

In a branch facility, you can e-mail information about production, inventories, and special problems as often as necessary.

If you need materials, you can contact suppliers instantly by fax or e-mail to place orders, arrange shipments, or solve problems.

If you're a retail manager, you can continuously receive sales and stock information from the store's cash register computers.

If you're a general manager who needs specialized information, you can use the World Wide Web to obtain that information from anywhere anytime. You can subscribe to services that give you up-to-the-minute weather conditions worldwide, stock prices on foreign exchanges, transportation and shipping schedules, and virtually any other type of data you need.

Faster, Faster! Keeping Up with Current Techniques and Methods

Information goes beyond simple facts and figures. Managers must have in-depth knowledge of the most effective and cutting-edge work methods.

You've been in your field for many years; you think you know your job and all the tricks of the trade. Do you really? "If it ain't broke, don't fix it" doesn't apply anymore. A certain method may work, but that's no guarantee that it can't be done better. Equipment that didn't exist a few years ago may improve production or quality today. Techniques may have been refined or totally changed. This is a dynamic world, and you should never stop learning. Continual learning makes you a better steward of the talents God has given you to change your world for the better.

You Can Teach an Old Dog New Tricks

Here's another outdated saying: "You can't teach an old dog new tricks." Well, it may be true of dogs, but it certainly isn't true of humans. Don't let your team members tell you they're too old to learn new things.

When computers first became an essential management tool, many older managers and workers resisted learning how to use them, claiming, "Computers are for young people; I'll never be able to master them." But they *did* learn. Today you'll find a computer terminal on virtually every desk in an office, whether that desk is used by a computer whiz, a 50-year-old executive, a twenty-something clerk, or a middle-aged secretary. They have *all* learned.

Talk the Talk— Communicating Like a Leader

Jesus Christ was the master communicator, and it's clear throughout the Gospels that he went to great pains to make sure he was understood. These days, *communication*—what you say and how you say it—can determine whether you succeed or fail.

Once you've improved your ability to communicate, you can more effectively present your ideas to your boss, your associates, your customers, your team, and even your friends and family. In this chapter, you'll learn some strategies to better your oral and written communication—a major step toward becoming a more successful team leader.

What You Say

Suppose you're addressing a group, or you're having a one-to-one conversation with an associate. Your choice of words and your delivery may determine your success or failure. That's why you should think out your message and how you plan to present it in advance. Sometimes you'll have to think on your feet with little or no time to prepare, but more often than not, you can prepare—even on short notice.

Know Your Subject

On the job you'll usually communicate with others about subjects you're thoroughly familiar with. Be that as it may, you should review the facts to be sure that you have a handle on all the information and are prepared for questions.

From time to time, you may be asked to report on matters with which you are unfamiliar. Your company may want to purchase a new type of computer software, for example, and ask you to check it out. Here's how you should start tackling the assignment:

- Learn as much as possible about the subject.
- Know 10 times more than you think you ought to know for the presentation.
- Prepare notes about the pluses and minuses of the proposed purchase, solution, and so on.
- Whether you will make this report to one person or to a group of managers or technical specialists, be prepared to answer questions about any subject that might come up.

That's the Spirit

An important part of preparation is prayer. Jesus himself (God the Son) spent hours in prayer and meditation before facing the crowds and communicating the truth.

Avoiding Stumbling Blocks

Unless your audience is familiar with it, don't use *jargon*—those special initials, acronyms, and words used in your field or company and nowhere else. A statement such as, "We booked the perp on a 602A," for example, won't mean anything to someone who's not a police officer.

Know Your Audience

Half of good communication is understanding your audience. Choose words that your listeners will easily comprehend. If the people you address come from a technical background, you can use technical terminology. But if you're an engineer presenting a proposal to the finance department, it's your responsibility—not your audience's—to ensure that the message is clear. If you can explain it in layperson's terms, do so. If you have to use technical language, take the time to explain and repeat terminology.

How You Say It

No matter how well thought out your message is, no one will understand it if you don't express it clearly and distinctly.

Following are the five most common problems people have with speaking clearly:

- **Mumbling.** Do you swallow word endings? Do you speak with your mouth almost closed? Practice in front of a mirror. Open up those lips.
- **Speaking too fast.** Whoa! Give people a chance to absorb what you're saying.
- **Speaking too slowly.** Speak too slowly, and you'll lose your audience. While you plod, their minds wander.
- **Mispronouncing words.** Not sure how a word is pronounced? Look it up.
- **Speaking in a monotone.** Vary the inflection of the tone and pitch of your voice.

> **Avoiding Stumbling Blocks**
>
> Do you use "word whiskers," those extra sounds, words, and phrases peppered throughout speech? You know what they are—"er," "uhhhh," and "y'know" are just a few. They distract you (and others) from your thoughts. Listen to yourself, and shave off those "whiskers."

> **Power Principles**
>
> Voice-mail programs give you the opportunity to listen to your message before making it final. Take advantage of these options. The more you listen to yourself, the better you'll hear how you sound to others. It will help you determine how to speak more clearly.

Have You Ever Really Heard Your Own Voice?

You don't hear yourself as others hear you. Record your voice and listen how you talk to others in person or on the phone. All you need to do to correct most of these problems is to be aware—then you can begin to eliminate them.

Adding Video to the Audio

An old Chinese proverb says that a picture is worth a thousand words. People remember more of what they see than what they hear, and they remember even more of what they see and hear simultaneously. If people *see* something when you present your message (that is, if you use visual aids), it makes your message that much clearer, more exciting, and, most important, more memorable.

That's why TV is such an effective tool: It brings together, in a *simulcast*, both the video and the audio elements of a message. A perfect example of how this works is *Sesame Street* on public television. But you don't need

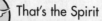

That's the Spirit

Jesus masterfully used images to illustrate his messages: Vines, seeds, sheep, and grain are just a few examples of objects he used to communicate truth to his largely agrarian audience.

a TV camera to be able to simulcast. Simply apply the philosophy behind simulcasting to your own presentation. These relatively inexpensive and easy-to-use techniques can help you broadcast your message more effectively:

- Use graphs or charts to clarify figures.
- Use photos, drawings, or diagrams to illustrate points.
- Use flow charts to describe processes.

Your company should also have many of the following visual aids available to you for larger group presentations:

- **Flip charts and chalkboards.** These are the least expensive and easiest items to use.
- **Overhead projectors.** Use these items to display prepared transparencies, which you can draw on and augment as you talk.
- **Slide presentations.** Colorful and dramatic slides can emphasize important points.
- **Videos or films.** Here's a much more expensive aid, but it's worth it, particularly if your presentation will be repeated several times.

Even if you never make group presentations, you still can simulcast your message to an audience of one:

- Flip charts and chalkboards are just as easy to use and as effective whether your audience is 1 or 100.
- Use your yellow pad (or any color pad you like). Anything that can be drawn on the flip chart can be drawn on a pad of paper.
- Charts, diagrams, and photos can be prepared before any meeting. Emulate salespeople who have successfully used these tools to make sales. Placed in acetate folders, usually in a loose-leaf binder, these items make an attractive visual aid.

Are You Really Listening?

Suppose one of your colleagues brings a problem to you and asks for help. You begin listening attentively, but before you know it, your mind is wandering. Instead of listening to the problem, you're thinking about the pile of work on your desk, the meeting you have scheduled with the company vice president, or the scuffle your son got into at school. You hear your colleague's words, but you're not really listening.

It happens to all of us. Why? Our minds can process ideas 10 times faster than we can talk. While someone is talking, your mind may race ahead. You complete the speaker's sentence in your mind—often incorrectly—long before he or she does. You "hear" what your mind dictates, not what's actually said.

This is human nature. But that's no excuse for being a bad listener. Read on to learn how to listen more effectively.

That's the Spirit

In Mark 8:18, Jesus laments that his disciples have "ears but fail to hear." They had just seen him feed 4,000 people with 7 loaves of bread. Now when he is commenting on the Pharisees' sin and lack of faith, they're still stuck on bread (v. 16). Significantly, Jesus characterizes this failure to listen as a hardness of the heart (v. 17).

Sorry, I Wasn't Listening

Now suppose your mind was wandering and you didn't hear what the other person said. It's embarrassing to admit you weren't listening, so you fake it. You pick up on the last few words you heard and comment on them. If you make sense, you're lucky. But you may have missed the real gist of the discussion.

When you haven't been listening, you don't have to admit, "I'm sorry, I was daydreaming." One way to get back on track is to ask a question or make a comment about the last item you did hear: "Can we go back a minute to such-and-such?"

Another method is to comment this way: "To make sure I can better understand your view on this, please elaborate."

Five Tricks to Make You a Better Listener

You *can* become a better listener. All you have to do is make a few changes in your work environment and in your approach to listening—a small effort with a big return.

- **Eliminate distractions.** The greatest distraction is probably the telephone. You want to give the speaker your full attention—*and the phone rings.* Answering the call not only interrupts your discussion but also disrupts the flow of your thoughts.

  If you know you'll be having a lengthy discussion at your desk, arrange for someone else to handle your calls, or set your voice mail to pick up right away. If this isn't possible, get away from the telephone. Try an empty conference room.

- **Get rid of excess paper to reduce distractions.** If your desk is strewn with paper, you'll probably end up skimming them and realize too late that you're reading a memo instead of listening. Put those papers away in a drawer. Or go to a conference room and take only the papers that are related to your discussion.

- **Don't get too comfortable.** Some years ago I was discussing a situation with another manager. As was my custom, I sat in my comfortable executive chair with my hands behind my head. Maybe I rocked a little. Fortunately, I caught myself before I dozed off. Ever since then, I've made a point of sitting on the edge of my chair and leaning forward rather than backward when I engage in discussions.

> **def·i·ni·tion**
>
> **Interpret and Apply**
>
> An **active listener** not only pays close attention to what the other party says, but this person asks questions, makes comments, and reacts verbally and nonverbally to what is said.

- **Be an active listener.** An *active listener* doesn't just sit back with open ears. An active listener asks questions about what's being said. You can paraphrase or ask specific questions about specific points. This technique not only enables you to clarify points that may be unclear, but it also keeps you alert and paying attention.

- **Be an empathetic listener.** Listen with your heart as well as with your head. Empathetic listeners not only listen to what other people say, but they also try to feel what other people are feeling when they speak. In other words, put yourself in the speaker's shoes.

- **Take notes.** It's impossible to remember everything said in a lengthy discussion. Take notes, but remember not to take stenographic transcriptions. If you're concentrating on what you're writing, you can't pay full attention to the conversation.

Jot down key words or phrases, and write down figures or important facts—just enough to remind you of the principal points that were made.

Immediately after a meeting, while the information is still fresh in your mind, write a detailed summary. Dictate it into a recorder, enter it into your computer, or write it in your notebook—whichever is best for you.

Body Language: The Silent Signals

People communicate not only through words, but also through gestures, facial expressions, and movements. Wouldn't it be great if you could buy a dictionary of body language?

Unfortunately, no such dictionary could exist because body language isn't standardized like verbal language. Some gestures—a nod or a smile—may seem universal, of course, but not everyone uses body language as you do.

Wise Counsel

Body language is a lot more important than people think. Take a hint from top salespeople: They make a practice of carefully studying the body language of a prospect during the first few minutes of the interview. They note how the prospect's expressions often emphasize what is really important to him, perhaps adapting their pitches accordingly. All of us can benefit from following this practice. It will enable us to become better communicators, whether we are the speaker or the listener.

When people nod as you speak, for example, you might assume they're agreeing with you. But some people nod just to acknowledge that they're listening. When someone folds his arms as you speak, you might think his action is a subconscious show of disagreement. But it could simply be that your listener is just cold!

What You Send Might Not Be What's Received

Communication works like a two-way radio: two parties sending messages and responding to each other. Sometimes, however, the message that's received may not be exactly the same as the message that was sent. Perhaps there's interference—static that may be generated from either end of the connection.

What causes that "static" in direct conversations? It might be rooted in your own mind. Everything you say and hear is filtered through your brain and influenced by the attitudes you've acquired over the years. The following list details some of those attitudes.

- **Assumptions.** You've seen this—for example, you know the solution, and you assume that the listener knows as much about it as you do. So you give instructions based on the assumption that the person has the know-how, even though he or she may not. The result is that you don't give adequate information. Static!

- **Preconceptions.** People tend to hear what they expect to hear. The message you receive is distorted by any information that you already have about the subject. So if the new information is different from what you expect, you might reject it as being incorrect. Listen and evaluate the new information objectively instead of blocking it out because it differs from your preconceptions. On the other hand, when communicating with others, try to learn their preconceptions and be prepared to jump a few hurdles.

- **Prejudices.** Your biases for or against a person influence the way you receive his or her message. If you greatly admire the speaker, more than likely you'll be inclined to accept whatever he or she says. If you fervently dislike the speaker, you'll discount anything that's said.

  Biases also affect the way subject matter is received. People turn a deaf ear to opposing viewpoints on matters they have strong feelings about.

> **That's the Spirit**
>
> Seek from God the spiritual gift of discernment. Body language may not always be what it seems. For instance, the body language of Judas was a welcome kiss of greeting, but Jesus knew it was betrayal. Likewise, we may pick up on body language or other cues that an individual may be misleading us.

Channels—The Message Distorter

Remember the game of "telephone" we played as children? One person whispers a message to the next person, who then whispers it to the next, and so on. By the time it gets back to the originator, the message is usually entirely different.

This happens in real life whenever messages must be filtered through several people. Your company may require that you go through channels to deliver information; by the time you receive a message, it may have been distorted by a variety of interpretations. For effective communication, try to eliminate—or at least minimize—the use of channels (especially with routine matters that don't involve policy changes). One advantage of the flatter organizational structure is that it has fewer channels.

Conducting Effective Meetings

An effective way to exchange information is through meetings. But meetings can be a big waste of time if they're not organized properly.

Avoiding Stumbling Blocks

When people who are usually invited to meetings are not invited, they may worry: "Why wasn't I asked? Is the boss giving me a hidden message? Am I on the way out?" Avoid this concern by explaining beforehand your new policy and why you instituted it.

Power Principles

In establishing the sequence of topics at a meeting, put the most complex ones at the beginning of the program. People come to meetings with clear and less distracted minds and are able to approach deeper matters more effectively early on.

Have you ever left a meeting thinking, "What a waste of time. I could have accomplished so much more if I had spent this past hour at my desk!" In a recent survey, over 70 percent of the people interviewed felt they had wasted time in the meetings they had attended.

There is hope. Meetings can be made productive. In the following sections, I'll discuss a few ways to conduct your meetings more efficiently.

Players Only

Invite only appropriate participants. Some managers hold staff meetings on a regular basis—sometimes weekly or even daily. Quite often, many of the people who attend are not involved in the matters that are discussed. By inviting only those who can contribute to the meeting or will be affected by what is discussed, you can avoid wasting others' time and keep the meetings briefer.

What's on the Agenda?

Prepare an agenda. An agenda is key to the success or failure of a meeting. Plan your agenda carefully, covering all matters that you want to discuss. By determining in advance not only what subjects will be addressed, but also the order in which they will be covered, you'll make the meeting run more smoothly.

At least three days before the meeting, send the agenda to all people who will attend. This will allow them to study the topics of discussion and prepare their contribution.

Stick rigidly to the agenda. Don't allow people to bring up topics not on the agenda. If anyone tries, point out that unless it's an emergency, it cannot be discussed at this meeting. Suggest that it be placed on the agenda for the next meeting.

Let's Hear It

Attendees should be encouraged to study the agenda and be prepared to discuss each item. If you need specific data to make a point, organize it into easy-to-follow visuals (for example, charts or handouts) and bring it to the meeting. Encourage discussion and create an atmosphere in which people can disagree without fear of ridicule or retaliation.

Wise Counsel

Provide "takeaway" photocopies of diagrams, flow charts, or whatever data you bring to the meeting. Distribute the copies to everyone at the meeting to ensure that they have a clear and permanent representation of the subjects you discuss. The focus of a meeting should be on expanding, demonstrating, and clarifying information—not introducing brand new concepts, particularly technical, or complex material.

If you are the leader, ask questions that stimulate discussion. Be open to questions and dissension. It's better to have people butt heads during the meeting than let them stew over their problems over a long period of time.

The Dominator

It's tough when one person notoriously dominates meetings, especially when he or she airs personal pet peeves and is always distracting. Here are some tips on how you, as a meeting leader, can attempt to keep such a person quiet:

- Before the meeting, suggest to the person, "I know you like to contribute to our meetings, and I appreciate it; but we have a limited amount of time and some of the other people want a chance to present their ideas. So let's give them a chance to talk, and you and I can discuss your issues after the meeting."

- If the dominator still insists on over-running the meeting, wait until he or she pauses for breath— it is inevitable—and quickly say, "Thank you. Now let's hear what Sue has to say."

- Announce that each speaker has only three minutes to make his or her point. Be flexible with others, but be strict with the dominators.

Ending the Meeting

At the end of the meeting, after all the items on the agenda have been covered, the leader should summarize what has been accomplished. If any team members received assignments during the course of the meeting, have them indicate what they understand they will be expected to do and when they will do it.

Take Minutes

Take notes so that there is no misunderstanding of what has been decided at a meeting. These need not be detailed transcripts of the entire discussion, but a summary of the decisions made on each issue. After the meeting, distribute copies of the minutes not only to the attendees, but also to all people who may be affected by what was determined. The minutes will serve as a reminder to the participants of what was decided and as a communication to those who didn't attend.

Conferences, Conventions, and Retreats

In addition to team- or department-level meetings, managers often participate in company-wide conferences or conventions. These are more elaborate than local meetings; if you are asked to make a presentation at one of them, you should prepare it carefully. Tips on making presentations of this sort will be discussed in Chapter 10. A relatively recent innovation in company communications is the *retreat*. A group of managers is invited to a facility away from the company offices—usually

That's the Spirit

Jesus often pulled his disciples aside for a type of retreat or conference, away from the crowds. These were the times in which he communicated directly to them, and they grew closer to him.

a resort hotel—to relax and informally discuss company problems. You'll play golf or tennis, take nature walks, go canoeing, build campfires, or splurge on buffets. The hope is that staff members will loosen up and be more creative in presenting ideas and more receptive to receiving them.

If you are invited, of course, you should accept—it's less an invitation than a command. Sure, have fun. Participate in the discussions. But prepare what you will say and be businesslike in your demeanor. Dress informally but not loudly. Watch what you say.

Getting the Most Out of Conventions or Conferences

Most managers who attend conferences often complain that they get little benefit from them. Here are 10 steps that will help make meetings more meaningful to you:

1. **Plan and prepare.** Most conferences and conventions are announced months in advance. Usually an agenda accompanies the announcement. Study it carefully. Does any subject listed require special preparation? You may want to read a book or an article on unfamiliar subjects to help you comprehend and contribute to the discussion. You may want to re-examine your company's experience in that area so you can relate what is being discussed to your own organization's problems.

Avoiding Stumbling Blocks

When attending a convention or retreat, don't relax completely. Don't think for a minute that your offhand remarks will be considered "off the record." Everything you do and say will be noticed by the powers that be. All the more so, times away from the office are occasions for consistency and integrity.

2. **Don't sit with your colleagues.** You can speak to them anytime. Here is your chance to meet new people. Make a point of sitting with different people at meetings, especially at luncheon or dinner discussions. You can pick up new ideas and make new contacts who may be valuable resources for information long after the conference. Be humble and realize that God can give you opportunity to learn from anyone.

3. **Open your mind.** You go to conferences and conventions to learn. To get the most out of what a speaker says, keep your mind open to new suggestions. They may be different from what you honestly believe is best, but until you hear it all and think it through objectively, you won't really know. Not all new ideas are good ones, but they should be listened to, evaluated, and carefully and objectively considered.

4. **Be tolerant.** Prejudice against a speaker—whether it be because of appearance, voice, or attire—keeps many an attendee from really listening to what is discussed or from accepting the ideas presented. During a conference break, I overheard one participant tell another, "This meeting is a waste of time. How can a woman tell us men how to market machine tools? She ought to stick to housewares or cosmetics." Sexism prevented him from acquiring information that could have been important to his company.

5. **Take notes.** Note taking has two important functions. It helps organize what you hear while you are at the conference, which leads to more systematic listening. It also becomes a source for future reference. The same skill can be employed on Sunday mornings as you listen actively to your pastor.

6. **Ask questions.** Don't hesitate to query a speaker when the opportunity arises. A lot of truth in the Gospels came as Jesus responded to questions that his disciples asked. Even so, don't waste other people's time with trivial questions.

7. **Contribute ideas.** Nobody expects you to say anything that would damage your firm or its competitive position, but most discussions are not of this nature. They're designed instead to promote the exchange of general ideas. The experience of one organization helps others. By contributing ideas, you provide richer experiences for everyone else—and for you.

Power Principles

Keep a record of the names and addresses of the speakers you hear at a conference or convention. Also list the names and addresses of people you meet at these events.

8. **Summarize.** After the meeting, review your notes while the meeting is still fresh in mind. Write or dictate a report on the conference for your permanent files.

9. **Report.** Report on what you have learned to your boss or others in your organization who might find the information valuable. By sharing what you have learned, you add to the value your firm receives from sending you to the convention.

10. **Apply what you have learned.** If you don't do anything with what you learned at the conference, it has been a waste of time and money. It's the same principle as what we know to be true in our Christian walk. We can read the Bible forever, but if we don't apply its truth, we haven't gained anything.

Open Your Ears, Open Your Mind

"Let the wise listen and add to their learning, and let the discerning get guidance." (Proverbs 1:5) This instruction from the introduction to Proverbs seems pretty straightforward at first glance—even a little on the obvious side. If you want to be wise, listen and get guidance. But consider who it is that should be doing the listening and getting of guidance: It's the already wise. These are the people who have attained, and yet it is they that the Scriptures instruct should be listening and counseled. Shouldn't they be doing the talking and the counseling, if they're so wise?

But consider this: Don't many of your team members have much more insight into what goes on in a company than you realize? That's why you should continually ask your staff for ideas about cutting costs, improving techniques, and implementing innovations. As Proverbs declares, the wiser you are, the more willing you'll be to seek advice.

My Mind Is Open, but Their Mouths Are Shut

Managers often complain that they're ready to listen to ideas, but no one makes any suggestions. Whose fault is that? It's not likely that team members don't have any ideas—it's more likely that you just haven't established a climate of receptivity.

At a seminar I gave in Paterson, New Jersey, a participant named Stan came up to see me afterward. "I manage a tax service and have seven skilled accountants working for me. I run meetings at which I ask for their ideas, and I know that they must have some good ideas, but I can't get them to come up with them. What am I doing wrong?"

Power Principles

When you solicit ideas from your team members, never present your view first. Because of your position, what you say may influence what team members had planned to say. Listen with an open mind. Their comments may give you new insights into the problem and result in a better solution.

I arranged to attend one of Stan's meetings, in which he presented a problem, suggested a solution, and then asked whether anyone had ideas that might also apply. He turned from one group member to another, and the typical response was, "No, I go along with what you said."

In a discussion with the accountants after the meeting, I learned that, in the past, if they had suggested any ideas that were different from what Stan had presented, he had greeted the idea with sarcasm or outright rejection. "Why disagree?" they asked. "It won't do any good."

Keeping an Open Door Open

Barbara supervised 12 clerks and boasted that her door was always open to staff members. But when one of the clerks would walk in, the look of annoyance on Barbara's face signaled that visitors were not welcome. It didn't take long for them to recognize that the door was open only in theory.

Some managers say that they want to be available to their associates but that there is so much work to do, they can't let people barge in whenever they feel like it. One solution is to have a partially open door. Set aside certain hours during which anyone is welcome to come in without an appointment to discuss problems, make suggestions, or just kick around ideas. In this way, you can plan your time so that your work gets done and your associates still have the opportunity to bring you their concerns.

Managing by Walking Around (MBWA)

You can learn a great deal by walking around. If you're always in your office or hiding behind the papers on your desk, how can you expect to know what's going on?

You have to get out there with your associates, talk to them, and develop their confidence.

It's not just walking around; it's what you do when you walk around. Lou made a practice of walking around the factory floor and stopping to speak to some of his employees—usually the same old-timers whom he had known for years. He asked how they were doing and about their families. It was good for morale, but he never learned anything of real value.

Carmen also walked around her department, but she took a different approach: Before her tour, she reviewed which projects were being performed, the assignments each person had, and the work problems she was particularly concerned about. The questions and comments she presented to her colleagues were specific. Her MBWA-style paid off for her: Her associates knew that she wanted to hear their ideas.

Rejecting Ideas Without Causing Resentment

Suppose Keesha comes to you excited about a great idea she believes will help the department, but in your opinion, her idea isn't practical. You know she will not only be upset if the idea is rejected, but she may also wonder why she even bothered to suggest anything. She may not ever make another suggestion. But you know that just because this idea wasn't a good one doesn't mean that her future ones won't be winners.

Rather than reject a poor suggestion, ask questions about it. With good questioning, you can get people to rethink their ideas and see the weak points they had initially overlooked. They will then reject their own bad ideas without your having to make a single negative comment.

Encourage Idea Sharing

Some people are bubbling with ideas and can't wait to share them. But many people need some prodding to get them to bring their suggestions to you. Consider your position a unique opportunity to minister to people—to encourage and build another up.

Various programs have been developed to make it easier for employees to bring their ideas to the company's attention. Some, such as suggestion boxes, have been around for a long time. This section discusses others that have been introduced more recently.

Feeding the Suggestion Box

Suggestion boxes have been around for decades. Do they generate good ideas, or are they just receptacles for gripes and grievances?

Suggestion systems can be as good as you want them to be. All it takes is a sincere commitment and a real effort to make them work. Companies have received from employees many suggestions that have enabled them to solve difficult problems, eliminate waste, improve quality, create new products, and save people millions of dollars annually.

The use of an employee suggestion form (see the following) encourages people to participate.

Suggestion Form

Contributor: _____ Date: _____

Department: _____ Team Leader: _____

Situation: _____

_____

_____

_____

Your suggestion (use additional pages if necessary): _____

_____

_____

_____

Estimate of first year's savings: _____

Other benefits to be derived: _____

Please attach supporting documents to this form.

You will receive acknowledgment and comments from the Suggestion Committee within 10 working days. Thank you for your suggestion.

Power Principles

Make suggestion programs exciting by incorporating some of these rewards:

- Run periodic special award contests.
- Conduct a lottery. All persons who make suggestions participate in a drawing for a big-screen TV.
- Have a monthly or quarterly luncheon for all winners.
- Send award winners' photos to local newspapers.

Follow my suggestions to help ensure the success of your suggestion program:

- Make sure senior management is fully behind the program.
- Publicize the program with creativity and flair.
- Make awards commensurate with the value of the suggestion. Many companies determine the amount of the award as a certain percentage of the money the company earns or saves.
- Acknowledge all suggestions promptly. Otherwise, participants lose interest in the program and are loath to make suggestions in the future.
- Have all suggestions evaluated by a suggestion committee and, where applicable, technical specialists. The committee should be empowered to accept or reject suggestions expeditiously.
- Make decisions and notify the contributor as soon as possible.
- Give public recognition to persons receiving awards—in the company newspaper, on bulletin boards, and at staff meetings.

That's the Spirit

"By insolence comes nothing but strife, but with those who take advice is wisdom." (Proverbs 13:10)

Eyeing Ideas for "I" Meetings

The letter *I* in "I" meetings stands for *idea*. Several days before a meeting, the people who will attend are given the agenda (usually with only one or two items). They are asked to think about the matters to be discussed and be prepared to present at least one idea about each item.

At the meeting, the ideas are presented and discussed. Because the participants often approach problems from different angles, they're likely to offer a variety of ideas.

Unlike brainstorming (discussed later in this chapter), in which the sole purpose is to generate ideas with no critiques or discussions, suggestions made in "I" meetings are discussed in detail, and decisions about their viability are made.

Running Around in Quality Circles

The Japanese people mostly attribute the high quality of their products to *quality circles*. Workers, usually without management participation, are free to discuss any and all aspects of their work. They are given access to any information they feel is necessary to their discussions.

> **Interpret and Apply**
>
> A **quality circle** is a group of employees who voluntarily meet on a regular basis to discuss ideas for improving the quality of their products or services.

Because the meetings are informal and managers don't oversee them, ideas flow freely and are then passed on to management. A high percentage of these suggestions are accepted and instituted. Although the concept of "quality circles" was conceived to discuss quality problems, these discussions have expanded over the years to productivity, performance, the working environment, and other aspects of business.

> **Wise Counsel**
>
> The concept of quality circles didn't originate in Japan. It originated right here in the United States in the 1950s but failed to catch on then. When workers were asked to participate in quality circles, the typical response was, "It's not my job. Someone else is responsible for quality." Today, most people recognize that quality is everyone's business.

Focusing on Focus Groups

Market researchers developed *focus groups* to learn about typical consumers' reactions to a company's product or service. Many consumer product manufacturers have focus groups try out a product and then discuss their opinions about it. Likewise, service organizations use focus groups to evaluate the service they are providing.

Over the past few years, human resources consultants have used this approach to reveal the true attitudes of employees about their company, their department, their managers, and specific aspects of their jobs.

Interpret and Apply

Focus groups, created to discuss how proposed company changes will affect workers, represent a broad cross-section of employees.

Although focus groups are most effective when restricted to specific areas, they can also be used as a means of identifying basic problems that can be explored in other groups. It is absolutely essential that no member of management observe the meeting in progress or view or hear tapes later. Anonymity of the participants is key to frank discussion. But it's okay to study written transcripts that don't identify who said what.

Confidential Employee Surveys

Employee attitude surveys have long been used to determine employee morale and locate problem areas. In recent years, these surveys have been refined and have become quite sophisticated diagnostic tools.

To obtain honest and meaningful information from employees, surveys, like focus groups, must be conducted by an impartial outsider. Surveys can range from a series of broad questions about company policies or employee satisfaction (or lack thereof) to specific questions about special matters.

Inasmuch as such surveys should be designed to fit each company's special needs, they should be developed and conducted by organizations geared for that purpose. Getting the most from an employee survey goes beyond just obtaining information. A lot of planning has to go into the design of an employee survey, and it is best if it is geared toward a specific industry. For instance, a survey that is designed for use by a publisher would not be appropriate at all for use by a trucking company.

Avoiding Stumbling Blocks

It's not a good idea to try to conduct your own survey. Unless the employees truly believe that the information they give will be kept confidential, you'll get only what they think you want to hear.

Some of the best employee surveys are specially designed by a consulting firm that understands and specializes in the industry being examined. In addition, once you have answers to the questions asked, they must be interpreted intelligently, or else you haven't really learned anything. In essence, this is something that must be done by specialists.

Trials and Tribulations of the Town Meeting

Town meetings are open-ended meetings to which all employees are invited and encouraged to express their thoughts and ideas to management. Generally, this is not a good idea. Companies that run town meetings often find that they become little more than gripe sessions. People with personal agendas tend to dominate the meetings.

Stimulating Creativity

"If it ain't broke, don't fix it." Wrong! Today's world is tough and competitive. You can't wait for things to break before fixing them. If you're not constantly coming up with better ideas—better ways to do things—your competitors will overwhelm you. Use constructive discontent to look at everything you're doing. Keep asking yourself, and encourage other people to ask themselves, "Is there a better way?"

It's easy to get into a rut: You become so comfortable with the status quo that you resist change. Change hurts. If you change the way you physically do something, new muscles are brought into play—and it hurts. If you change a mental process, you get real headaches. That's why so many people resist new ideas and avoid suggesting them.

Most people don't consider themselves to be creative. They assume that only a chosen few—inventors, artists, and writers, for example—have that talent. But all of us have the seeds of creativity within us. Those seeds just need to be developed.

> **That's the Spirit**
>
> Dissatisfaction is a tool God can use to motivate us to greater things.
> —John C. Maxwell

As a manager, you can establish a climate that nurtures those seeds. Then watch the creative ideas flow from the people in your department. By becoming aware and helping associates become aware of the five creative approaches that follow, you and your team members can dramatically increase the team's creativity levels.

One: Lateral Thinking—Looking at It Sideways

When you face a problem, you'll usually attack it logically—and that's good. But sometimes logical doesn't necessarily mean straightforward or direct. Often the best answer to a problem isn't right in front of you. You'll have to look at the problem from different angles to find the solution.

Alexander Fleming, a biologist, studied certain microbes. Periodically, when he selected a tray in which the microbes were kept for study, he'd find that the germs were dead. At first this was frustrating because he couldn't determine how to kill the germs if they were already dead. But then he redirected: Additional study proved that a mold that had developed in the tray had killed the germs. Thus came the discovery of penicillin. That's lateral thinking.

Training yourself to think laterally isn't easy. The first step is to be aware that problems aren't always what they seem and that solutions aren't always straightforward. For more pointers, take a look at the book *Lateral Thinking: Creativity Step by Step,* by Edward deBono. In it, deBono provides a detailed program to help you learn how to think laterally.

That's the Spirit

When Nicodemus came to visit Jesus at night (John 3), Jesus engaged the Pharisee by challenging him to think on a completely different level. The Jewish tradition dictated that the Law was the only way to salvation, but Jesus insisted that the only way human exclusion from God's kingdom could be resolved is to be "born again" (v. 3). Today the solution is so commonly understood that we can miss the creativity Jesus displayed by challenging Nicodemus to think outside of his box. The logic is wonderfully clear: If nothing can resolve the problem of the sinful state we're born into, then start over with a new (spiritual) birth.

Two: Being Flexible—Observation and Adaptation

Every day you observe things happening around you. Sometimes, by adapting lessons you learn in one context to other areas of your life, you can solve myriad problems.

While Jeff was waiting for his car to be serviced at a quick lube shop, he thought about his own company, which had a fleet of delivery vans. Whenever one of the vans needed servicing, a driver had to take it to the dealer's service center and leave it there for the day. His company lost four person-hours just for transportation every time a van was serviced—this, in addition to the van being out of service for the entire day. Jeff knew that if those vans could be serviced at a quick lube shop, his company could save a considerable amount of money. He made the suggestion. The company implemented it, saved thousands of dollars, and gave Jeff a substantial suggestion award.

Three: Modify, Modify, Modify

By modifying something you already have, you may come up with something new, different, or better. Victor Kiam, the CEO of the Remington Electric Shaver Company, recalls when one of the members of his office staff returned to work after undergoing surgery. She lamented how, in preparation for surgery, the nurse used a double-edge razor and nicked her three times. She said, "You should use a Lady Remington." Kiam brought that idea to his research people, who developed a modified Lady Remington, designed to be used as a surgical shaver. It's now doing well in the marketplace.

Four: Elimination—Getting Rid of Things

Most people think that in order to be creative, they have to invent something new. You can be just as creative by getting rid of things. Because most companies are bogged down with paperwork, a truly creative approach to paring the paper hassle would save companies considerable time and money.

Evaluate by asking the following questions of every form, record, and report that is generated on a daily, weekly, or monthly basis:

- **Is this paperwork really necessary?** Every month when Susan received a copy of a certain report, she skimmed it briefly and then immediately filed it away because it wasn't of much value to her. A careful look at the report revealed that although the report had had some use several years earlier, it had outlived its value. By eliminating the report altogether, the company saved time and money.

- **Can it be combined or consolidated with other forms?** Many forms or reports contain similar or even identical data in a different format. But if a computer database can be programmed to convert the same centralized data to different reports, this can free staff up for more productive work.

- **Can it be improved?** By redesigning a form, you can often make it easier to compile and understand.

- **Can it be reviewed electronically?** Specialized software for creating forms and reports lets you redesign or create better forms quickly on the computer.

Five: Brainstorming—Encouraging Group Creativity

A brainstorming meeting may be exciting, hectic, and totally chaotic, but it does generate ideas. The goal of brainstorming is to develop as many ideas as possible—not to critique, analyze, or discuss them or make decisions.

Suppose you are participating in a brainstorming session in which participants call out ideas that are hurriedly listed on a flip chart. Some of the ideas seem totally ridiculous, but no one scoffs, rebuts, or comments. No matter how stupid or inane an idea seems, it's listed on the chart.

Avoiding Stumbling Blocks

Brainstorming isn't appropriate for all types of problems. It works best when you're dealing with specific situations rather than with long-term policies.

Why is the group encouraged to bring out all these ideas, even the absurd ones? The psychological principle behind brainstorming is called triggering. Any idea, no matter how dumb it seems, can trigger more viable ideas in other participants' minds. By allowing participants to think freely and express their ideas without fear of criticism, brainstorming draws out a maximum number of valuable ideas from people. After the session, a committee analyzes the better ideas in more detail.

You Can't Do It All Yourself

Did you ever consider what a remarkable thing it was that Jesus called 12 disciples? After all, this was God the Son. If anyone was capable of doing the job himself, it would have been Jesus. And no doubt Jesus could have carried out his entire mission to save humanity all alone. Nevertheless, he trained the disciples and put them to work, often delegating responsibilities. And what was Jesus' purpose? It was the ultimate delegation: "Go and make disciples of all nations, baptizing them" and "teaching them." (Matthew 28:19–20)

There's an old Boy Scout hiking maxim that's worth noting: "A leader without followers is just someone out for a stroll." Being a leader isn't just about accomplishing the task; it's about leading others. In the business world, this means that a team leader has enough confidence in the team members to know that they'll carry out an assignment satisfactorily. True leaders delegate rather than succumb to another maxim that is generally poor advice: "If you want something done right, you have to do it yourself."

Don't Hesitate—Delegate!

Sure, there are certain things that only you can do, decisions that only you can make, and critical areas that only you can handle.

Many of the activities you undertake, however, can and should be done by others. This list discusses some of the reasons you may hesitate to delegate and explains why you should reconsider:

- **You can do it better.** That may be the case, but you should spend your time and energy on more important things. Each of your team members has talents and skills that contribute to your team's performance. By delegating assignments (even though it might take longer at first), you give team members the opportunity to develop and master skills, making your job easier later.

That's the Spirit

The disciples recognized the value, importance, and potential of the job Jesus was offering them. They realized here was a leader willing to use their abilities and creativity to do the same job he was doing.

—Myron Rush

- **You get a great deal of satisfaction from a certain aspect of the work, and you hesitate to give it up.** You're not alone. All of us enjoy certain things about our work and are reluctant to assign them to others. Look at the tasks objectively. Even if you have a pet project, you must delegate it if your time can be spent handling other activities that are now your responsibility as a manager.

- **You're concerned that, if you don't do it yourself, it won't get done right.** You have a right to be concerned. The following section explains how to minimize this risk.

Who's Gonna Do the Work?

You know the capabilities of each of your associates. When you plan their assignments, consider which person can do which job most effectively. You can use the assignment to build up another person's skills. The more team members who have the capabilities to take on a variety of assignments, the easier your job is for you. You should train one or more team members in several areas so you can delegate work in those areas when necessary.

Tell 'Em What to Do—The Right Way

After you give detailed instructions to one of your team members, your usual question is probably "Do you understand?" And the usual answer is "Yes."

But does the employee really understand? Maybe. Rather than ask "Do you understand?" ask "What are you going to do?" If the response indicates that one or more of your points isn't clear, you can correct it before the employee does something wrong.

When it's essential for an employee to rigidly conform to your instructions, give a quiz. Ask specific questions so that both you and your team member completely agree about what he or she will do. Otherwise, you can just get some general feedback.

Tailor the way you make assignments to the preferences of the person to whom you're delegating. Some people like to have responsibilities spelled out explicitly, while others prefer simple, concise instructions. Some people prefer e-mail, and others would rather have you delegate in person.

Make Sure They Understand—and Accept—Your Instructions

Your instructions must be both understood *and* accepted by your team member. Suppose that on Tuesday morning, Janet, the office manager, gives an assignment to Jeremy with a deadline of 3:30 that afternoon.

To gain acceptance, let your team member know just how important the work is. Janet might say, "Jeremy, this report must be on the director's desk when she comes in tomorrow morning. She needs it for an early morning meeting with the executive committee. When do you think I can have it?" Jeremy may think, "This is important. If I skip my break, I can have it by 5:00." By letting people set their own schedules within reasonable limits, you get their full commitment to meeting or beating a deadline.

But suppose that Janet really did need that report by 3:30—so that it could be proofread, photocopied, collated, and bound. To get the report completed on time, she could have assigned someone to help Jeremy.

Be realistic when you assign deadlines. Don't make a practice of asking for projects to be completed earlier than you need them; people will stop taking your deadlines seriously.

Control Points—Your Safeguard

A control point is the point at which you stop a project, examine the work that has been completed, and correct any errors before they blow up into catastrophes.

Avoiding Stumbling Blocks

Some managers make decisions in every phase of an assignment and look over everyone's shoulders checking for dotted *i*'s and crossed *t*'s. When you micromanage, you stifle creativity and prevent team members from working at their full potential.

Power Principles

When people bring you a problem, insist that they bring with it a suggested solution. At best, they will solve their own problems and not bother you. At the very least, they'll ask you, "Do you think this solution will work?" which is much easier to respond to than "What do I do now?"

A control point is not a surprise inspection. Team members should know exactly when each control point is established and what should be accomplished by then. At these points, the errors can be detected and corrected before the work continues. Otherwise, the errors will be perpetuated throughout the entire project.

Provide the Right Tools—Delegate Authority

You can't do a job without the proper tools. Providing equipment, computer time, and access to resources is an obvious step, but giving away *authority* is another story. But if a job is to be done without your micromanagement, you must give the people doing the job the power to make decisions. If they need supplies or materials, allot them a budget. If a job might call for overtime, give them the authority to order it. If you have to be around to make every decision, the work will get bogged down.

When You Delegate, You Don't Abdicate

Team or workgroup members almost always have questions, seek advice, and need your help. Be there for them, but don't let them throw the entire project back at you. Let them know that you're available to help, advise, and support, but not to do their work.

Putting Delegation to Work

Now that you know the principles of delegation, you're ready to apply them on the job.

To help you systematize your approach to delegation, use this sample delegation worksheet. You may photocopy it or adapt it to your needs.

Delegation Worksheet

Delegated to: _____

Date of assignment: _____ Deadline: _____

Brief description of assignment: _____

_____

Communication:

Assignee's comments: _____

_____

_____

Areas that must be clarified _____

Control points:

First control point will be on _____ at _____

Phase to be completed: _____

_____

Performance standards: _____

_____

_____

Date this phase completed: _____

(Use separate pages for each subsequent control point.)

Assignment completed: _____ Date: _____

Comments: _____

_____

_____

How we can make this person more effective in the next assignment:

_____

_____

Delegating to Teams

When an organization is structured into teams, work should be delegated and assigned as a team activity. When people have some control over the assignments they get, they approach their work with enthusiasm and commitment.

When your boss gives you a complex project, present it in its entirety to your team. You should discuss with your team how to break the assignment into phases. Most members will choose to handle the areas in which they have the most expertise. If two members want the same area, let them iron it out with each other, stepping in only when diplomacy is necessary.

Certain phases of the assignment are bound to be tough or unpleasant. No one's really going to volunteer to do them. Have your team set up an equitable system for assigning this type of work. Just as God says in his word that he doesn't show favoritism, neither should you or your team.

As team leader, be sure that every member of your team is aware of everyone else's responsibilities as well as his or her own. In this way, everyone knows what everyone else is doing and what kind of support he or she can give or receive from others.

To keep everyone informed, create a chart listing each phase of the assignment, the person handling it, deadlines, and other pertinent information. Post the chart in the office for easy referral.

That's the Spirit

Acts 6 recounts a crisis in leadership—some of the practical responsibilities for serving the church were about to keep the apostles from their primary concern: "the ministry of the Word of God" (v. 2). The obvious solution was to delegate to seven wise leaders. The results were exciting. "The word of God spread. The number of disciples in Jerusalem increased rapidly." (v. 7)

Delegating by Using Teams

Before companies began using the team concept, work was done interdepartmentally. Predictably, this process would often result in bottlenecks. If one department fell behind, it would cause delays in all the others.

The multidepartmental team (also called a *cross-functional team*) can successfully handle projects that require coordination among many diverse workgroups within a company. An effective team has these characteristics:

- It is composed of representatives from all relevant internal departments, such as sales and production. Team members are usually chosen by the team leader in coordination with managers of the involved departments.

- Outside representatives, such as customers, suppliers, and subcontractors, are invited to participate in team discussions. Although these people aren't members of the team, their input is important in helping the team accomplish its goal.

- Production schedules are determined based on customers' needs. Team members are given detailed information about these needs and are encouraged to deal directly with customers to keep up-to-date on necessary adjustments.

- Delivery of materials is arranged on a just-in-time basis. To avoid unnecessary inventory costs, arrangements are made for delivery of materials and supplies as close as possible to the time they'll be used.

- Work assignments are planned collaboratively and control points are established. Some projects require teams to meet daily to coordinate and maintain attention to the assignment. Other projects require only occasional meetings to check on progress and deal with problems.

The key to the success of multidepartmental programs is communication. Team members are encouraged to communicate in person, on the telephone, or by writing, faxing, or e-mailing each other on a timely basis. Problems can then be addressed without delay.

Project Management

When companies are faced with special types of projects, usually one-time tasks (such as introducing a new product to the market, moving to a new location, or developing a new product or service), they often create a project management team rather than assign it to one or more operating departments.

This new group handles all matters related to the project. Project managers have the authority to obtain from various departments in the company all necessary personnel, equipment, and anything else to complete the assignment. Project team members are often temporarily relieved of their regular duties for the duration of the project.

The person chosen to be *project manager* is usually a senior or middle manager who has expertise in the activities the project involves. Some of the project manager's first tasks are listed here:

- Assemble a multidepartmental team that includes representatives from various parts of the organization to plan and implement the project.

- Together with these representatives, plan the project and set timetables for each phase.

- Work with team members to coordinate the work of everyone involved, from the inception of the design phase, to the final distribution, to customers. The people involved may include engineers, production supervisors, marketing and sales staff, and shipping and distribution personnel.

The result is that you get cooperation in place of turf wars. Rather than time-wasting red tape, you get fast decisions. By crossing over traditional departmental barriers, project managers can get quick action, shift gears when necessary, and react immediately to urgent problems.

That's the Spirit

When Nehemiah began his grand project of rebuilding the Jerusalem wall, he first called together "the officials" who represented the leadership of various family groups (Nehemiah 2:16–17). Being the good project manager that he was, he involved a diverse and broad representation: Eliashib the High Priest and his fellow priests covered the Sheep Gate (3:1), the sons of Hassenaah handled the Fishgate (v. 3), Joiada and Meshullam took care of the Jeshanah Gate (v. 6), and on and on the list goes. Nehemiah got "buy-in" by delegating broadly.

Using the Computer as a Scheduling Tool

As work scheduling becomes more complex, computers will be integral to helping you keep the details organized.

Scheduling programs, such as Microsoft Project, enable you to define the various project tasks and their relationships to one another. Microsoft Project lets you concentrate on major phases of a project or on specific detailed tasks. It also enables you to allocate and track resources and to set working hours and days for groups and individuals. The program alerts you to deviations from the schedule so that you can take immediate action.

When you use this type of software, it's easy to see whether your project is progressing as planned. You know which tasks must be given special attention to avoid delaying the completion of a project.

Microsoft Project also has a variety of report formats that you can use to communicate your progress to your own staff, customers, and anyone else involved.

Managing Multiple Priorities

If you're a typical twenty-first-century manager, you're probably loaded down with more work than it seems possible to do—and so are your team members.

Avoiding Stumbling Blocks

Putting in more hours, bringing more work home, and going to the office on weekends may help, but it often results in stress, fatigue, and low morale, which can reduce performance and productivity. Don't forget that most people have families, other interests, and the need to rest and refuel. And for good reason–God himself modeled the value of rest when he rested from the work of creation on the seventh day. (See Genesis 2:2-3.)

What can you do when members of your team have other assignments that are equally important or when your team is facing several high-priority tasks that must be completed in the same time frame?

Communicate, Communicate, Communicate

You can't pull rank. It used to be that you could force your priorities on others because you were higher on the totem pole. Occasionally, this is still acceptable, but in most progressive organizations such power plays are discouraged.

Work it out. Talk to team members and to other team leaders to schedule work that will enable all of you to make the best contribution you can to your organization. This process takes diplomacy and a willingness to compromise.

Working Smarter Beats Working Harder

A limited number of hours is available for work; no matter how you look at it, there are only 24 hours in a day. For most people, the eight-hour workday is a mere pipe dream. Many people spend 10 or 12 hours at the office and then take work home with them at night. There's a limit, however, to the amount of time a person can spend working.

Overwork *does* exist. In the past few years, as more companies downsize, over-working has become a serious problem. Employees who remain in an organization after a downsizing have to take on their ex-colleagues' assignments in addition to their own workload.

> **Power Principles**
>
> When you say "no" to an assignment, explain how taking on the assignment would inhibit completion of other higher-priority projects. Suggest alternative solutions.

As you learned in Chapter 5, you should seek new and creative approaches to your work—that is, work smarter, not harder. Ask yourself: What kind of work can be eliminated? Which work processes can be re-engineered? Which can be delegated? The time you spend learning about new approaches will pay off through expedient performance.

Don't Be Afraid to Say No

You can't do everything. At times, your team gets so bogged down with work that taking on another assignment would simply be impossible. How can you turn it down diplomatically?

Sometimes you can't. The project may have a high priority and must be completed. In that case, re-examine all your other projects. Determine which of them can be put on the back burner until you complete the new assignment. Often, you can just reschedule. Or maybe the project can be done more effectively by another team. Know your limitations. This is the time to be prayerfully seeking God's guidance. He will either give you the grace and strength to complete the task or the wisdom and direction to find support.

Part 2

The Supervisor as Coach

Your team is in place. Now comes the real work: molding those men and women into a dynamic, interactive, high-performance unit. That's what a coach does for athletic teams, and that's your job now.

How do you do it? By helping the members of your team develop their God-given gifts to optimum capacity. You have to keep your team aware of your organization's goals and on top of the latest methods and techniques that will enable them to reach those goals. You have to help them learn what they don't know and perfect what they *do* know. Our spiritual counterpart is the apostle Paul, who tells us in Ephesians 4:7, "God has given each of us a spiritual gift according to the generosity of Christ." In verse 12, Paul says that leaders have a responsibility to equip their followers to do God's work and to build up the church.

In this part of the book, you'll pick up some suggestions for the training and development of the people on your team.

Chapter

7

Developing Your Team for Optimum Performance

God is unchanging. But he created this world to be constantly changing, constantly growing. (Of course, sin brought in another dynamic of change as well.) The point is, nothing in this world stays the same for long. The way we approach our jobs, the way a job is performed, and even the type of work we do change with the times. As a team leader, you must keep up with these changes and help team members learn how to do their jobs and keep up with changing methods and techniques.

Planting the Training Seeds

It's your job to make sure your team members have the know-how to do their jobs. New associates may bring with them skills they acquired through education and not experience. It's a plus, of course, if a new team member has done similar work in another company, but even work experience isn't enough to eliminate the need for training. Every organization has its own way of doing things. To ensure consistency in the way your group works, all new associates should be given basic job training or retraining.

When's the Harvest?

New people may need basic training, but training and development aren't limited to newcomers. All members of your team need ongoing training. They should continually acquire new techniques and renew established skills. And as a follower of Christ, you should especially be interested in encouraging self-development, including in the workplace.

As a leader and a coach, you are the guide and stimulus of your team's growth. By working closely with each of your team members, you can suggest areas in which additional training will be helpful and point out skills they should acquire. You can also provide the resources for this process.

How much time, effort, and money should you invest in training? There's no question that well-trained, high-performance teams are major ingredients in a company's success, but (as mentioned in Chapter 2) there must be a balance between the P (potential of people) and R (results desired).

> **Avoiding Stumbling Blocks**
>
> Reward your people with the opportunity of further career education. Provide books, conference attendance, tapes, and speakers that will enhance them.
>
> —John Maxwell

Few companies have unlimited training budgets—companies aren't universities. People in professional and high-tech jobs must acquire necessary skills before joining an organization. A company's responsibility is to help these people adapt their knowledge to meet its particular needs.

Some jobs, however, are unique to a company. In such cases, the company is the only source employees have for training. The amount of time and money a company spends on training, then, depends on the complexity of the tasks that need to be performed.

America is moving rapidly from a production-based to a service-based economy. The required skills differ, and the need to train the people who perform them presents new challenges to management. The trainers—team leaders and managers—are the coaches who will develop the skills necessary for their team's optimum performance.

Train for What?

Training may be important, but it is only cost effective if the selected training areas pay off in higher productivity and a better bottom line.

Too often, companies implement unnecessary training programs, ignoring the more valuable areas in which people would actually benefit from some training. Before choosing any training programs, the company should conduct a needs analysis. Professional training experts apply systematic approaches to needs assessments, but you can also make some basic assessments on your own.

Ten Questions About Your Training Needs

Study the jobs involved and ask yourself questions like these:

1. What is the gap between desired and actual performance?
2. Is the problem caused by lack of technical skills?
3. Is the problem caused by employees' attitudes?
4. Can you close the gap through supervisory attention, or do you think special training is needed?
5. If you do require training, which employees need the training?
6. Do you have the internal capability to provide the training? If so, who will do it and when?
7. If not, and you choose to go outside, what sources are available?
8. What performance results should you expect from the training?
9. What is the cost of the training?
10. What financial benefits will result?

Once you have the answers to these questions, you can determine the type of program to institute. If you choose to do the training internally, prepare to be the best instructor you can be. Techniques and tools of effective instruction are covered in Chapter 8.

Wise Counsel

Training people is often a one-way process. The teacher presents information and hopes the student absorbs it. When training is replaced by learning, the emphasis is on developing the capability of trainees to identify and solve problems, to seek knowledge, and to take the initiative in continuing self-development.

—Erwin S. Stanton

Keeping Up with the State-of-the-Art

The fundamentals of a job must be taught from the start, and then continued training to teach new technologies should be standard procedure. But that's not enough. The following list shows five ways to bring your training and development up-to-date:

- Instead of teaching employees how to deal with specific problems, give them a general understanding of how to identify and solve all problems.

- Place the ultimate responsibility for learning on the individual (or, in team learning, on the team). The person who conducts the training is a facilitator: Rather than spoon-feed information to trainees, this facilitator guides them through the process and summarizes and reinforces the resulting insights.

- Make sure that people who will learn together share a common vocabulary, are trained to use the same analytical tools, and have communication channels available so they can work together and with other people or teams within an organization.

Avoiding Stumbling Blocks

Steer clear of training programs that promise miracles. Only God can work those. If they sound too good to be true, they *are* too good to be true. Your best bet is to use well-established, proven training programs.

- To learn to solve problems, trainees should be encouraged to tap resources in other departments or outside the company, such as customers, suppliers, and trade or professional associations. But in such times of need, seek God's provision first. After all, he can provide for all of your needs on the job too. (See 2 Corinthians 9:8.).

- Avoid having professional trainers do the training. Let people from all job categories (managers, team leaders, human resource specialists) be the facilitators. This expands training resources and helps develop future leaders.

In-House Universities—Training Medium of the Future

Have you heard of Hamburger University? It's no joke. McDonald's created it to train its management people, and it was the forerunner of many other "company universities." So why was a university created to teach people how to flip a Big Mac? If that was all there was to managing a McDonald's outlet, it would be considered overkill. McDonald's recognized early on that developing managers who know how to lead teams, market products, and increase sales pays off in making its units profitable.

In an article titled "Five Top Corporate Training Programs" in *Successful Meetings* magazine, Robert Carey says that a number of other companies have converted their training departments into autonomous schools. According to the American Council on Education (ACE), more than 40 of these company universities have been established in the United States. This section looks at some of the most successful of these "universities."

At Walt Disney, Training Is Show Biz

Disney University isn't a campus, but a process for training all employees of Walt Disney World Resorts. Facilitators for the training are Disney employees themselves. They share with trainees their own personal experiences working for Disney. But what makes this program unique is that trainees are allowed to mingle among the visiting crowds at the parks and observe Disney employees in action. The result is that Disney's front-line attrition rate is only 15 percent, compared with 60 percent for the rest of the hospitality industry.

Saturn Company: GM's Training for the Next Century

The key to Saturn's structure is its use of teams. The goal of the Saturn University training program is to teach employees to operate as continuously learning, fully independent work teams. The teams are responsible for their own development. The teams manage their own budgets, order their own materials, and gauge their own educational progress, with each team member being responsible for creating a training and development plan.

Significantly, half of all Saturn training is in interpersonal relations and communications. And the best example of Saturn's commitment to education is that all executives, including its CEO, teach at Saturn University.

Motorola University

Motorola, an award-winning international electronics manufacturer, is committed to customer service. Motorola University was created to make sure all employees keep

Wise Counsel

Motorola University invites other companies to learn about its training. Write to Motorola University at 2 Century Center, 1700 East Golf Road, Schaumburg, IL 60173, or call 708-538-4404.

their technical skills sharp, but that was only the beginning. Motorola programs also help trainees develop creativity and leadership, work in teams, and improve customer relations.

The program's success has resulted in Motorola's amazing growth in a highly competitive industry—not just in the United States, but also in the global marketplace. The training program has become a model for many other organizations.

Finding Training Expertise Outside the Company

When should you go outside the company for help in training? When others can do it better. Review your needs assessment. Determine what type of required training you cannot do yourself. Then look for the organization that can do it for you.

Wise Counsel

The National Organization of Executive Secretaries offers periodic seminars on developing management skills for secretaries and executive assistants. For information, write to 900 South Washington St., Suite G13, Falls Church, VA 22046, or call 703-237-8616.

If the training need is on computers or technical equipment, your best source may be the manufacturer or software provider. These firms usually have training facilities. Either they send trainers to your office or offer classes at their own offices. Costs vary. Many suppliers offer free training with a purchase; others charge per hour or day.

Training in the soft skills is more complicated. You can implement in-house programs in selling, leadership, self-confidence, communications, public speaking, and more. Or send team members to public seminars and classes. (Programs are offered by individual consultants, college professors, training organizations, and others.)

Eight Tips for Picking the Right Trainer

1. Select a firm with professional credentials. The firm should be a member of the American Society for Training & Development (see Appendix C), or should be affiliated with a university or appropriate professional associations.

2. Ask managers of other companies for referrals. If they have used training organizations for similar problems, their recommendations will be valuable.

3. Check out the firms you are considering with other companies in your industry or area. Even if these other companies haven't used the training firms you're considering, they may know of others that have.

4. Ask for references. Get the names of several past and present clients. Make sure you speak with clients who used the service several years ago. Ask them about the long-term value they feel the training has offered. Ask if they would use the firm again.

Power Principles

Many companies that have regular needs for people with certain skills team up with local community colleges to train people—often providing financial aid, equipment, materials, and instructors.

5. Sit in on a current training class. If the firm gives public programs, either attend a session yourself or send one of your managers. If the type of program you want isn't offered publicly but is at another company, ask the company's permission to attend.

6. Ask to see a random selection of past program evaluations. Look for patterns of positive and negative factors.

7. Make sure the instructor is an expert in the field you need help with. Interview the principal of the firm and the assigned instructor, making sure he or she has more than a superficial knowledge of your need.

8. Be wary of programs that advertise training "gimmicks" and claim to give your employees motivation or improved interpersonal skills, even drawing upon New Age–type world views. Indeed, much New Age thinking is now found in the business world, and discernment and avoidance is needed. These programs may be truly fun and exciting, but they rarely provide long-term benefits.

Using Local Schools and Colleges

Some training can be provided inexpensively through local schools. These facilities are especially helpful with training in basic skills, such as English as a second language, computers, typing, and business practices. Some companies, such as Eastman Kodak, arrange for the schools to send teachers to company facilities to conduct classes after working hours. Many community colleges develop special programs to meet the needs of companies in their communities.

Likewise, many universities offer undergraduate and graduate degree programs that can be valuable to local employees. They also have nondegree courses in their continuing education divisions designed for people who either don't have a degree or already have a degree in one area and want to acquire knowledge in other areas.

Companies can encourage employees to participate in such programs by paying directly for them or reimbursing tuition.

Bells Ring, Lights Flash, but Does the Training Work?

Often the training program generates excitement among the participants. They enjoy the class, are amused by the instructor's stories, and are stimulated by the case studies, games, and interactive programs. Great! But have they learned what they were sent to learn?

Over the years, many senior executives have expressed skepticism about the value of training because they could not quantify the results. Attempts to measure the effectiveness of training programs were generally done superficially, usually by asking the trainees to fill out a questionnaire reflecting their reaction to the program.

In 1959, Donald L. Kirkpatrick, now professor emeritus at the University of Wis-consin, first proposed a model for measuring training programs. This model was recently revised and updated in his book *Evaluating Training Programs: The Four Levels.*

Level 1: Using the traditional trainee evaluation forms. Using questionnaires to get immediate feedback from trainees allows you to gauge their reaction to the program. You'll learn the trainee's feelings about course content, instructor effectiveness, and whether the course met the trainee's expectations.

Power Principles

A company's training investment is most likely to pay off when the training department is held accountable for results, used only when it is the appropriate tool, and linked to the company strategy.

Wise Counsel

A recent variation of Kirkpatrick's four levels of training evaluation is Jack J. Phillips's Level 5— Measurement of ROI, or return on investment. Here, you evaluate whether the monetary value of the results exceeds the cost of the program.

Level 2: Determining what the trainee learned. Just as schools have always tested students on what they learned in class, you can test what your employees learned during training. Administer a written or oral exam, or ask for a demonstration of skills acquired. Follow up a few months later to see how much of the material the trainee has retained.

Level 3: Evaluating the application of learned skills to the job. This can be a significant tool in determining the value of training. Have the trainees appliedto their jobs what they learned during training? With hard skills, you should be able to assess application by checking for such things as reduction in number of rejects and increase in productivity. Of course, it is much more difficult to measure application of soft skills. Behavioral scientists have developed instruments to measure this, but such studies must be conducted by specially trained professionals.

Level 4: Tying training to the bottom line. Did the training result in a measurable improvement in business results?

Chapter

8

Training Tools and Techniques

God has placed you in a position of leadership—that means he also called you to train those whom you lead. In most organizations, training is done on the job by team leaders and supervisors—not professional trainers. Training is not an innate talent. It can be learned. In this chapter, I discuss several successful techniques that can be used in most types of skill training.

The Four P's

Training cannot be a haphazard process. It must be planned and systemized. Many organizations have used an effective and simple four-step training program for several years. Job-instruction training (JIT), a systematic approach to training people to perform tasks, involves four steps: preparation, presentation, performance, and post-work.

Preparation

Preparation is both physical and psychological. All physical equipment and facilities necessary for training should be in place before you begin. After you begin, you don't want to be interrupted by having to look for items you need.

In the psychological part of the process, you should tell a trainee before the training begins what will be taught, why it's performed, and how it fits into the overall picture. When people can see the entire picture, not just their small part in it, they learn faster and understand more clearly, and they're more likely to remember what they've been taught.

Presentation

You can no longer say to a trainee, "Just watch me and do what I do." If it were only that simple. Work today is much too complex to learn just by observation. The following four steps can guide you in showing someone how to perform a task:

1. Describe what you're going to do.

2. Demonstrate step by step, explaining each step and why it's done. (For example, "Notice that I entered the order number on the top right side of the form, to make it easy to locate."

3. Have the trainee perform the task and explain to you the method and reason for each step.

4. If the trainee doesn't perform to your satisfaction, have him or her repeat the task. If the employee performs well, reinforce the behavior with praise or positive comments.

Performance

After you're satisfied that a trainee can do a job, leave the person alone and let him or her do it. The trainee needs an opportunity to try out what he or she has learned. Mistakes probably will be made, but that's to be expected. From time to time, check out how things are going and make necessary corrections.

Post-Work

The post-work step is important because people tend to change what they have been taught. This is where a strong dose of godly patience can be crucial! Careless people may skip some steps in a procedure, causing errors or complications. Smart people may make changes that they believe are better than what they were taught—caution them not to make any changes until they have discussed them with you. They often may not be aware of the ramifications of their suggested changes.

Schedule post-work discussions of new assignments three to four weeks after the presentation step. At that time, review what the associate has been doing; if changes have been made intentionally or inadvertently, bring the person back on track.

Training Is a Team Activity

Just because you're the team leader doesn't mean you have to train all your team members. The training function should be shared by everyone on the team. Some organizations encourage an entire team to share in the task of training new members; others assign one person to act as a mentor. A note of caution: A person who knows the job best isn't always the most qualified person to train others.

Job know-how *is* essential for the person who will do the training, but it's only part of the picture. Look for these additional factors:

- **Personal characteristics.** Patience, empathy, and flexibility are good qualities to look for—and ones that all Christians should pursue.

- **Knowledge of training techniques.** Just as Jesus trained the apostles to train church leaders, it is wise to provide training for trainers, to build up their communication skills.

- **A strong, positive attitude toward the job and the company.** If you assign a disgruntled person to do your training, that person will inject the trainee with the virus of discontent. Philippians 2:14 tells us, in everything we do, to stay away from complaining and arguing.

Avoiding Stumbling Blocks

Practice does *not* make perfect. If people practice doing things wrong, they become perfect in doing things wrong. Practice makes *permanent*. When you train associates, periodically check out what they're doing. If it's wrong, correct it immediately, before it becomes permanently ingrained as a bad habit.

Scheduling Training

When planning training, determine whether the training will be done on or off the job. On-the-job training is done at the work site during regular working hours. Off-the-job training is conducted in a classroom or a special facility rather than at the regular place of work, and it has many advantages over on-the-job training:

- **People learn faster,** since no other work interferes with the learning process.
- **It's usually conducted by a professional trainer** who has the know-how, personal skills, and no other duties that distract.

Power Principles

Carefully plan the sequence in which you will present the subject. Begin with the simple stuff and work up to complex subjects. Build a foundation before you attempt to construct the framework.

- **It doesn't interfere with production,** since trainees are in a classroom and not on a job site.

Despite these major advantages, off-the-job training has a limitation: It isn't cost effective unless you're training several people at the same time. Another limitation is that you can't really learn the full scope of a job outside the job environment. Therefore, off-site training generally enables you to train only for a particular task or skill, not for the entire job. Many companies use a combination of on- and off-site training.

Setting the Training Schedule

When you prepare a training schedule (see the following on-the-job training schedule), indicate the subjects that must be covered, determine how long it should take, and allot the necessary time. Also, give the trainer enough flexibility to handle any

Avoiding Stumbling Blocks

Never purchase a training tape before you preview it. Most companies that sell tapes charge a fee for the preview, but it's worth it.

snags that could arise, as well as training aids and clear direction regarding training methods that should be employed.

Whether you or an associate is assigned to do the training, review the training schedule before you begin. Be sure that everything to be learned is scheduled. The sequence of the subject matter is often a problem, so be sure to check it, too. You should introduce new subjects only when the trainee is ready to learn them.

On-the-Job Training

Job: _____

Trainer: _____ Trainee: _____

Equipment necessary for training: _____

_____

_____

Time scheduled Day/Hour	Subject	Training Methods	Training Aids	Completed

"They Just Don't Get It"

Everyone responds differently to being taught new things. Some people are slow to learn, some are reluctant to change their ways and resist training, and some believe they're not good at learning and give up easily.

Slow Learners

Margaret, the team leader, was about to give up on Mark, who was trying hard to learn new material but just couldn't quite get it. Margaret asked a colleague for help with the problem: "When Mark worked in your department, did he have difficulty learning new things?"

"Yes," the other team leader responded. "He's a slow learner, but after he did learn the material, he became one of my best workers." Margaret followed up: "What did you do to help him?" He responded, "I watched his learning patterns and recognized that he needed to have the tasks broken down into smaller segments. Then we worked to bring them together. Also, he responded best when I gave him immediate feedback about his performance."

The Learning Curve

Have you ever made great progress in learning something new, only to realize that your mind suddenly seems to stop? You can't move beyond a certain point, but why?

The human mind can absorb only a limited amount of new information at any time. At some point in the learning process, you have to stop and integrate the new material with what you already know. While this process is in place, you're at a plateau: Nothing new can enter your system. After the new material is absorbed, however, your mind opens again and—boom!—off you go. This process is known as the *learning curve*.

Whether you're the learner or the teacher, keep the learning curve in mind. When you or your trainee seem to be unable to go beyond a certain point, *stop*. Wait an hour or a day or longer. Depending on the complexity of the material and the learner's background, the duration of the plateau varies.

> **Power Principles**
>
> Being a slow learner doesn't mean that a person is stupid. Pray about it, be patient, and try different approaches! Slow learners often can develop into productive team members.

The Know-It-All

You've run into know-it-alls. You can't tell them anything. They believe that they know best and oppose any type of change.

But change they must. Because know-it-alls resist learning new things, you have to learn how to overcome their attitude:

- Listen to their objections. Point out the advantages of the new changes and how they will make the system more efficient, less expensive, or easier to maintain.

- Get other team members to back you up.

- Use patience, reinforcement, and diplomacy to make your point. Words can either build up or tear down. As Proverbs 18:4 says, a person's words can be life-giving water.

The Fear of Learning

How often have you heard someone say, "It's too hard for me—I'm too old to learn new things"? Eric was a bookkeeping machine operator for 20 years. Then his company replaced its old Burroughs machines with PCs—he was devastated.

When the computer company's trainer began the training program, Eric froze. He didn't seem to absorb even the basic elements of his work. Eric's request for a transfer to another department was denied because computers were used everywhere. Eric was at his lowest when Lillian, one of the other bookkeeping machine operators, took him aside. "Eric, you *can* learn. I'm older than you, and I learned to use the PC. Try it. I'll help you. *All* of us will help you." The help and support of his peers gave Eric the incentive to learn. Now he's a productive PC operator and proudly boasts about his new skills.

Avoiding Stumbling Blocks

Make sure any training manual you write or approve is written to the level of the trainees and is clear, concise, and complete.

Training and Development Techniques

Today's leaders have available to them a variety of aids and techniques to facilitate their training efforts. Some have been around for years; others were developed more recently.

Training Manuals—Gobbledygook or the Real Stuff?

Training manuals, or "do it by the numbers" handbooks, are helpful for teaching routine tasks. Unfortunately, training manuals can be poorly written and confusing;

some are laced with technical terminology intelligible only to the engineers who wrote them.

Because jobs today are becoming less routine, training manuals are often inadequate—to the point that they even stifle creativity. Don't rely on a book because it's easy; instead, think out new and possibly better approaches to training.

Interactive Computer Training

Many companies have developed a variety of interactive computer programs to train employees. Such programs were initially designed for use in schools to enable students to learn at their own pace. But because most companies have their own ways of doing things, generic programs, such as the ones used by schools, haven't been of much value. But some generic programs, such as those that teach basic accounting skills and various computer operations, can be an asset to any organization. Also, consider customizing generic programs to meet your own requirements.

The Internet—the School of the Future

The personal computer has moved training from the classroom to the desk, the kitchen table, and even the lap of each individual.

Universities and private organizations offer courses and individual study programs on hundreds of subjects. You can study a foreign language, learn basic or advanced math, acquire technical know-how, and even obtain a college degree. The Internet makes it possible for students to engage in classroom interaction, even when they're participating from home.

Teleconferencing

Sometimes the most effective way to train or retrain staff members is to hold classes that bring together employees from several locations. This is a common practice among national and global organizations. It's also one of the most expensive ways to train.

One way to reduce the cost and time involved is teleconferencing. Using specially designed computer and TV equipment, participants can see, hear, and interact with the instructor and each other without going far from their base. Larger organizations may have teleconferencing technology available on-site. Smaller companies can use the services of teleconferencing firms that can set up such conferences wherever needed.

CD-ROMs

Interactive programs are also available in CD-ROM format. Walk into any computer store, and you will find a variety of standard courses on CD-ROM. These can be used at the workplace or given to employees to use at home.

Case Studies

A *case study* is a description of a real or simulated business situation presented to trainees for analysis, discussion, and solution.

Case studies are used in graduate schools, seminars, and corporate training programs to enable trainees to work on the types of problems they're most likely to encounter on the job. The studies are often drawn from the experiences of real companies. The experience of working out these types of problems with a team and in a classroom, instead of learning by trial and error, pays off (with fewer trials and less costly errors).

> **Avoiding Stumbling Blocks**
>
> To make case solving most effective, design cases that are related to the job. Make them complex and challenging, and make their solutions necessitate collaboration and teamwork.

Role Playing

In today's companies, most jobs require interaction with other people. Perhaps the best way to train people for this type of interaction is through role playing. As in case studies, role playing should be based on realistic situations a trainee may face on the job.

Effective role playing must be carefully structured. Participants should be briefed on the goals of the exercise, and each participant should be given a specific part to play. Don't give people scripts—improvisation makes the exercise more spontaneous and allows for flexibility. Just make sure you establish limits so that participants don't stray from the goal of the exercise.

To get everyone—not just the players—involved, give each role to a group of people. The group studies and discusses how the role should be played. Then one member of the group is appointed to play the role. The other group members may step in to supplement the primary player. For example, if the person playing the role of a personnel interviewer fails to ask a key question, one of the members of that group can intervene and ask the question.

After the role playing is completed, all the groups critique what has transpired and discuss what they've learned from the experience.

Using Video

Probably the most dramatic innovation in training and development is the use of video as a training tool. Check video catalogs; you'll find tapes that cover a variety of subjects.

Video tapes, like training manuals, are most appropriate for training people to do routine jobs. For situations in which flexibility and initiative are necessary, customizing videotapes to meet your own needs is a more effective option. This list describes some ways to use customized video to enhance the effectiveness of your training programs:

- **Tape demonstrations.** For work of a physical nature (most factory or maintenance jobs and some clerical jobs), a good demonstration is an important part of the training. You can tape yourself or one of your team members performing the job. Show the tape in real time to demonstrate the pace at which a job should be carried out. Use slow motion to better explain each step of the task.

- **Tape job performance.** One of the best ways to help people recognize exactly what they're doing on the job is to videotape them at work and then let them review the tape.

- **Tape team meetings.** One employee's team leader videotaped several team meetings. By studying the tapes, the employee noticed that she tended to push her ideas across and was sometimes rude to other team members. She told her team leader that until she saw the tape, she didn't realize the way she came across. She agreed to attend a human relations training course.

- **Tape role playing.** Videotaping role playing and reviewing the tapes makes the tool even more effective.

- **Tape presentations.** There's no better way to improve your oratory skills than to study videos of your practice deliveries.

Using Audio

One of the best ways to train people whose jobs require lots of telephone use—telemarketers, customer service representatives, order clerks, credit checkers—is to record telephone conversations. You can purchase a component that connects the telephone to a voice-activated tape recorder (or even an answering machine), but be sure it is legal in your state. Tape several conversations, and then review them with each team member.

Cross-Training

When teams are the operating units in an organization, it's helpful for everyone on a team to be able to perform the work of any other member. The whining comment "It's not my job" is no longer valid. Predictably, the biblical concept of doing for others what you would have them do for you makes good business sense as well.

In cross-functional or multidepartmental teams, this capability isn't always feasible: For instance, a team consisting of people from marketing, engineering, and finance doesn't easily lend itself to cross-training.

Most teams, however, are made up of people who do similar work. One sales support team consists of order clerks, customer service representatives, and computer operators. All are trained in every aspect of the team's work and can move from job to job as necessary.

Preparing for Advancement

Training isn't limited to teaching job skills. Training team members to become team leaders is an important aspect of organizational development.

The Cadet Corps

For many years, training for management positions was limited to people who were on a special management track. They usually were hired as management trainees after graduating from college and went through a series of management training programs within an organization, often supplemented by seminars, courses, and residencies at universities or special training schools.

One of the most commonly used cadet programs was job rotation. After basic orientation, trainees were assigned to work for a short period in each of several departments. The objective was to give them an overview of the company so that when they moved into regular positions, they would have a good concept of the entire operation.

Makes sense? Sometimes. In many companies, the time spent in each training assignment was not long enough to give the trainees any more than a superficial knowledge. They wasted the time of the department heads, and the regular team members—knowing that the trainees would be gone shortly—often resented their intrusion. Resentment was compounded by people's feelings that these cadets were of a privileged class and would someday be their bosses without having worked their way up.

Everybody Is a Potential Manager

In recent years, the special management track has been supplanted by team development, in which training for management is open to any team member. And why not? Even the military has learned that graduation from military academies isn't essential to be a top leader. (Two of the recent Chairmen of the Joint Chiefs of Staff—Colin Powell and John Shalikashvili—weren't West Pointers.) Companies have recognized that latent leadership talent exists in most people and can be developed in them. (Chapter 9 discusses some of the programs that companies have used to encourage people to move up in their careers.)

Interpret and Apply

def·i·ni·tion

A **mentor** is a team member assigned to act as counselor, trainer, and "big brother" or "big sister" to a new member. The Apostle Paul mentored both John Mark and Timothy during his journeys. (Not all mentoring is successful or easy, though, as was evidenced by Paul's falling out with John Mark. [Acts 15:37–39])

Mentor, Mentor—Where Is My Mentor?

It's a well-known fact that when a high-ranking manager takes a less experienced employee under his or her wing—becomes that person's *mentor*—the protégé not only has a head start for advancement, but he or she also will acquire more know-how about the work, the workings of the company, and the "tricks of the trade" than others.

Why shouldn't everybody have a mentor? Why leave it to chance that some senior managers choose a protégé while others do not? Why not make mentoring a job requirement—not only for senior executives, but for all experienced team members? By structuring a mentoring program and assigning the best people on your team the responsibility of mentoring a new member, you take a giant step forward in encouraging productivity and growth in the newcomer.

A structured mentoring program requires that chosen mentors be willing to take on the job. Compelling someone to be a mentor is self-defeating. Not everybody is interested in or qualified for this assignment. New mentors should be trained by experienced people in the art of mentoring.

Wise Counsel

"As iron sharpens iron, so one man sharpens another." (Proverbs 27:17) Both the mentor and the mentored benefit from the process of mentoring. Those who are mentored learn the new skills, while mentors sharpen their skills in order to pass them on. It heightens the mentor's sense of responsibility as he guides his protégé through the maze of company policies and politics. It also makes the mentor more effective in his interpersonal relationships.

Ten Tips for New Mentors

If you're a first-time mentor, you're probably unsure of how to deal with this new responsibility. If you have had your own successful experience with a mentor, use that as a guide. If not, seek out a member of your organization who has a reputation as a great mentor, and ask that person to be your mentor in mentoring.

In any case, here are 10 tips to start you on the right track:

1. Know your work. Review the basics. Think back on the problems you've faced and how you dealt with them. Be prepared to answer questions about every aspect of the job.

2. Know your company. One of the main functions of a mentor is to help the trainee overcome the hurdles of unfamiliar company policies and practices. More important, as a person who has been around the organization for some time, you know the inner workings of the organization—the true power structure: company politics.

3. Get to know your protégé. To be an effective mentor, take the time to learn as much as you can about the person you are mentoring. Learn about his or her education, previous work experience, current job, and more. Learn his or her

goals, ambitions, and outside interests. Get accustomed to his or her ways of communicating in writing, verbally, and, most important, nonverbally. Paul mentored Timothy and knew his family background as well as his strength and weaknesses.

4. Learn to teach. If you have minimal experience in teaching, pick up pointers on teaching methods from the best trainers you know. Read articles and books on training techniques.

5. Learn to learn. It is essential that you keep learning—not only the latest techniques in your own field, but also developments in your industry, in the business community, and in the overall field of management.

6. Be patient. Your protégé may not pick up what you teach as rapidly as you would like.

7. Be tactful. You are not a drill sergeant training a rookie in how to survive in combat. Be kind. Be courteous. Be gentle—but be firm and let the trainee know you expect the best.

8. Don't be afraid to take risks. Give your protégé assignments that will challenge his or her capabilities. Let the person know that he or she won't succeed in all the assignments, but that the best way to grow is to take on tough jobs. We learn through failure, after all.

9. Celebrate successes. Let the trainee know you are proud of accomplishments and progress.

10. Encourage your protégé to be a mentor. The best reward you can get from being a mentor once the need for mentoring is done is having your protégé carry the process on by becoming a mentor.

Laying the Foundation for Self-Training

Not long ago, when you were trained for a job, you were considered fully trained after you mastered the skills and functions of the job. This training was augmented by occasional technology updates. But now, just a few years later, many formerly routine and highly structured jobs are dynamic and flexible.

Look at the position of "secretary." It used to connote a woman taking dictation, making appointments for her boss, answering the phone, filing papers, and acting as a gofer. Today that secretary is more of an executive assistant. He or she may prepare the agenda for a meeting, supervise clerks, compile information and write reports, and make important business decisions. It's a considerably different job. Traditional secretarial training isn't adequate preparation for this type of work.

Training must be replaced by learning. The difference between training and learning is that training is a one-way transfer of information from trainer to trainee. Learning involves not only absorbing information, but also knowing how to identify potential problems, seeking the knowledge and information that are necessary to solve problems, and creating new concepts. This process is the focus of modern training and development.

When Do You Graduate? You Don't!

"Of making many books there is no end, and much study wearies the body." (Ecclesiastes 12:12) There's so much to learn and so little time. Even if we limit what we learn to material that's relevant to our jobs, there's no way we can ever learn it all. It can make you tired just thinking about it.

But you must never weary of learning! Successful people make a practice of allocating time to keeping up with developments in their fields, no matter how busy they are.

This chapter discusses some of the things you can do to help yourself and your team members develop skills that will facilitate success both in your current jobs and in the future.

The need for training never ends. The following list of reasons can help you understand why:

- As technology changes, you have to keep up with the state of the art in your field.

- Changing circumstances in your company or industry require your team to acquire knowledge in unfamiliar areas.

- You and your team members want to strengthen your weaknesses and add to your strengths, not only to do a better job now but also to prepare for career advancement.

Wise Counsel

Too many people stop learning because they have come to believe that you go through 12 years of school and then you go to college for 4 years and then your education is over. But good education really does nothing more than prepare you to stretch and learn for the rest of your life.

—John Maxwell

Upgrading Current Job Skills

It's essential for job survival that you keep up with the latest developments in your field. You must be on the cutting edge of technology and other developments, and, as team leader, you must ensure that your team members are trained in those areas.

Sharpening the Saw

Just as good carpenters must keep their saws sharpened, good managers must keep their tools and those of their teams in tip-top condition. To do this, set up a program for yourself and for your team members to continually develop current skills and acquire additional ones. In your program, make sure to do the following:

- Identify the skills of each team member.
- Investigate new equipment and methods.
- Determine which additional skills are necessary.
- Arrange for training in these areas.

Becoming a Better Presenter

You or another member of your team may be called on to make a presentation to another team, a vendor, a customer, or even a higher-level management committee.

People who communicate well one-on-one often freeze when they have to speak to a group. Others may do well when they're talking to their own team, but they are on tenterhooks when they have to address others.

Overcoming a fear of public speaking is best accomplished by getting up and doing it. One man learned this the hard way when, almost beside himself, he hurriedly rushed through a presentation, fumbled for words, and—even though he knew the answers—was unable to respond to their questions. A manager who attended the meeting called the man aside and said, "When I had to make my first presentation, I was just as nervous as you. But I did something about it. I joined Toastmasters."

Toastmasters offers many benefits, including the opportunity to network and learn discipline, leadership skills, and how to think on your feet. Look in the phone book, or call Toastmaster's International at 1-800-993-7732 to find the chapter nearest you.

Avoiding Stumbling Blocks

When giving a presentation that includes slides, never look away from your audience to read from the slides. Keep in front of you what is on the slides so that you can refer to the information without turning away from the group.

More formal training is also available. Most universities and community colleges have public speaking courses, and public schools offer adult education programs. These classroom presentations are often videotaped and followed by critiques. Some companies retain private training organizations, such as Communispond, to run in-house programs on public speaking. Others hire experts to personally coach managers or associates in presentation preparation. For that matter, your pastor has to prepare for public speaking week after week and is an excellent resource.

Learning a Foreign Language

If your company is expanding into the global market, knowing a foreign language can be a significant asset. Although businesspeople in most countries speak English, you'd be at a great advantage if you could conduct your business in your overseas associates' native tongues.

Universities and special training centers throughout the country conduct intensive language programs. Pioneered by the U.S. State Department, these programs teach foreign languages by immersing participants in English-free environments. Some intensive programs have produced fluent speakers in various languages within three weeks, with the added benefit of cultural training.

If you have the discipline to work on your own, audio tapes and CD-ROM language programs can teach you a language. But access to a teacher and interaction with classmates are much more effective in helping you learn a new language.

Using Other Programs

A variety of training and development programs can be valuable to you and your organization. The following list shows some of the types of available programs:

- **Computer literacy.** As a team leader, you may realize that you and your team members would benefit from learning how to use new computer software. Arrange for it to happen.

- **Writing skills.** One of your team members may express an interest in improving her writing skills. If your company provides an in-house writing program, or if a local school has a similar course, send the team member to it. Your company's tuition-reimbursement plan may pay for this type of program.

- **English-language skills.** If one of your team members is a new immigrant and better English skills could increase his or her value to your team, help the person locate a suitable program.

- **Dale Carnegie course.** If the aggressive behavior of one of your team members is affecting your team's work, discuss the matter with the person and suggest this or a related program to improve his or her interpersonal relations.

Improving Your Long-Term Career Opportunities

As a result of the flattening of organizational structures, career paths that were formerly common roads to company advancement have changed radically. A young person used to be hired at an entry-level position and—with diligence, hard work, and a little luck—could move gradually up the company hierarchy. But younger counterparts entering the workforce in the twenty-first century don't have such an easy path into management. The opportunities for career growth are still available, but the road to management is much different now. As Proverbs 19:20 tells you, "be wise and get all the advice and instruction you can."

You Can Earn More Money

Although it's not the only reason, many people seek advancement for the financial reward that comes along with it. With fewer management-level positions required in a flattened structure, many companies have adjusted their compensation systems, to keep good people from quitting and to encourage good work from all team members.

That's the Spirit

Fairly compensating (and not exploiting) associates is a significant concern for the godly manager: "Look! The wages you failed to pay the workmen who mowed your fields are crying out against you. The cries of the harvesters have reached the ears of the Lord Almighty." (James 5:4)

Avoiding Stumbling Blocks

Profit-sharing plans are sometimes based on formulas so complex that employees cannot understand them and often feel frustrated.

The traditional method of paying employees was to establish base pay for a job. Employee performance was evaluated annually, and most workers received some type of raise, either a cost-of-living adjustment or a higher amount for good performance. Employees usually continued to receive this salary until their next review. However, long-term employees were paid significantly more than newer—and perhaps more productive—people, rewarding for longevity rather than for performance.

This system is being replaced in many organizations by a system of pay based on performance. All team members, regardless of tenure, are paid a base salary. Additional income comes in the form of bonuses or profit sharing, measured in some companies by a team's productivity.

A more common system is some variation of profit sharing. If a company makes a profit, all employees share in it. If they don't, no one receives a bonus. Bonuses based on profit are distributed either quarterly or annually to serve as an incentive for employees to be concerned about production, quality, waste, and customer satisfaction.

A growing form of the profit-sharing plan is an ESOP, or employee stock-ownership plan, in which employees are given the opportunity to buy shares in the company and become its true owners. Inasmuch as their employees are their own bosses, in a sense, they'll knock themselves out to satisfy customers.

Keep in mind that money is a primary reason why people seek advancement. They're satisfied as long as they have the opportunity to make as much or more money through the compensation system as they might have made by upgrading their position. As Scripture advises, "work brings profit and mere talk leads to poverty." (Proverbs 14:23)

What's Keeping You Back?

Karen's goal was to move into a leadership position within her field of marketing. Her bonuses were more than satisfactory, but that wasn't enough: She was ready for team leadership. Looking around, she noticed that her team leader and others were doing fine work and weren't about to move up, either in or out of the organization. It seemed that she was stalled in her career.

Unusual? Not at all. One of the major challenges to management is what to do with high-potential, ambitious people such as Karen who are frustrated because of a lack of upward mobility.

If you can't depend on moving step by step up the ranks in your current department or job category, you have to seek other channels that may help you reach your goal. Two successful approaches are horizontal growth and outsourcing.

Stepping Sideways on the Way Up

Karen asked her team leader and her human resources manager what she could do to move into a more responsible role. Karen met with a career counselor who told her that people able to function in several areas have more career opportunities than people who specialize in only one. Karen then took additional training courses in aspects of the business outside marketing. She was given in-house training in operations and enrolled in outside classes in computer technology and finance. She was then assigned to a cross-functional team in which she was able to interrelate with specialists in other departments.

Power Principles

If opportunities for vertical growth in your company are limited, encourage team members to acquire skills in other areas. By helping people broaden their backgrounds, you help them grow in their careers and become even more valuable to your organization.

By expanding outside her specialty, Karen participated in horizontal growth, opening several doors that may lead her to higher management spots.

The Outsource Option

Part of the restructuring process has involved outsourcing. In this process, a company subcontracts work that formerly had been performed in-house to outsiders. This allows the company to get the work done less expensively and also frees company management to concentrate on areas in which it is most competent.

Robert had been in the traffic department of his valve company for 17 years. He had moved up to the number two position in the department and reported to the vice president for distribution. One day he heard a rumor that the company was planning to eliminate the traffic department and subcontract it to an outside source.

Robert confronted his boss, who verified that the company was seriously considering that option. But he noted that the move was at least a year away and asked him to consider being the subcontractor. Because Robert knew as much about traffic as anyone in the company, the boss suggested that the company would probably become Robert's first customer and that he was then likely to get additional customers. The boss also suggested that Robert continue in his present job during the transition period but begin the process of developing his new company on his own time. In this way, he could keep things moving smoothly during the transition and be ready to begin functioning as a subcontractor immediately when the new system went into effect.

Companies planning to outsource are often happy to assist one of their own employees in becoming a subcontractor. They can then work with someone they know and trust and who knows their special problems. This process offers ambitious people a career opportunity that the company cannot provide internally.

Being an independent entrepreneur isn't for everyone. Risks are involved: You have to raise capital, lease workspace, purchase equipment, and hire staff members. And there's always a risk that it won't work out. Being your own boss may sound appealing, but it often involves longer hours and harder work than being employed by a company. In addition, you have to provide your own benefits. Contractors aren't covered by a company health plan, pension fund, or group insurance. People who feel more comfortable under a corporate umbrella may find it difficult to adapt to being in business for themselves.

Developing Team Leaders

Organizational flattening has led to the elimination of many middle-management positions and has reduced the number of layers within companies. But companies will always have a CEO, senior officers, and some middle managers. And the chief source for filling these openings will be team leaders.

Any member of a team is a potential team leader, and any team leader is a potential higher-level manager. The selection and development of team leaders can therefore be the single most important personnel activity a company undertakes.

Power Principles

If your goal is upper management, prepare for it now. Tomorrow's leaders won't be specialists—they'll have experience in several management functions and probably in more than one industry. They'll be comfortable working with computers, statistics, financial and marketing figures, and international business relations. They'll also have superior communication and public relations skills.

Identifying Potential Team Leaders

As a team leader, *you* are the most important source for identifying potential team leaders in your company. This list shows some things you should remember as you evaluate your fellow team members:

- Be a keen observer of their behavior, skills, and personalities.
- Know the goals of each person, and help each one clarify his or her career goals.
- Give each person an opportunity to lead a project, make a report, or chair a meeting.
- Encourage them to take in-house training and enroll in seminars or educational courses.
- Keep your managers aware of your team members' abilities and goals.

Preparing People for Advancement

As mentioned in Chapter 6, the restricted "management track" approach to promotion has been supplanted in most organizations by a more open attitude. To accomplish this openness, most companies have instituted management-development programs or arranged for management candidates to take outside training. Some programs begin by having employees consult with human resource specialists trained in career counseling. They can develop a plan of action to provide internal training and offer recommendations for outside schooling.

This list mentions some of the available management-development programs:

- **Special skills.** Training in areas such as statistics, computers, and specific technical fields.

- **Leadership.** Seminars and courses in psychology, applied leadership, and management techniques through either in-house or outside sources.

- **Problem-solving and decision-making.** Effective seminars and special programs such as the ones offered by Kepner-Tregoe (Princeton, New Jersey).

- **Graduate degrees** in management or a technical specialty. Tuition reimbursement.

Another way to facilitate training for yourself or team members is to purchase materials that people can study on their own time, such as audio or video tapes or CD-ROM programs (and, although it may seem old-fashioned, books).

Introducing the T & D Meeting

A team meeting for T & D (training and development) can be an easy and effective vehicle for ongoing learning—or it can be a complete waste of time. A well-thought-out training meeting can reinforce old knowledge and introduce new ideas. It can serve as a means of getting feedback about how earlier training has been applied and as a guide to what changes should be made. It also gives team members an opportunity to participate in the training process.

Prepare for training meetings by following these suggestions:

- **Set clear objectives.** State clearly the purpose of the meeting: to teach participants a new method, perfect a technique, or develop skills.

- **Choose the method to be used.** You can choose, for example, a demonstration followed by practice, a participatory workshop, or a problem-solving discussion.

- **Assemble training aids.** Use flip charts, an overhead or slide projector and slides, handouts, videos, computers, and other items to make your meetings more "user friendly."

- **Use your team members as trainers.** Take advantage of the expertise of your own team members by allowing them to lead the discussion about different aspects of the material. This technique not only provides information and expertise that you may not possess yourself, but it also leads to a more participatory atmosphere.

- **If it's helpful, arrange for backup instructors.** If your background in what's being taught isn't adequate, bring in an expert to conduct the meeting or at least to assist.

Tips for Conducting Better Training Meetings

Conducting a training meeting is a challenge to a team leader. Meetings must be informative (team members leave knowing more), exciting (they participate), and motivating (they leave wanting to apply the knowledge).

Power Principles

A team leader's role in T & D includes the following tasks:

- **Communication:** Ensure that team members are made aware of information that affects their jobs.
- **Observation:** Keep tabs on team members to identify training needs.
- **Assessment:** Measure accomplishments against goals.
- **Counseling:** Work with team members to shore up strengths and strengthen weaknesses.
- **Helping:** Train team members to develop their full potential. As believers, we're called to help everyone, whether in our business or not, to be the best they can be by serving them.

Here are some suggestions for making your meetings more effective:

- **Treat team members as knowledgeable people,** not as schoolchildren. Team members are adults who are willing to learn.
- **Avoid lecturing.** A lecture is deadly. Make the meeting a participatory experience for all who attend.
- **Don't just repeat what's in the training manual or handouts.** Team members can read it for themselves. You're there to expand, illustrate, and elucidate.
- **Prepare for each session.** You should know 10 times more about the subject than you present at the meeting.

- **Keep the sessions short.** Keep them short, but not so short that the material can't be adequately covered.

- **Use drama and humor.** Use your imagination to keep attendees awake, alert, and excited about what they're learning. Learn from your pastor's use of interesting stories and illustrations.

- **Use visual aids.** Use appropriate materials to augment what is spoken.

- **Set aside the last five minutes of each session for a summary**. Be sure to clear up any misunderstandings made obvious by participants' questions and comments. If a class lasts more than a day, spend 10 or 15 minutes summarizing the preceding day's discussion.

Part

3

Understanding and Complying with Equal Employment Laws

"Everyone must submit himself to the governing authorities, for there is no authority except that which God has established. The authorities that exist have been established by God." (Romans 13:1) God's command through the apostle Paul is about as direct and clear as one could expect—obey laws.

"Christians are responsible for being law-abiding citizens who cooperatively go about their work in society." (1 Thessalonians 4:11–12) That means you're responsible for knowing the laws so that you may abide by them.

The problem is, like all laws, the laws governing equal employment opportunity are subject to interpretation. What appears clear and simple, therefore, easily becomes vague and complex.

This part of the book looks at these laws and provides you with some suggestions and guidelines.

Chapter 10

How Equal Employment Opportunity Laws Affect Your Job

Justice in the workplace must be a profound concern for the Christian manager. Jeremiah warned, "Woe to him who builds his palace by unrighteousness, his upper rooms by injustice." (Jeremiah 22:13) So practicing justice at work is not merely a matter of legal expediency; it's a matter of choosing righteousness over sin.

But as sincere as you may be for practicing justice, its application can be tough to discern—especially when it comes to equal opportunity laws. As a manager, these laws affect most of the decisions you make about the way you hire, supervise, compensate, evaluate, and discipline personnel.

This chapter looks at these laws and discusses some of the problems that have plagued other employers and what you can do to avoid similar troubles.

What the Laws Say—An Overview

The laws governing equal employment affect every aspect of your job as a manager. This begins even before your first contact with an applicant and governs all your relations with employees, from interviewing candidates to separating from the company, and sometimes even after that.

The main federal laws that apply to equal employment are shown in this list:

- The Civil Rights Act of 1964, as amended, prohibits discrimination in employment on the basis of race, color, sex, religion, or national origin. The section of the law that covers employment (Title VII) is the Equal Employment Opportunity (EEO) law and is administered by the Equal Employment Opportunity Commission (EEOC). The EEOC also administers the Age Discrimination in Employment Act (ADEA) and the Americans with Disabilities Act (ADA).

- The Age Discrimination in Employment Act of 1967, as amended, prohibits discrimination against individuals 40 years of age or older. Some state laws cover all persons over the age of 18.

- The Americans with Disabilities Act of 1990 prohibits discrimination against people who are physically or mentally challenged.

- The Equal Pay Act of 1963 requires that an employee's gender not be considered in determining salary (equal pay for equal work).

Most states have similar laws. Because some state laws are stricter than the federal laws, make sure that you know what your state requires.

In addition, several presidential executive orders require that certain government contractors and other organizations receiving funds from the federal government institute affirmative-action programs to bring more minorities and women into the workplace (see Chapter 11).

It's important to remember that an employer isn't obligated to hire an applicant just because he or she is in a protected category (such as a person covered by the ADA). An employer can still hire another, better qualified candidate. But the employer cannot use discriminatory information to *exclude* a candidate who is otherwise most qualified for a job or promotion. Therefore, managers must avoid doing, asking, or saying anything that could possibly be construed as discriminatory.

What to Watch for When Hiring

Suppose you have an opening in your department and you ask personnel to line up some potential interviewees. To find the ideal candidate for your team, you tell personnel: "We're an aggressive, hard-hitting bunch of young guys. Get me a sharp, up-and-coming recent college grad. Most of my boys are Ivy Leaguers, so that will be an asset. And, oh yes, no hippies—get me a clean-living churchgoer."

How many violations of the equal employment laws are in that statement? Let's review it:

- **"Young guys."** Violates the prohibition of both age and sex discrimination. Avoid terms that even hint at gender, such as "guys" or "boys."

- **"Recent college grad."** "Recent" usually means "young." Specifying *or even implying* that a candidate be "young" violates the age discrimination laws.

> **Avoiding Stumbling Blocks**
> Consult an attorney to clarify any actions you take under EEO laws.

- **"Ivy Leaguer."** Discriminates against people who, because of their race or religion, have chosen to attend primarily minority colleges or religion-sponsored schools.

- **"Churchgoer."** In this context, this phrase violates the prohibition against religious discrimination. (Certain scenarios involving religious organizations are exceptions if they meet specific criteria.)

"I Didn't Know That Question Was Illegal"

Every team member must be thoroughly familiar with EEO laws because an improper question from any interviewer can lead to a formal complaint. To test yourself, take the following quiz.

The quiz answers are based on federal law, but states interpret laws differently.

What Do You Know About EEO?

To function as a manager today, you must be thoroughly familiar with various state and federal laws concerning equal employment opportunity. To help you measure your knowledge of these laws, we have prepared the following quiz. It covers only a few of the key factors in the laws, but it should give you some insight into understanding this important area.

Answer Yes or No:

On an application form or in an interview, you may ask ...

1. "What are the names of your nearest of kin?" _____

2. "Do you have a permanent immigration visa?" _____

3. "Have you ever been arrested?" _____

Indicate whether each of these help-wanted ads is legal:

4. "Management trainees: College degree; top 10 percent of class only" _____

5. "Accountant: Part-time opportunity for retiree" _____

6. "Sales: Recent college graduate preferred" _____

Other areas:

7. Companies may give tests to applicants to measure intelligence or personality as long as the publisher of the test guarantees that it is nondiscriminatory. _____

8. A company may refuse to employ applicants because they are over 70. _____

9. A company may refuse to employ an applicant if she is pregnant. _____

10. A company may ask whether a woman has small children at home. _____

A company may indicate an age preference if ...

11. It is for a training program. _____

12. Older people cannot qualify for the company pension program. _____

13. The job calls for considerable travel. _____

Miscellaneous questions:

14. A company may specify that it requires a man for a job if the job calls for travel. _____

15. A company may specify that it requires an attractive woman to greet customers and visitors. _____

1. **No.** You cannot ask about next of kin because the response may show national origin if the name differs from the applicant's. You may not even ask whom to notify in case of emergency until after you hire an applicant.

2. **Yes.** Immigration laws require that legal aliens working in the United States have a permanent immigration visa (green card).

3. **No.** Courts have ruled that because ethnic minorities are more likely than non-minorities to be arrested for minor offenses, asking about an arrest record is discriminatory. You *can* ask about convictions for felonies (see the section "Criminal Records," later in this chapter).

4. **No.** Unless you can substantiate that students from the top 10 percent of their class have performed significantly better than students with lower grades, this ad isn't job related.

5. **No.** Because most retirees are over the age of 60, specifying a "retiree" implies that persons between the ages of 40 and 60 are not welcome. The Age Discrimination in Employment Act protects persons older than 40 against discrimination because of their age.

6. **No.** The phrase "recent college graduate" implies youth. As noted, even the implication of "youth" violates the terms of the ADEA.

7. **No.** The Supreme Court, in *Griggs* vs. *Duke Power Co.*, upheld the EEOC's requirement that intelligence and personality tests must have a direct relationship to effectiveness on the job for the specific job for which the test is used. Because only the company using the test can verify this relationship, it must be validated against each company's experience.

8. **No.** The Age Discrimination in Employment Act prohibits discrimination against people who are 40 years or older. There is no top age limit.

9. **No.** Pregnant women may not be refused employment unless the work might endanger their health (such as heavy physical work or exposure to dangerous substances). Employers cannot ask an applicant whether she is pregnant or comment that the company doesn't hire pregnant women. If a pregnant woman were rejected, she would have to prove that the reason for the rejection was her pregnancy.

10. **No.** Because men aren't usually asked whether they have small children at home, it has been interpreted as a means of discriminating against women.

11. **No.** Training programs may not be limited to young people.

12. **No.** Participation in a pension program is not an acceptable reason for age discrimination.

13. **No.** Ability to travel is not related to age.

14. **No.** Ability to travel is not related to gender.

15. **No.** A company's desire to have an attractive woman as a receptionist doesn't make it a bona fide occupational qualification (see the following section).

Every manager who hires people should, ideally, score 100 percent on this quiz. Failure to comply with any one of these rules may result in complaints, investigations, hearings, and penalties.

Bona Fide Occupational Qualifications (BFOQs)

For some positions a company is permitted to specify only a man or only a woman for the job. Clear-cut reasons must exist, however, for why a person of only that gender can perform the job. In the law, these reasons are referred to as bona fide occupational qualifications, or BFOQs.

If a job calls for heavy lifting, it's legitimate to require that all applicants—both men and women—pass a weightlifting test, but you cannot specify male only. Furthermore, if a job calls for driving a forklift truck with the operator occasionally being required to do heavy lifting, you cannot accept only physically strong candidates if the lifting is only a small part of the job. For instance, a smaller woman can be capable of performing the major aspect of the work, and other people can be assigned to handle the lifting.

> **That's the Spirit**
>
> Stay within proper boundaries in terms of sharing your Christian beliefs. Don't do it on company time and don't be coercive. Most of all, witness by the way you live, even more than by the words you pray.

Suppose that you have always had an attractive woman as your receptionist and that the job is now open. Is this a BFOQ for a woman? Of course not. There's no reason that a man—with the personality for the position—cannot be just as effective.

Things I'd Like to Know but Can't Ask

The "lawful and unlawful" questions in the following table are presented as general guidelines that apply under federal laws and the laws of the strictest states. To ensure that you're in compliance with legal requirements and interpretations in any specific state, however, check with local authorities and an attorney specializing in this field.

Legal and Illegal Pre-Employment Questions

Subject	Lawful	Unlawful
Age	"Are you 18 years or older? If not, state age."	"How old are you?"
Arrest record	"Have you ever been convicted of a crime? (Give details.)"	
Birth control	None.	
Birthdate	None. (After person is employed, proof of age for insurance or other purposes may be requested.)	Requirements that applicant submit birth certificate
Birthplace	None.	
Citizenship	"Are you a citizen of the United States? If not a citizen of the United States, do you intend to become a citizen of the United States? If not a citizen of the United States, have you the legal right to remain permanently in the United States?" (See Chapter 9.) "Do you intend to remain permanently in the United States?"	
Disability	"Do you have any impairments physical, mental, or medical) that would interfere with your ability to perform the job for which you have applied?"	
Driver's	"Do you possess a valid driver's license?"	

continues

Legal and Illegal Pre-Employment Questions *(continued)*

Subject	Lawful	Unlawful
Education	Inquiry into applicant's academic, vocational, or professional education and schools attended.	None.
Experience	Inquiry into work experience.	None.
Gender	None.	Any inquiry about gender on application form or interview. "Do you wish to be addressed as Mr., Miss, Mrs., or Ms.?"
Language	Inquiry into languages applicant speaks and writes fluently.	"What is your native language?" or any inquiry into how applicant acquired ability to read, write, or speak a foreign language.
Marital status	None.	"Are you married, single, divorced, or separated?" Name or other information about spouse. Where spouse works. "How many children do you have?" "How old are your children?" "What arrangements have you made for child care when you're at work?"
Military experience	Inquiry into applicant's military experience in the Armed Forces of the United States or in a state militia. Inquiry into applicant's service in specific branch of United States Armed Forces.	Inquiry into applicant's general military experience (for example, a military unit of another country).
Name	"Have you ever worked for this company under a different name?"	Original name of applicant whose name has been changed by court order or otherwise. Maiden name of married woman.

Subject	Lawful	Unlawful
	"Is any additional information (a change of name or use of assumed name or nickname) necessary to enable a check of your work record? If yes, explain."	"Have you ever worked under a different name? State name and dates."
National origin	None.	Inquiry into applicant's lineage, ancestry, national origin, descent, parentage, or nationality. Spouse's nationality. "What is your native tongue?"
Notify in case of emergency	None.	Name and address of person to be notified in case of an emergency. (This information may be asked only after an applicant is employed.)
Organizations	Inquiry into applicant's memberships in organizations that the applicant considers relevant to ability to perform job.	"List all clubs, societies, and lodges to which you belong."
Photograph	None.	Requirement or option that applicant affix a photograph to employment form at any time before being hired.
Race or color	None.	Complexion, color of skin, coloring.
Relatives	Names of applicant's relatives other than spouse already employed by company.	Names, addresses, number, or other information concerning applicant's spouse, children, or other relatives not employed by company.
Religion or creed	None.	Inquiry into applicant's religious denomination, religious affiliations, church, parish, pastor, or religious holidays observed. Applicants may not be told "This is a Catholic (or Protestant or Jewish) organization."

> **That's the Spirit**
>
> God himself has compassion on those who are marginalized because of poverty, race, or gender. He tells the Israelites in Jeremiah 7: 5–6, "It will be merciful only if you stop your wicked thoughts and deeds and are fair to others; and if you stop exploiting foreigners, orphans, and widows."

Marriage and Children

In your desire to obtain as much information as you can about an applicant so that you'll make the right hiring decision, you may ask questions that seem important but that violate equal employment opportunity laws. The most frequently asked illegal questions relate to marriage and child care.

Suppose your team puts in a great deal of overtime—often on short notice. One applicant is a married woman (you noticed the ring on her finger), and you think that you have to know whether she has children at home. You reason that everyone knows that women with children have to pick them up at day care and can't work overtime. Another applicant isn't wearing a ring. Maybe she's divorced. Maybe she has children. You have to find out in order to know her availability, right?

Wrong, in both cases. Of course it's important to know whether applicants can work overtime on short notice, but you cannot assume their availability to work based on their responsibility for child care. In many families, the father picks up a couple's children from a day care facility. The inability to work overtime isn't limited to child-care matters. Anyone—single or married, man or woman—may not be able to work overtime for many reasons.

> **Power Principles**
>
> Steer clear of interview questions that even hint at relating to a person's race, religion, national origin, gender, age, or disabilities.

How do you deal with this issue? You tell both men and women applicants about the overtime and then ask whether that will be a problem.

Here's a good rule of thumb: Don't ask questions of one gender that you wouldn't ask of the other. "Okay," you think, "I'll ask both men and women about their children, and then I'll be safe." Nope, even this method can be interpreted as discrimination. Because while both a man and woman may give the same answer, our interpretations may differ.

Here's another good rule of thumb: Don't ask applicants any questions about marriage or family. Period. These types of questions elicit information that may be used to discriminate against women.

Criminal Records

You cannot ask applicants whether they have ever been arrested. Surprised? You shouldn't be. In our judicial system, after all, a person is innocent until proven guilty. You can ask about *convictions* for a felony; however, you cannot refuse to hire a person solely on the basis of a conviction—unless it's job related. You might, for example, disqualify an applicant from a cashier's position if he was convicted for theft, but not if he was convicted for disorderly conduct.

Lie Detector Tests

Employees handle cash or confidential information in many companies, so employers want to do their best to weed out dishonest people. For years, companies used polygraphs to screen applicants for sensitive jobs, but no more! A federal law now restricts the use of these lie detector tests.

Exempt from this law are government agencies, defense contractors, companies providing armed security guards, and a few others.

Although lie detector tests are not legal in the hiring process, they can still be used as part of an investigation for theft, embezzlement, industrial espionage, and similar offenses. Before using polygraphs for any purpose, check with your attorney to ensure compliance with all applicable federal, state, and local laws.

> **That's the Spirit**
>
> It is true that young people have a lot of energy and persistence. But older people have experience and wisdom on their side. "The glory of the young is their strength; the gray hair of the experienced is the strength of the old." (Proverbs 20:29)

> **Wise Counsel**
>
> The majority of complaints filed with the Equal Employment Opportunity Commission deal with age discrimination.

Age Discrimination

The one equal employment law that will eventually cover you and everyone else is the Age Discrimination in Employment Act. Despite common misperceptions, studies have shown that seniors are at least as productive and creative, are more reliable, and make better judgments and decisions than their younger counterparts.

Avoiding Age Discrimination in Hiring

Even though most company application forms don't ask a person's age or date of birth, and although most people omit that information from their resumés, it's still easy to guess an applicant's age range within a few years. A team leader who prefers that young people join his or her team may overlook potential members who could be of great value to the team, based solely on age.

When you interview older applicants, avoid the stereotypes that may keep you from hiring highly qualified people for the wrong reason:

- **"The applicant is overqualified."** The term "overqualified" is often a euphemism for "too old." Some people may have more know-how or experience than a job requires, but that doesn't necessarily mean that they won't be productive. Judge the person as an individual, not as a member of an age group.

- **"The applicant made more money in the last job."** If the amount of salary your company can offer is a factor in your hiring decision, discuss it with the applicant—he or she should be the one to determine whether the salary is satisfactory. And a younger person is no less likely to jump if a better paying job comes along.

- **"This person won't fit in with my team."** Make that determination on the basis of the candidate's personality, not his or her age.

Power Principles

Your team will benefit from a mix of men and women of all ages and various cultural backgrounds.

Encouraging Retirement

One method companies use to cut costs when they downsize is to compel higher-paid workers (who are most often older men and women) to retire early. Under current law, employees cannot (with a few minor exceptions) be forced to retire, no matter how old they are, unless they're not capable of performing their work.

Although forcing out older workers is illegal, companies often persuade people to retire by offering them bonuses, benefits, or other rewards. You can use this strategy as long as you do it in good faith and according to the law. Because it's a legal matter, an attorney should prepare the appropriate documents.

The Americans with Disabilities Act (ADA)

The newest and probably least understood civil rights law is the Americans with Disabilities Act (ADA). This section discusses some of the highlights of the law and how it applies to you as a manager. Your company must adhere to this law if it has 15 or more employees.

What You Can Do—What You Don't Have to Do

The ADA makes it illegal to discriminate in hiring, in job assignments, and in the treatment of employees because of a disability. Employers must make *reasonable accommodation* so that these people can perform the essential duties of their jobs.

This accommodation can vary from building access ramps for wheelchair users to providing special equipment for people who are seeing- or hearing-challenged, unless this type of accommodation is an *undue hardship* for the company. Undue hardship is usually defined in monetary terms. If an applicant who uses a wheelchair applies for a job with a small company, the cost of building an elevator or a ramp to give access to the floor on which the job is located may be a financial hardship. Because of this undue hardship, the company could reject the applicant or provide a less expensive accommodation, if possible. If the same applicant applied for a job in a more affluent company, however, it may not be considered undue hardship to do the necessary construction.

Accommodation doesn't always require expensive construction. The hypothetical examples in this list examine some other ways to meet this requirement:

- The small company you work for wants to hire as an accountant someone who uses a wheelchair, but the accounting department is on the second floor of your building. Assuming that this would qualify as an *undue hardship* for your company, why not let him work on the ground floor? His work could be brought to him. It may be an inconvenience, but it would qualify as reasonable accommodation— and it would enable you to hire this particular competent accountant.

- A highly skilled word processor operator is legally blind and walks with the aid of a white cane. She can transcribe from dictated material faster and more accurately than many sighted people can. You want to hire her, but you're concerned that in case of a fire or other emergency she would be a danger to herself and others. The accommodation you can make is to assign someone to escort her in case of an emergency.

- An assembler in a factory was badly injured in an automobile accident, and his job requires him to stand at a workbench all day. When he was ready to return to work, he was unable to stand for long periods. Accommodations should be made. A high stool could be provided so that the employee could reach the workbench without having to stand. Or his hours might be adjusted so that he could work part time on that job and do other work that didn't require standing for long portions of the day.

Must I Hire Substance Abusers?

Alcohol and drug users are considered disabled under the ADA. If a person can perform a job satisfactorily, a previous record of alcoholism or drug addiction is not reason enough to refuse hiring or to discipline or terminate a current employee. If an applicant is still addicted, however, and the addiction manifests itself in a recent history of poor attendance or poor performance, you can reject or discipline the person—not because of the addiction, but because of poor work habits.

It's legal to discipline employees who use drugs or alcohol in the workplace or who report to work under the influence of an illegal substance.

The Plus Side: Utilizing the Talents of Physically and Mentally Challenged People

Many companies have found that people who are mentally challenged can do routine and repetitious work and not be bored by it. These people are often capable of learning much more than you might expect. It takes more patience, and some tasks may have to be simplified, but trainees who master these tasks retain the skills and often improve on them. Coaches who are specially trained to work with mentally challenged people are available in many communities.

AIDS in the Workplace

You may be concerned about hiring people who have AIDS (Acquired Immuno-deficiency Syndrome) or retaining employees who have become infected with this disease. The courts have ruled that people with AIDS are covered by the ADA. If your team members see this policy as a problem, point out that all medical reports show that HIV is not spread by casual contact. To overcome this unjustified fear, follow the example of many companies that have instituted HIV/AIDS–awareness programs.

> **That's the Spirit**
>
> Some managers, in the name of Christianity, might be tempted to discriminate against those who suffer because of moral failing, such as drug users or those with AIDS. Remember that while we are called to shun sin, we must always love sinners. Furthermore, in the workplace, our responsibility is job performance. That means we have a moral obligation to obey both company policies and the law. And always, as we do so, we must be a good example by showing compassion.

Ouch! What Happens When You Violate the EEO Laws?

After hearings before state or federal agencies responsible for enforcing civil rights laws, if a company is found to be in violation of these laws, any or a combination of the following penalties may be invoked:

- If the complainant is an applicant, you may be required to hire that person with back pay to the date of the interview. If no job is available, a financial settlement will be negotiated.

- If the complainant is a discharged employee, you may have to reinstate that person with back pay from the date of termination.

- If the complainant has been denied a promotion, raise, or other benefit, you will be required to make that person "whole" (promote or give him or her the raise or benefit retroactively).

Wise Counsel

When the Civil Rights Act of 1964 was introduced in Congress, it covered only race, color, religion, and national origin. An opponent of the act added sex discrimination to it because he believed that such a radical provision would make the law unpassable. As they say, the rest is history.

- If it's a class action, in which a pattern of discrimination is found, all parties to the class action may be awarded a financial settlement (frequently hundreds of thousands of dollars).

- In addition to financial penalties, companies have been required to institute an affirmative action plan to correct imbalances of minorities or women in the organization.

- Government contractors who violate the law or executive orders may lose their contracts or be banned from receiving future contracts.

- Companies that don't comply with orders from administrative agencies can be prosecuted in the courts and fined. Executives who defy the orders can be jailed.

- Companies can be sued by persons whose rights have been violated under these laws. Damages may be awarded for lost pay. In addition, companies can incur punitive damages, which can amount to tens or even hundreds of thousand dollars.

Chapter 11

EEO Problems on the Job

"If anyone considers himself religious and yet does not keep a tight rein on his tongue, he deceives himself and his religion is worthless." (James 1:26)

For the believer, such cruelty as that which characterizes harassment or discrimination is nothing short of contrary to the nature of Christ. After all, in Christ there can be no discrimination by race, gender, or status (Galatians 3:28). So, we who claim to have Christ-like minds (Philippians 2:5) must likewise see no such distinctions—within or without the church.

But even assuming that a Christian leader will have a Christ-like attitude toward another gender or race, there still is the difficulty of managing others who have nothing resembling Christ's indiscriminate love. How to manage in these circumstances, and do so according to the law—that's the challenge of this chapter.

During the first 20 years these laws were in effect, most complaints were made in the areas of hiring and firing. Although complaints in these areas are still prevalent, more complaints over the past 10 years have involved on-the-job problems, such as sexual harassment and the treatment of minorities and women in the workplace.

Guarding Against Sexual Harassment

You've read about it in the papers; you've heard of it on television: The president of a famous cosmetics company is accused of sexually harassing 15 female employees, and the company pays the women $1.2 million in an out-of-court settlement. Then a U.S. senator is forced to resign because he is accused of sexually harassing at least 26 women who worked for him.

It's not only company presidents and senators who are accused of sexual harassment. Organizations of all sizes and types have faced charges brought against them by both female and male employees claiming sexual harassment.

Wise Counsel

In 1998, the Mitsubishi Company settled a sexual harassment suit by agreeing to pay $34 million to 360 women who had been harassed in their plant in Normal, Illinois. The women reported that they had been fondled by male workers; propositioned by supervisors; called crude, sexually explicit names; subjected to viewing pornographic graffiti on the walls, and generally mistreated. Complaints to management were ignored.

The Supreme Court Says ...

In 1998, the Supreme Court handed down two decisions related to sexual harassment. In one case, the court ruled that a company can be forced to pay damages to workers who are sexually harassed by a low-level supervisor, even if the company knew nothing of the harassment.

The court said the general rule is that companies and public employers are automatically liable for a supervisor's sexual harassment. But if sued, companies can sometimes defend themselves by proving that they have a strong policy against sexual harassment and respond quickly to complaints. They must also show that the victim failed to complain. But the burden of proof remains on the employer. The court said, in effect, that companies must prove their innocence when a worker claims sexual harassment on the job. When in doubt, the company is liable.

In another case, a Chicago woman claimed that her boss made repeated comments about sex, urged her to wear shorter skirts, and told her that she was not "loose enough" to suit him. He commented that he could make her life very hard or very easy.

After a year, the woman quit and sued the company, Burlington Industries. The U.S. Court of Appeals in Chicago held Burlington liable for the supervisor's harassment, even though no specific job consequence had been involved. The Supreme Court agreed. Although the woman had not suffered a tangible job employment action at the hands of her employer, Burlington was still subject to vicarious liability for her manager's action. To defend itself, the company would have had to prove that it had "exercised reasonable care" to prevent harassment in the workplace.

What Is Sexual Harassment?

The commonly accepted definition of sexual harassment isn't always the same as the legal definition. The legal definition of sexual harassment covers much more than just demanding sexual favors for favorable treatment on the job (naturally, these types of demands are included).

> **Power Principles**
>
> As a general rule, short of giving the traditional handshake, avoid physical contact in the work place (even with those colleagues whom you know well). Don't hug, don't pat, and certainly don't kiss. Remember the platinum rule (refer to Chapter 2): "Do unto others as they would have you do unto them."

Here's the way the courts and the EEOC define sexual harassment: Any unwelcome sexual advances or requests for sexual favors or any conduct of a sexual nature when …

- Submission is made explicitly or implicitly a term or condition of initial or continued employment.
- Submission or rejection is used as a basis of working conditions, including promotion, salary adjustment, assignment of work, or termination.
- Such conduct has the purpose or effect of substantially interfering with an individual's work environment or creates an intimidating, hostile, or offensive work environment.

But what does this mean in plain English? This section looks at how this concept works on the job.

"Explicit" Is Clear, but What's "Implicit"?

"Wait a minute," you say. "If a guy tells a woman she's attractive, *that's* harassment?" It depends on what is said and how it is said.

That's the Spirit

In 2 Corinthians 13:12, Paul tells the Christians there to greet one another with a holy kiss. This is a part of Eastern culture even today and has pure motives. But of course in our culture, and certainly in that of the workplace, this has different connotations and should be avoided.

The comment "That's an attractive dress" is different from the comment "That dress is sexy." The statement "I like your new hairdo" is acceptable, but the statement "Wearing your hair like that excites me" is not.

Consider Randy, for example. He's a "toucher." When he greets people, he grasps their hands, pats them on the back, and gives them hugs. He's also a kisser—he often pecks women on the cheek. Randy was shocked when he was called into the human resources office and told that some of the women in his department had complained. In Randy's eyes, these were acts of friendship, but to the women who complained, they were unwelcome.

That's the Spirit

Christians are called to stick out at times—to even appear foolish by the world's standards. This especially is true when it comes to the crass jokes and sexual remarks of colleagues. Even standing by and saying nothing, or worse, simply laughing it off, communicates approval, whether you intend to or not. The hard reality is that often what we fail to do is as much a compromise to our witness as overt actions—what some have called the "sin of omission."

What Is "an Intimidating, Hostile Work Environment?"

As noted in the legal definition, sexual harassment isn't limited to demands for sexual favors: It also includes conduct that creates an intimidating and hostile work environment.

As an example, Ken's team has always been all-male, and now two women have been added to his group. Some of the men resent this "intrusion" and are making life unpleasant for the female team members. The men make snide remarks, give the women incorrect information that causes them to make errors in their work, and exclude them from work-related discussions. No actions are taken that can be interpreted as "sexual" in nature, but this still qualifies as sexual harassment. The men have created a hostile work environment for the women.

As another example, Tina works in a warehouse. She is offended by the street language some of the men use. When she complains, she is told, "That's the way these guys talk. They talked this way before women worked here, and they're not going to change now. Get used to it."

Men and women alike are offended by this kind of language. Because dirty language can create "an offensive work environment," it can be legal grounds for a complaint.

If you're faced with a similar situation, talk to the people (or person) using the inappropriate language. Point out diplomatically that such behavior is unprofessional and offensive to both women and men. Inform them that such behavior can cause legal problems for them and the company. Tell them that if they continue to use street language, they will be subject to disciplinary action.

Dating, Romance, and Marriage on the Job

Cathy was perplexed. Dennis, one of her team members, had gone out a few times with Diane, who worked in another department. It had never developed into a romance, but Diane continually bugged Dennis to go out with her again. Diane went into Dennis's office several times a day to talk with him, even though Dennis didn't welcome her visits. Diane's constant attention interfered with his work. The next time Diane visited Dennis, Cathy called her aside and told her that social visits were not permissible. Diane never returned, but she continued to harass Dennis by telephoning him after work.

Is the company off the hook? Not yet. Even though the harassment has ceased on the job, because both Dennis and Diane are employed by the same company, the company has an obligation to stop Diane from bothering Dennis. Cathy should discuss the situation with Diane's manager and, if necessary, with the human resources department. If Diane continues her harassment, she should be appropriately disciplined.

Avoiding Stumbling Blocks

Why lose productive workers because of an archaic rule against spouses working at the same company? Most married couples work well together and have enough control over their own lives not to bring their personal problems into the workplace.

That's the Spirit

Priscilla and Aquila, a husband-wife team, were listed as co-workers with Paul. (See Romans 16:3).

But dating isn't always unwelcome. Many romances that start on the job end up in marriage. So, what effect does it have on your team when two associates become romantically involved? This situation can be a delicate one. Some companies, fearing that closely related people working together will lead to complications, prohibit parents, children, siblings, and spouses from working on the same team or even in positions in which they must interrelate.

> **Power Principles**
>
> Companies can protect themselves from charges of sexual harassment by clearly notifying all employees that the behavior will not be tolerated and by establishing and publicizing a procedure for dealing with complaints. This policy should be administered by a senior executive, and all complaints, if true, should be quickly investigated and corrected.

Relationships other than spousal relationships are not covered by law, and companies are left to deal with them at their own discretion. But when it comes to marriage, there are additional complexities. If a company prohibits married couples from working together and two team members marry, which one should leave the team? Some companies base their policy on rank (the lower-ranking spouse leaves) or salary (the lower-paid spouse leaves). Because the man might more likely be the higher-ranked or higher-paid employee, this policy discriminates against women. If this type of policy exists in your company, the best way to deal with it is to let the couple make the determination about which one will leave.

Discrimination based on marital status isn't expressly prohibited by federal law, but it is barred by interpretation of the sex discrimination clauses by the EEOC. Some states do have specific laws prohibiting discrimination based on marital status.

Caution: The Harasser Can Be Anyone

Suppose one of the salespeople who comes into your office makes a point of telling off-color jokes to the female workers. Some of them think he's hilarious, but you notice the look of disgust on the faces of others. Although no complaints have been made, you see that the behavior is creating an offensive work environment. The salesperson doesn't work for your company, but you still have an obligation to do something about it.

The courts have ruled that an employer is responsible for the offensive behavior of all its employees (regardless of whether they're in management) and even non-employees when the employer or its agents (that's you, in this case) know about it or should have known about it.

Speak to the person on whom that sales rep calls. Tell him or her to discuss the matter with the sales rep. If the undesirable behavior continues, the company has an obligation to tell the salesperson that it cannot continue doing business with him.

Note that your company is responsible not only when it knows about the offensive behavior but also *when it should have known* about it. This point is a delicate one. How are you supposed to know about everything that might happen? You can't, of course, but if you're observant, you should know a great deal about what transpires.

Ten Steps to Prevent Sexual Harassment Charges

Take the following steps to prevent sexual harassment charges:

1. Establish a formal policy prohibiting sexual harassment. Clearly indicate all actions that could be construed as harassment and what steps employees should take if they are harassed. Appoint a senior executive to administer the policy.

2. Publicize the policy through bulletins, articles in the company newspaper, regularly scheduled meetings, and training programs.

3. Make it easy for complainants to bring matters to the attention of management. Post notices throughout your offices detailing to whom and how employees should bring up their complaints.

4. Investigate all complaints—no matter how trivial or unjustified they appear to you. Keep written records of all findings (memos, reports of interviews, and statements from the complainant, the person accused, and witnesses).

5. Never terminate or threaten complainants or potential complainants.

6. Don't make rash decisions. Analyze all the facts. Consult your attorney (remember, the matter may wind up in court).

7. Take action. If the complaint is justified, correct the situation. Depending on the case, this may include requiring the harasser to apologize, ordering a cessation of the acts that led to the complaint, adjusting the salary, promoting or changing the working conditions of the persons who have suffered, or, in flagrant or repeated offenses, firing the harasser.

8. If the investigation finds that the complaint was not justified, explain the decision carefully and diplomatically to the complainant. Keep in mind that if he or she is not satisfied, a charge can still be filed with appropriate government agencies or brought to court.

That's the Spirit

Ephesians 5:4 says there should be no foolish talking or course jesting (off-color jokes) among believers.

9. Don't look for easy ways out. Transferring the harasser to another department may solve the immediate problem, but if the harasser repeats the offense in the new assignment, the situation is compounded.

10. If a formal complaint is made to the EEOC or a state equivalent—even if you feel that the complaint is groundless—treat it seriously.

Religion in the Workplace

The law requires you to make reasonable accommodation for a person's *religious practices*, unless doing so results in undue hardship on your company.

def·i·ni·tion

Interpret and Apply

According to the EEOC, **religious practices** include not only traditional religious beliefs, but also moral and ethical beliefs and any beliefs an individual holds "with the strength of traditional religious views."

Sometimes accommodation is easy. Suppose that your company is open seven days a week and that members of your team take turns working on Saturdays and Sundays. One of your employees, David, who is Jewish, can never work on Saturdays. Just schedule him for Sunday work. Now imagine that you're not open on Sunday but that you have other employees who can work Saturdays; then you're still required to excuse David from Saturday assignments. The other employees may resent having to work on Saturday, but the unhappiness of other employees doesn't qualify as "undue hardship."

If your business is small and there aren't enough people qualified to cover the Saturday shift, it may be considered an undue hardship, and you would not have to hire David.

Here are two other religious considerations in the workplace:

- **Observing religious holidays.** Employees must be given time off to observe their religious holidays, although you're not required to pay them for these days. These holidays are usually considered excused absences and are charged against personal or vacation days.

- **Proselytizing on company premises.** Margaret, a devout Christian, believed that she had been called to evangelize her co-workers. She continually distributed tracts and other Christian literature. At the request of team members, her team leader asked her to refrain from this behavior. She refused, claiming that the religious accommodation law and the First Amendment gave her the right to proselytize. Margaret was wrong. Just as a company can prohibit political campaigning on company premises and during working hours, it can restrict religious behavior that disturbs other people in the workplace. As a Christian manager, this is certainly awkward, particularly when the would-be evangelist is a Christian. But there is a big difference between discussing your faith in a relevant context during break and irritating people regularly—no one has ever been harassed into the kingdom of God. For that matter, doing so on company time robs the employer of work for which he or she is paying.

Wise Counsel

Paul called upon you as a believer to "lead a quiet life, to mind your own business and to work with your hands, just as we told you, so that your daily life may win the respect of outsiders." (1 Thessalonians 4:11–12) Communicating faith in the workplace can certainly be a difficult issue, but Paul's instruction and emphasis upon winning the respect of employees certainly wouldn't seem to accommodate harassment.

Other Areas of Concern

It's not illegal to require people to obey a dress code, as long as the dress code isn't discriminatory. If women are prohibited from wearing shorts, for example, but nothing is done about the men's open shirts, it would not be considered equal treatment under the law. Prohibiting a Muslim woman from dressing as prescribed by her religion or an Orthodox Jew from wearing a yarmulke would also violate the law's religious provisions.

That's the Spirit

In I Timothy 2:9, Paul says that women should be modest in their appearance. They should wear decent and appropriate clothing and not draw attention to themselves. The same can be said for men. The point is, our appearance is also an important witness to the world.

Dress codes may vary within a company, depending on the type of work that's done. Dress codes for factory and warehouse workers are different from those of office employees and employees who deal with the public.

Don't overdo it. Even IBM has dropped its requirement that male employees wear dark suits, white shirts, and blue ties, and that women wear dark dresses or suits. As long as what an employee wears is in good taste, it should be acceptable.

Avoiding Stumbling Blocks

Unless the need to speak English is job related, you cannot require employees to speak only English in the workplace. Employees who normally speak a different language and who are more comfortable conversing in their native tongue cannot be compelled to speak English among themselves.

Another area of concern is smoking: If you want to stop employees from smoking in your work area, can you do it? Several states and local communities do have laws that restrict smoking in commercial buildings. But even in areas in which no local laws apply to this situation, many companies have either prohibited smoking or restricted it to specific areas.

In some companies that have no companywide policy, team members determine the smoking policy for their work area.

The Rules on Employment of Non–U.S. Citizens

You're worried. You continually read about companies that get into trouble for hiring illegal aliens (no, not Martians—people from foreign countries). You're almost afraid to hire anyone who has a foreign accent.

Not hiring someone because of this fear is illegal. You cannot discriminate against a person because he or she isn't an American. But you must ensure that an applicant is legally allowed to work in this country.

To prevent your company from inadvertently falling afoul of immigration laws, follow these guidelines:

- **Have all new employees (not just those you suspect are foreign) fill out an I-9 form.** You can obtain copies from the Immigration and Naturalization Service. This form should be completed *after* a person is hired. When a starting date is agreed on, the employee should be advised that he or she must submit proper documentation before being put on the payroll.

- **Have new employees provide documents to prove their identity.** You have to be sure that a new employee isn't using someone else's papers. Acceptable documents include a driver's license with photo, a school ID with photo, and similar papers.

- **Have new employees provide documents to prove citizenship.** These documents include a current U.S. passport, a certificate of naturalization, a birth certificate, or a voter registration card.

- **Noncitizens must have documents that authorize employment.** The most commonly used authorization is INS Form I-551, commonly called the "green card" (it originally was green, but now it's white). The employee's photograph is laminated to the card. In other cases—for example, with students who are allowed to work while in school—different forms are acceptable.

Working with a Multicultural Workforce

If your team consists of men and women who come from different cultures, it can lead to misunderstandings and conflicts. As the team leader, you cannot ignore this situation. Your job is to make your team a smooth-running, collaborative group. It isn't always easy to change a person's deeply ingrained perceptions. Newcomers to America must be taught American ways, and Americans must learn to understand the attitudes and customs of newly arrived immigrants.

That's the Spirit

"There is neither Jew nor Greek." (Galatians 3:28) Among believers there is no distinction between race. "You are all one in Christ Jesus," Paul insists. Certainly, for Christians, the principle of embracing all races extends beyond the church; however, our only hope for true unity is found within it—in God the Son.

Digital Equipment Corporation (DEC) has set up a program to address this situation. Small groups of employees meet regularly to explore people's assumptions and stereotypes about their own culture and those they have of others. This list shows some of the goals of DEC's program:

- To identify and eliminate preconceptions and myths about new ethnic groups in the company.

- To overcome the tendency of people to fraternize with people of only their own ethnic group. All DEC employees—Americans and new immigrants—are encouraged to make friends with people from other backgrounds.

- To become aware of assumptions that cause differences in the perception of other cultures and to take steps to correct them.

A large company such as DEC has resources that you may not have available, but with a little imagination and sensitivity, any team leader can adopt a similar program.

Coping with the Language Barrier

"How can I supervise these people when they don't speak English and I don't know their language?" You've heard this complaint over and over again. It's not a new phenomenon. A hundred or more years ago, when immigrants from Europe flooded this country, their supervisors were faced with the same problem. The usual approach then—and it still works—was to find employees who did speak the language and use them as interpreters. If the non-English speakers in your company are all from the same country, you can make an effort to learn enough of their language for basic communication. And, of course, many companies today offer English as a Second Language programs for their employees.

If you're worried about your non–English-speaking employees' abilities to understand instruction manuals, just have the manuals translated. Or think about using nonverbal tools, such as demonstrations, training films, and graphics, to train people to perform manual operations.

Other Types of Cultural Diversity

Decision makers must learn to accept the reality of diversity. This calls for abandonment of traditional stereotypes about workers—who they are, what they look like, and why they work. Rather than argue over whether to support diversity, direct your energy toward designing work systems that anticipate the varying and unique qualities of a diverse workforce.

> **Wise Counsel**
>
> Stereotypes are hard to break. San Diego State University has been ordering classroom furniture for more than 100 years. Only recently has it awakened to the reality that not all students are right-handed!

Second, develop more objective methods of personnel selection and appraisal. Instead of depending on traditional interviews—which often perpetuate biases—use methods that sample the applicant's ability to do the necessary work.

In addition, formal diversity programs have been developed in a number of companies, but they tend to be concentrated in larger organizations.

Affirmative Action

Under current civil rights laws, you're not required to give women or minorities any preferential treatment in hiring or promotion. Companies with government contracts or organizations that receive federal funds, however, fall under an executive order requiring them to establish formal *affirmative action plans* (AAP).

If your firm has an AAP, it was probably drawn up by a specialist in the legal or human resources departments. You don't have to worry about the technical aspects of this plan. All you have to know is the company's goals for staffing your department with various minority groups and women so that you can make every effort to comply with them.

If your department isn't in line with the affirmative action goals of your company, you should make an effort to hire or promote a qualified person from the group in which the deficiency exists.

Interpret and Apply

Companies that have government contracts in excess of $50,000 and more than 50 employees must have a written **affirmative action plan** committed to hiring women and minorities in proportion to their representation in the community in which the firm is located.

Recent Developments in Affirmative Action

California, Texas, and a few other states have passed laws to loosen their affirmative action practices. For example, colleges and universities are no longer required to engage in affirmative action in admission of students. In addition, these laws repeal affirmative action requirements for state and municipal positions and eliminate preferential treatment of minorities in awarding contracts. Acts have been introduced in Congress to change federal affirmative action policies, but they have not passed as of this writing.

Note that none of the state laws affects the private sector. The laws and executive orders discussed throughout this chapter still hold and are strictly enforced. Any changes that are made will be widely publicized.

Power Principles

Affirmative action is required only for African Americans, Hispanics, Asians and Pacific Islanders, Native Americans, and women.

Twelve Ways to Keep Alert to Your EEO Responsibility

Go along with the spirit as well as the letter of the law.

Offer women and minorities opportunities that were previously denied to them.

Open training programs to minorities, women, and the physically challenged, and encourage them, by offering counseling and support, to complete these programs.

Discipline should be administered equitably and should be carefully documented.

Be aware of you won biases and work to overcome any influence they may have on your job decision.

Use everyone's abilities optimally. Don't base you views about a person's abilities on age, sex, or race. Judge people not on what they cannot do, but on what they *can* do.

Set realistic performance standards based on what a job really calls for. Do no specify, for example, that a job calls for heavy lifting when most of the lifting is done mechanically.

Ignore stereotypes and judge people by their individual abilities, strengths, and weaknesses.

Never use racial epithets or slurs—even in just.

Encourage all people to deal with their co-workers as human beings, whether they're black or white; men or women; physically challenged or able-bodied. Mold them into a team.

Sex life and job life must be kept separate.

Support your company's equal-employment and affirmative-action programs fully in every aspect of your job.

Follow these suggestions. They add up to good business.

"I Need Time Off to Take Care of My Mother"

Congress passed the Family and Medical Leave Act (FMLA) in 1993, requiring companies with 50 or more employees to provide eligible employees with as much as 12 weeks of unpaid leave in any 12-month period for the following reasons:

- The birth or adoption of a child, or the placement of a child for foster care
- Care of a spouse, child, or parent with a serious health condition
- The employee's own serious health condition

To be eligible, the employee must have been employed by the company for at least 12 months and must request this leave at least 30 days before the expected birth or adoption of the child. When this notification isn't possible, such as with the onset of a serious illness of a family member, employees are required to provide as much notice as possible.

Both men and women are eligible for leave under this law. If both husband and wife work for the same employer, however, the total amount of leave is limited to 12 weeks for the couple.

The key provisions of the law make these requirements:

- After the employee returns from the leave, the company must provide the employee with the same position or with a position with equivalent pay, benefits, and other conditions of employment.
- Health insurance must be continued during the leave period and must be paid for in the same manner as though the employee were still on the payroll.

As with most laws, variations apply in special circumstances. For example, Dick's mother receives outpatient chemotherapy every Tuesday, and he brings her to the hospital on Tuesday and stays with her on Wednesday while she regains her strength. Although the law primarily calls for continuing periods of leave, special arrangements can be made so that Dick can take off the time he needs. If the type of work Dick does makes this arrangement unfeasible, however, the company has the right to transfer him temporarily to another job with the same pay and benefits that enable him to take the days off.

To obtain the details about how this law may affect you or a team member, check with your human resources department, legal department, or local office of the Wage and Hour Division of the U.S. Department of Labor (listed in the U.S. government pages of most local telephone directories).

Conflict between work and family obligations has become an inevitable aspect of modern work life, often resulting in absenteeism, work interference, job turnover, and other deleterious impacts. While conflict between work and family responsibilities cannot be eliminated, family leave and other work/family policies can make it easier for America's workers to fulfill their responsibilities as parents, family members, and workers.

Part
4

Choosing Team
Members

"He who walks with the wise grows wise, but a companion of fools suffers harm." (Proverbs 13:20). Scriptures are clear that the people with whom you regularly associate and work can have a significant influence upon not only your work, but also upon you yourself. Choose your team wisely.

It's your dream to build a dream team. Team leaders rarely have the opportunity to choose a full team, but from time to time new members are added as replacements for people who have left or because the team expands.

Choosing a new team member can be one of your most important acts as a team leader. You'll probably have to live with this person for a long time, so choose carefully and systematically—and use all the tools available to help you make the best decision.

The next time you have a vacancy on your team, you have an opportunity to hire someone who will bring you closer to the team of your dreams. This part of the book provides you with the know-how to do so.

Creating Realistic Job Specs

Maybe you're seeking to fill the position of a person who has left your team, and you already have a job description for that job. The easy way is just to use this existing job description, but that's not necessarily the best way. This is your chance to review the description in light of the changes that may have developed since it was originally written. Reanalyze the job. Treat it as though it were a brand new position. In this way, the new job description will reflect the current duties and activities of the job.

Creating a Good Job Description

Job descriptions are important. Even if you know the job requirements as well as you know the back of your hand, you still need a written job description to begin the hiring process. This description serves many useful purposes:

- **Hiring.** Develop realistic job specifications that enable you to seek out candidates who can do what a job requires them to do.

- **Training.** Determine what knowledge has to be acquired and which skills have to be developed in your training program.

- **Reference.** Devise a permanent source of reference concerning job duties for team leaders and members.

- **Performance.** Create a list of standards against which performance can be measured so that everyone knows just what is expected in a job.

- **Appraisal.** When a formal performance appraisal is made (see Chapter 19), the job description becomes a touchstone against which performance can be evaluated.

That's the Spirit

"The most important feature of any organization is the quality of the staff. ... After all, staffs that just happen get happenstance results!" (John C. Maxwell, *Be a People Person*, Victor, 1994, p. 147). If God has called you into a leadership position, then his desire is for you to be proactive and purposed in all you do. This includes choosing wisely the best people you can to build the best team you can.

Jesus was selective in choosing his team (of disciples). He knew their skills and how they would realistically fit with his ministry's needs. Likewise, you had better have a clear and realistic concept of what you need.

Critics are concerned that job descriptions stifle creativity and innovation. They fear that many people will take these descriptions too literally and be unwilling to do anything not specifically listed.

How often have you asked someone to do something other than his or her routine work and heard the response, "It's not in my job description"? All job descriptions should include the phrase "and any other duties that are assigned." The inclusion of this phrase doesn't mean that you have a servant who can be ordered to do any job that pops up. It means that you can assign duties that are at least job related.

Suppose that Don finishes typing a document, and you ask him to take it to the purchasing department. He refuses and says, "I'm an executive assistant, not a messenger. Delivering papers isn't in my job description." That's true: It's not specified, but it is a related duty.

> **That's the Spirit**
>
> You should not assign duties that are not job-related. But that doesn't mean **you** can't step in to fulfill a duty that isn't yours. Obviously you can't force someone to have a servant's spirit, but Jesus insisted that your own attitude must be that of a servant. In Jesus' time, a Roman soldier could compel some people to carry his load for a mile. So, even when the demand was unjust and demeaning, Jesus still insisted, "If someone forces you to go 1 mile, go with him 2 miles." (Matthew 5:41) You need to "go the extra mile," as the saying goes. Ironically, doing so will often encourage your people to do their best.

On the other hand, if you say, "Don, you're not busy now; please wash the windows," you're out of line. Your request falls under the phrase "other duties," but it isn't a reasonable extension of his regular work.

When Refilling a Position

The backgrounds of people who have been successful or unsuccessful in performing particular jobs should be a factor in your development of a job description, but not the primary factor. For instance, one previous employee's liberal arts degree or another's political background isn't necessarily related to what the job requires. To learn the key requirements, make a thorough job analysis.

When It's a Brand New Position

Suppose you have finally persuaded your boss to authorize the hiring of an additional member of your team. This position is a new one, so what exactly do you want it to cover?

If the new position is for another person who will perform exactly the same duties as other team members, you can use the same job description and specifications used by team members. In our ever-changing business world, however, a team's functions constantly expand, and new functions and responsibilities require different talents and abilities. You have to create a completely new job analysis.

Making a Job Analysis

The specialists who perform job analyses may be industrial engineers, systems analysts, or members of your human resources staff. If your company employs these people, use them as a resource. The best people to make an analysis, however, are those closest to a job—you and your team members. A job analysis should include a written description of the responsibilities that fall within a job (job description) and a written description of the skills and background required to perform a job effectively (job specification).

Four Techniques for Developing a Job Description

To make a realistic job description, follow the guidelines in this list:

1. **Observe.** For jobs that are primarily physical in nature, watching a person perform the job will give you most of the material you need to write the description. If several people are engaged in the same type of work, observe more than one performer. Even a good observer, however, may not understand what he or she is observing. Sometimes it involves much more than meets the eye.

2. **Question the performer.** Ask the people who perform a job to describe the activities they perform. This technique fleshes out what you're observing. It's a good idea to prepare a series of questions in advance.

 **Power Principles**

Don't base your job specifications on your version of an ideal team member. That person probably exists only in your mind. Be realistic.

3. **Question the supervisor or team leader.** If you are the team leader, review in your mind how you view the position, what you believe the performer should be doing, and the standards that are acceptable. If you're analyzing a job other than the ones you supervise, speak to the team leader or supervisor to obtain that person's perspective of the position.

4. **Make it a team project.** When work is performed by a team, job descriptions cover the work of the entire team. The best way to develop a complete job description is to get your entire team into the act.

The following job description worksheet is a helpful tool. Tailor the form you use to the type of job you're analyzing.

Job Description Worksheet

Job title: _____

Reports to: _____ Dept.: _____

Duties performed:

_____

_____

_____

Equipment used: _____

_____

Skills used: _____

_____

Leadership responsibility: _____

_____

Responsibility for equipment: _____

_____

Other aspects of job: _____

_____

Special working conditions: _____

_____

Performance standards: _____

_____

Analysis made by: _____ Date: _____

The Specs: What You Seek in a Candidate

After you know just what a job entails, you can determine which qualities you seek for the person who will be assigned to do the job.

The job specifications in some situations must be rigidly followed; others may allow for some flexibility. In civil service jobs or when job specs are part of a union contract, for example, even a slight variation from job specs can have legal implications. In some technical jobs, a specific degree or certification may be mandated by company standards or to meet professional requirements. On the other hand, if there's no compelling reason for the candidate to have a specific qualification, you may deviate from the specs and accept an equivalent type of background.

> **That's the Spirit**
>
> A primary purpose of a team "is to bring people together who can compensate for one another's weaknesses as they focus on using their own gifts, skills, and talents. Jesus [himself] modeled the church on this team approach to Christian service." (Ephesians 4:11–12)
> —Myron Rush

Most job specifications include the elements in this list:

- **Education.** Does a job call for college? Advanced education? Schooling in a special skill?

- **Skills.** Must the candidate be skilled in computers? Machinery? Drafting? Statistics? Technical work? Any of the skills necessary to perform a job?

- **Work experience.** What are the type and duration of previous experience in related job functions?

- **Personal characteristics.** Does a candidate have the necessary skills in communication, interpersonal relations, and patience? Does he or she have the ability to do heavy lifting?

Eliminating Good Prospects for the Wrong Reason

One of the most common problems in determining the specifications for a job is requiring a higher level of qualifications than is really necessary, thus knocking out potentially good candidates for the wrong reason. This problem frequently occurs in these areas:

- **Education.** Suppose that certain job specs call for a college degree. Is that degree necessary? It often is, but just as often having the degree has no bearing on a person's ability to succeed in a job. Requiring a higher level of education has more disadvantages than advantages. You may attract smart and creative people, but often a job doesn't challenge them, which results in low productivity and high turnover. More important, you may turn away the best possible candidates for a position by putting the emphasis on a less important aspect of the job.

- **Duration of experience.** Your job specs may call for 10 years of experience in accounting, but why specify 10 years? No direct correlation exists between the number of years a person has worked in a field and that person's competence. Lots of people have 10 years on a job but only one year of experience. (After they've mastered the basics of the job, they plod along, never growing or learning from their experience.) Other people acquire a great deal of skill in a much shorter period.

Rather than specify a number of years, set up a list of factors that a new employee should bring to a job and state how qualified the person should be in each area.

- **Type of experience.** Another requirement often mandated by job specs is that an applicant should have experience in "our industry." Skills and job knowledge often can be acquired only in companies that do similar work. In many jobs, however, a background in other industries is just as valuable and may be even better because the new associate isn't tradition-bound and will bring to a job original and innovative concepts.

Power Principles

To ensure that the person you hire can do a job, the job specs should emphasize what you expect the applicant to have accomplished in previous jobs—not just the length of his or her experience.

- **Preferential factors.** Some job specs are essential to perform a job, but other less critical factors could add to a candidate's value to your company. In listing preferential factors, use them as extra assets and don't eliminate good people simply because they don't have those qualifications.

- **Intangible factors.** Intangible factors can be as important (or even more important) than some tangible requirements. When you list the intangible requirements for a job, however, put them in proper perspective as they relate to a job.

If a job calls for communication skills, specify exactly which communication skills you need:

for example, one-to-one communication, the ability to speak to large groups, innovative telephone sales methods, or creative letter-writing skills.

Specs Are Guidelines—Be Flexible

Job specs can be so rigid that you're unable to find anyone who meets all your requirements. Sometimes you have to make compromises. Re-examine the job specs and set priorities. Which of the specs are nonnegotiable? For example, a candidate must have a degree in electrical engineering or else the work she performs cannot be approved by the government; a candidate must be a certified public accountant or he cannot conduct audits.

Some of the specs may be important but not critical. For example, although having a CPA degree may be a good credential, an internal auditor doesn't have to be certified. Likewise, although the specs for a job require knowledge of certain software, experience with different but similar software might do almost as well.

Suppose that your specs call for sales experience, but an applicant has no job experience in selling. As a volunteer, however, she was a top fund-raiser for the local community theater. That person may be able to do the job. In seeking to fill a job, a team leader should make every effort to meet the job specs but should also have the authority to use his or her judgment to determine when deviation from the job specs is acceptable.

What Do I Have to Pay to Get the Person I Need?

Another part of job analysis involves determining the pay scale for a job. Most organizations have a formal job-classification system in which various factors are weighed to determine the value of a job. These factors include level of responsibility, contribution of a job to a company's bottom line, type of education, and training and experience necessary to perform the job. Notice that the classification applies to a job, not to the person performing a job.

def·i·ni·tion

Interpret and Apply

To attract and keep good employees, your pay scale must be at least as high as the **going rate**, which is the salary paid for similar work in your industry or community.

The pricing of a job in smaller organizations is often done haphazardly: You pay what you have to pay in order to hire the person you want. But you must have some guidelines about what a job is worth so that you don't pay more than necessary or offer too little and not attract good applicants. You have to determine the *going rate* for a job you want to fill.

This list shows some of the sources for obtaining information about the salary scales in your community or industry:

- **Trade and professional associations.** These groups conduct and publish periodic salary surveys. Members of these associations can discern how their pay scales compare with those of other companies in their field and in their geographic area. These surveys are best used when you seek salary information for specialists in your industry or profession.

That's the Spirit

Taking your time to identify the raw talent for the right position will allow the candidate to reach his or her full potential. "Do you see a man skilled in his work? He will serve before kings; he will not serve before obscure men." (Proverbs 22:29)

- **Chambers of commerce.** Some chambers of commerce publish salary surveys for their locations. Because these surveys include a variety of industries, you can obtain salary information about jobs that exist in a variety of companies, such as computer operators and clerical personnel.

- **Employment agencies.** These agencies can inform you about the going rate for any type of position in which they place employees.

- **Networking.** Ask people you know who are managers in other companies in your community or industry. They often are willing to share information about going rates.

Once you have a clear understanding of what the job is worth, you are in a position to negotiate the specific starting salary with the candidate. In some cases, there is no negotiation. You make an offer and the candidate takes it or leaves it. However, when the salary is flexible, there may be some give and take.

Most people are offered a moderate increase over their current salary when hired for a new job. Occasionally, a higher increment is warranted for improved credentials, an advanced degree, or a professional license that the candidate has received since starting the previous job.

Sometimes applicants are unrealistic about what they can obtain. It is advisable to let the applicant know the salary range early in the interviewing process. If the candidate is totally out of line, he or she will withdraw or be eliminated before additional interviewing time is wasted. If the candidate is within range and is being seriously considered, the negotiation should take place before a final offer is made.

Throughout the interview, identify what is important to the applicant—for example, opportunity to accomplish his or her goals, advancement, or creative freedom. Show how those things can be attained on the job. In your negotiation, this often will persuade a candidate to accept a lower starting salary. Emphasize not just the salary, but also the benefits package, the frequency of salary reviews, and opportunities for advancement. Most candidates do not make the decision to accept or decline an offer based on salary alone.

Choosing Your New Team Member

On many levels, Jesus' selection of his disciples is not particularly comparable to the challenge you face in interviewing and choosing team members. Clearly, being God the Son, Jesus had a capacity for understanding people in ways that we cannot approximate. Nevertheless, Jesus did choose the 12 out of thousands of options. He knew what he was looking for.

From what we know of their years following Jesus, as recounted in the Gospels, it wasn't merely expertise or even reputation that Jesus was looking for in his followers. We can only speculate what Jesus saw in Peter and Andrew, for instance, when he chose them. But there was something he discerned about them when he said, "Come, follow me. And I will make you fishers of men." (Matthew 4:19) They immediately accepted the job, and they stayed with it the rest of their lives. Jesus didn't force them—they came of their own free wills because Jesus had somehow connected with them in a way that was compelling.

You have a job opening on your team, and you've prepared the job description and job specs. Now you're ready to screen applicants. While the position you're seeking to fill is not quite comparable to being a disciple of Christ, you do have the comparable challenge of selecting from a crowd a person who is the right fit and then compelling that person to come.

This chapter explains how to recruit personnel and provides some tips for evaluating application forms and resumés, as well as conducting interviews that will give you meaningful information on which to base your hiring decisions.

Your Best Bet May Be Close By

People who already work for your company may make valuable members of your team. They may work at jobs in which they don't use their full potential, or they may be ready for new challenges. Joining your team would be a move up for them. Even if an opening isn't an immediate promotion, a lateral transfer might enable that person to take a step forward in reaching career goals.

Taking Advantage of Internal Transfers

Not every transfer is a promotion, but it's often an opportunity for someone to learn, gain experience, and take a step forward in preparing for career advancement.

Seeking to fill a team vacancy from within a company has many advantages:

- People who already work in your company know the "lay of the land." They're familiar with your company's rules and regulations, customs and culture, and practices and idiosyncrasies. Hiring these people rather than someone from outside your company saves time in orientation and minimizes the risks of dissatisfaction with your company.

- You know more about these people than you can possibly learn about outsiders. You may have worked directly with a certain person or observed him or her in action. You can get detailed and honest information about a candidate from previous supervisors and company records.

Avoiding Stumbling Blocks

The practice of restricting promotions to current employees tends to perpetuate the racial, ethnic, and gender makeup of your staff. Companies whose employees are predominantly white and male and who rarely seek outside personnel have been charged with discrimination against African Americans, other minorities, and women.

- Offering opportunities to current employees boosts morale and serves as an incentive for them to perform at their highest level.

- An important side effect is that it creates a positive image of your company in the industry and in your community. This image encourages good people to apply when jobs for outsiders do become available.

Realizing the Limitations of Promoting Only from Within

Although the advantages of internal promotion usually outweigh the limitations, there are disadvantages to consider:

- If you promote only from within, you limit the sources from which to draw candidates, and you may be restricted to promoting a person significantly less qualified than someone from outside your company.

- People who have worked in other companies bring with them new and different ideas and know-how that can benefit your team.

- Outsiders look at your activities with a fresh view, not tainted by overfamiliarity.

Searching for Applicants Internally— the Company Job Bank

You can't possibly know everyone in your company who might be qualified for a position on your team. But your human resources (HR) department should.

If a job is a promotion or a position that will give an applicant a raise in pay or more challenging work, look first at your own team. You know these women and men best, and one of them might fit the bill.

If no one on your team is suitable or interested in the position, discuss the opening with someone from your HR department. Go over the job specs with that person. He or she can suggest possible candidates from within your company.

Some companies have formalized this process by using these two methods:

1. **Job banks.** A search of this computerized list of the abilities of all employees should turn up qualified candidates for your screening.

2. **Job postings.** Many companies post the specs for available positions on bulletin boards and sometimes on electronic bulletin boards. By doing this, companies

inform women and members of minority groups, who might not have been considered, about the availability of these jobs.

Recruiting and Selection

In addition to searching for candidates within your company, the HR department may help you *recruit* from outside sources. It may advertise the opening, contact employment services, visit colleges (for trainees), or use executive recruiters (often called "headhunters") for higher-level positions.

Before the actual recruiting begins, the team leader and the members of the HR team review the job specifications to coordinate the process. As expert as HR people may be in their specialty, however, they cannot do the job alone. A team leader's knowledge of the job and the team's personality is necessary to ensure that the best-qualified candidates are sought out and considered.

Applicants, Applicants, Where Are the Applicants?

"Good help is hard to find" is one of the oldest laments in business and still one of the most valid. Today, more than ever, retaining human talent is essential for fast-growing, fast-changing companies.

Due to the high level of downsizing in the late 1980s and 1990s, the attitude of employees toward their employers has changed. Loyalty to companies was eroded when companies showed they were not loyal to their employees. Attracting and keeping employees by financial incentive alone does not work. The most desirable employees expect solid compensation, but they also look for intangible benefits, such as growth opportunities, greater flexibility and self-direction, more personal satisfaction, and a more family-friendly workplace.

Getting the HR Department to Work for You

If you work for a large organization, chances are good that you do not do your own recruiting. You work through the human resources or personnel departments.

Naturally, you're not their only client. Other team leaders and managers are bugging them to fill their jobs. In this job market, they have their hands full.

But that's no excuse, as far as you're concerned. You need to fill those vacancies. Some suggestions follow:

- Make friends with the HR staff—not just when you need people, but as a regular practice.

- Offer to help by contacting people you know.

- Offer to screen resumés from ads. This saves time and work, and you will have to look at the resumés anyway sooner or later.

- Give prompt reactions to anybody these departments refer to you. One of the biggest gripes HR people have about team leaders is their stalling on making decisions.

Routine Sources for Job Applicants

If you work for a company that does not have a human resources or personnel department, you may have to dig up candidates on your own.

Even if a job is hard to fill, don't overlook the standard sources for recruiting applicants. These are tried and true methods:

- **"Help wanted" ads.** The most usual source for hiring is ads in local newspapers for routine jobs. These ads are read by local residents who are seeking positions. However, if your job is hard to fill and you are willing to relocate people from other areas, your best bet is to advertise in trade or professional journals.

- **Private employment agencies.** Most of these agencies have files of applicants who are immediately available and can match them against your job specs, enabling you to fill the job quickly. Because they screen applicants before referring them, you will see only qualified people and won't waste time interviewing countless unqualified people. Most employment agencies require the employer to pay a fee, which may range from 10 to 20 percent of the annual salary paid to the employee, and even more for technical and management jobs.

- **Headhunters.** Executive or technical recruiters differ from employment agencies, in that they put their efforts into identifying and going after specific candidates who are usually currently employed and not actively seeking jobs. These firms usually work on higher-paying positions. Some firms charge a flat fee, paid whether they fill the job or not; most take a nonrefundable retainer and a percentage of salary if they succeed in filling the job.

- **State employment services.** All states have an employment or job service that can recommend applicants for your jobs. You certainly should list your jobs with the local office of this agency. Often state services also provide testing and other screening facilities.

- **School-affiliated employment services.** High school, college, and technical or specialized school employment services are excellent sources for recruiting people with little or no experience.

Finding Qualified People for Hard-to-Fill Jobs

Your first move is to tap the resources you have on hand—your current staff. Most people in technical and other specialized work have friends and acquaintances in their own fields. They belong to professional associations, keep up with classmates, and attend conventions. Ask them for referrals. Some companies have formal programs in which rewards are given for referrals that result in a hire. Another source is placement committees of appropriate professional associations.

Wise Counsel

Don't forget to utilize Christian job-placement organizations. There are several on the Internet, such as InterCristo. You can also network among Christians at church or in your small group or Bible study. However, if you work for a secular organization, you should not utilize these exclusively.

The Internet

If your company doesn't have a web page, get one. This is a particularly effective tool for recruiting computer specialists and other technically trained people. Several websites also carry classified ads or even match applicants with job openings (for a fee).

Job Fairs

These are sometimes organized by trade associations or private recruiting firms. They tend to specialize in specific types of jobs. Companies may rent a booth at the fair to attract the applicants, provide people with job information, and even conduct preliminary interviews. Some larger firms conduct their own job fairs.

Train People

Another approach is to hire willing and adaptable people and then train them in the particular skills required to do the jobs. Some firms seek community college, vocational school, and high school graduates who don't plan to go to college and then train them for entry-level positions.

Retirees, Part-Time, and Share-Time Workers

Some employers are asking retirees to consider working part-time; others are luring mothers of young children back to the work force early by helping with day care. Others arrange for two people to share a job, with each person working part-time. This allows for continuity in the work and gets jobs done.

Importing Foreign Workers

Employers are bringing into the United States as many foreign computer specialists and other technicians as they can. But by law, there are limits placed upon how many special visas can be issued annually to such workers during a government fiscal year, which runs from October 1 to September 30.

Filling Sales Jobs

Another area in which many companies have difficulty in finding good people is sales. Here are some ideas to help find sales staff:

- **Rethink your job specs.** Too many companies limit their search to people with experience selling the same products they sell. Unless your product is highly technical, product knowledge can be acquired rapidly.

- **Ask purchasing agents.** Buyers and purchasing agents often are impressed by sales reps who call on them. Sometimes they learn that one of these people is seeking a change. Suggest that they refer that person to you. Don't limit your requests to people who work for competitors. People who sell other products to that buyer may be good prospects for you.

- **Ask your own salespeople.** Salespeople spend a good deal of time waiting in the anterooms of buyers' offices. They get to meet and chat with other salespeople calling on that buyer. Ask them to look out for people they believe would be a good addition to your staff. You may offer them a bonus if their referrals are hired.

- **Salespeople who call on you.** You have an excellent opportunity to size up personality, approach, and technique when a salesperson makes a presentation to you. Feel out how that person perceives his or her current opportunities. Perhaps the salesperson can better meet personal long-term goals in your firm.

Resumés: Separating the Wheat from the Chaff

The resumé is the applicant's promotional piece telling you why he or she should be hired. It is not necessarily an objective recap of qualifications.

You may receive hundreds of resumes in response to an ad. It can take hours of your time to read them and make your preliminary judgments. You can save time and uncover hidden problems in resumés by following these guidelines:

- Establish some "knockout factors." These are job requirements that are absolutely essential to performing the job. They include necessary educational qualifications or licenses, or perhaps crucial experience.

- Select key aspects of the job and screen for them.

- Look for gaps in dates. Many people who have had short-duration jobs leave them out of their resumé. Some signs to watch for are:

  1. Specifying years only rather than month and year (as in 1995–1998 for one job and 1991–1995 for the previous job). It may mean only a short period of unemployment between jobs, but it may also mean that a job held for several months between the listed jobs was omitted from the resumé.

  2. Listing number of years worked instead of dates. This may also be a coverup for gaps in work history. And it could indicate the applicant's attempt to emphasize older jobs when more recent work experience is not relevant to the job being sought.

  3. Giving more space on a resumé to older positions. This may be because an applicant simply updated an old resumé instead of creating a new one—which could be a sign of laziness. Or, it may just mean that the more recent jobs were of lesser pertinence than previous ones.

  4. Overemphasis on education for experienced applicants. If a person is out of school five or more years, the resumé should primarily cover work experience.

None of these is necessarily a knockout factor; the list simply suggests further exploration in the interview.

All Candidates Should Complete an Application Form

Except when applying for the most routine jobs, most applicants provide resumés of their background and experience. In addition, most companies require all applicants to complete an application form.

You may wonder why an application form is necessary when you have a resumé. You need it! As pointed out already, resumés are an applicant's sales pitch—designed to make you want to hire him or her. A resumé can hide undesirable aspects of a person's background or overplay positive factors. An application form provides you with the information *you* need to know, not what the applicant wants you to know.

Because all the information requested on the application form is the same for all applicants, it complies with the equal employment opportunity laws. In addition, it helps you compare applicants' backgrounds when you make your hiring decision. Make sure that all applicants complete the form, even if they provide a detailed resumé.

Be sure to study an application to get a better idea about a candidate's background before you call the person in for an interview.

Like every aspect of the hiring process, an application form must comply with equal employment laws. In today's litigious society, you would think that most companies would be conscious of this situation and have these forms reviewed carefully by legal experts. I'm amazed that even now—30 years after the EEO laws went into effect—I see application forms that ask for age, marital status, number of children, dates of schooling (which can identify age), and other illegal questions.

The following sample application form is typical of those used by many companies. You have to use the form your company provides, of course, but if you plan to revise it, this sample may give you some guidelines. In addition to the questions asked in the sample, companies often add questions that are of particular concern to them. Remember that the form should meet your needs while complying with appropriate laws. (The terms of employment and other matters mentioned at the end of the employment application are discussed in Chapter 22.)

Application for Employment

Date: _____

Name: _____ Social Security number: _____

Address: _____

City, State, ZIP: _____ Phone: _____

Position sought: _____ Salary desired: _____

EDUCATION

Level: _____ School/location: _____ Course: _____

Number of years: _____ Degree or diploma: _____

College: _____

Other: _____

_____

EMPLOYMENT RECORD

1. Company/Address: _____

   Dates: _____ Salary: _____ Supervisor: _____

   Duties: _____

   _____

   _____

   Reason for leaving: _____

   _____

2. Company/Address: _____

   Dates: _____ Salary: _____ Supervisor: _____

   Duties: _____

   _____

   _____

   Reason for leaving: _____

   _____

3. Company/Address: _____

   Dates: _____ Salary: _____ Supervisor: _____

   Duties: _____

   _____

   _____

   Reason for leaving: _____

   _____

How were you referred to this company? _____

Are you 18 Years of age or older? _____

If you're hired, can you provide written evidence that you are authorized to work in the United States? _____

Is there any other name under which you have worked that we would need in order to check your work record? (If so, please provide.) _____

APPLICANT'S STATEMENT

I understand that the employer follows an "employment at will" policy, in that I or the employer may terminate my employment at any time or for any reason consistent with applicable federal and state laws. This employment-at-will policy cannot be changed verbally or in writing unless authorized specifically by the president or executive vice president of this company. I understand that this application is not a contract of employment. I understand that the federal government prohibits the employment of unauthorized aliens; all persons hired must provide satisfactory proof of employment authorization and identity. Failure to submit such proof will result in denial of employment.

I understand that the employer may investigate my work and personal history and verify all information given on this application, on related papers, and in interviews. I hereby authorize all individuals, schools, and firms named therein, except my current employer (if so noted), to provide any information requested about me and hereby release them from all liability for damage in providing this information.

I certify that all the statements in this form and other information provided by me in applying for this position are true and understand that any falsification or willful omission shall be sufficient cause for dismissal or refusal of employment.

Signed _____

Preparing for an Interview

Too often you have a pleasant interview with an applicant and learn little more than basic information. An interview shouldn't consist of just a casual conversation: You should be prepared to ask questions that enable you to judge an applicant's qualifications and give you insight into that person's strengths and limitations as they apply to the job.

To ensure that you get the information you want, make a list of pertinent questions *before* you meet with a candidate:

- **Review the job description.** Prepare questions that bring out an applicant's background and experience in the functions of that job.

- **Review the job specifications.** Prepare questions to help you evaluate whether an applicant's background and skills conform with what you're seeking.

- **Review a person's application (if available) and resumé.** Some of the information you need may be gleaned from these documents. Prepare questions that expand on what's in those documents.

Questions You Should Ask

Structure interviews so that you don't forget to ask important questions. You usually should explore the five areas in this list:

Avoiding Stumbling Blocks

When you use a list of questions, don't stick only to the questions on the list. Listen to the answers—not only to what an applicant says, but also, more important, to what he or she does *not* say. Follow up with probing questions to elicit more detailed information.

1. **Education.** Does an applicant have the requisite educational requirements or other background that would provide the necessary technical know-how?

2. **Experience.** Inquire about the type and length of pertinent experience. Ask not only "What did you do?" but also "How did you do it?" You can determine from an applicant's answers whether he or she has the type of experience that's necessary for a job.

3. **Accomplishments.** It's important to learn what an applicant has done to make him or her stand out from other qualified candidates.

4. **Skills.** Learn the special skills an applicant can bring to a job.

5. **Personal characteristics.** The job specifications should indicate the personal characteristics necessary for doing a job. During an interview, try to identify, in addition to these characteristics, other personality factors that may affect the applicant's compatibility with you and your team members.

The following list of interview questions can guide you in preparing the questions you want to ask a job candidate. Questions similar to these, tailored to the job involved, can provide a great deal of meaningful information.

Interview Questions

Work experience

(Add specific questions to determine job knowledge and experience in various aspects of the job for which you are interviewing.)

Describe your current responsibilities and duties.

How do you spend an average day?

How did you change the content of you job from when you started it until now?

Discuss some of the problems you encountered on the job.

What do you consider to be your primary accomplishment in your current job (or previous jobs)?

Qualifications other than work experience (helpful questions for applicants with no direct work experience)

How do you view the job for which you are applying?

What in your background particularly qualifies you to do this job?

If you were to be hired, in which areas could you contribute immediately?

In which areas would you need additional training?

In what way has your education and training prepared you for this job?

Weaknesses

Which aspects of your previous job did you do best?

In which areas did you need help or guidance from you boss?

In which areas have your supervisors complimented you?

continues

---

continued

Motivation

Why did you choose a career in this area?

What do you seek in a job?

What's your long-term career objective?

How do you plan to reach this goal?

Of all the aspects of your last job (or jobs), which did you like most? Least?

What kind of position do you see yourself in five years from now?

What are you looking for in this job that you're not getting from your current job?

Stability

What were you reasons for leaving each previous job?

Why are you seeking a job now?

What were your original career goals?

How have these goals changed over the years?

Resourcefulness

Describe some of the more difficult problems you have encountered in your work.

How did you solve those problems?

To whom did you go to for counsel when you couldn't handle a problem yourself?

What's your greatest disappointment so far in your life?

In what way did this disappointment change your life?

Working with Others

On what teams or committees have you served?

What was your function on this team (or committee)?

What did you contribute to the team's activities?

How much of your work did you do on your won? As part of a team?

Which aspect did you enjoy more? Why?

What did you like best about working on a team? Least?

Conducting an Interview

Most job applicants are nervous or at least somewhat ill at ease in an interview. To make an interview go smoothly, put applicants at ease. Welcome them with a friendly greeting and a smile and a handshake, and offer a cup of coffee or tea. Introduce yourself and begin the discussion with a noncontroversial comment or question based on something from an applicant's background. For example, starting out with, "I noticed that you graduated from Thomas Tech; two of our team members are Thomas grads," ensures an applicant that you're familiar with the school and are favorably inclined toward its alumni. After you "break the ice," you're ready to move into the crux of an interview and ask the questions you have prepared.

When the Applicant Is Holding Back

Have you ever had the feeling that an applicant is hiding something or is reluctant to talk about a particular aspect of his or her background? These three techniques may help open these closed doors:

1. **Use silence.** Most people cannot tolerate silence. If you don't respond after someone has finished talking, he or she will usually fill in the gap by adding something more. ("I have experience in mass-mailing software." [Silence.] "I did it once.")

2. **Make nondirective comments.** Ask open-ended questions, such as, "Tell me about your computer background." An applicant will tell you whatever he or she feels is an appropriate response. Rather than comment on the answer, respond with "Uh-huh" or "Yes," or just nod. This technique encourages applicants to continue talking without giving any hints about what you're seeking to learn.

That's the Spirit

As Christians, God gives us the spiritual gift of discernment. Pray during your interview that you can discern the applicant's abilities and character as he or she responds.

3. **Probing questions.** Sometimes applicants can be vague or evasive in answering questions. Probe for more detail, as in this example:

Interviewer: For what type of purchases did you have authority to make final decisions?

Applicant: Well, I know a great deal about valves.

Interviewer: Did you buy the valves?

Applicant: I recommended which valves to buy.

Interviewer: Who actually negotiated the deal?

Applicant: My boss.

When the Applicant Tries to Dominate the Interview

Have you ever interviewed an applicant who tried to take over the interview? Instead of answering the questions asked, he tells you what he wants you to hear. Sometimes an applicant will rephrase your question so he can answer it in a manner favorable to him. For example, you say, "Tell me about your experience selling to department store buyers." The response: "Department store buyers are not as difficult to deal with as small store owners." The interviewee then expands on his experience in that market.

To overcome this, when the applicant pauses for breath, quickly interrupt by rephrasing the original question. "I see your point, but what experience have you had selling to department store buyers?"

Avoiding Stumbling Blocks

After an applicant has answered your question, *wait five seconds before asking your next question.* You'll be amazed at how many people add new information—positive or negative—to their original response.

When the Applicant Is Too Nervous

Applicants are often nervous at an interview. Once you help someone overcome the initial nervousness, you may find that you have an excellent candidate. Here are some suggestions to help:

- Don't start with a challenge: "What makes you think you can handle this job?" Put the applicant at ease. If he appears nervous, start with some small talk.

  Pick something nonthreatening from the application to comment on.

- With young applicants out for a first job, be supportive. Comment about their nervousness. Once it is verbalized, it often dissipates. Reinforce it with a comment such as, "I can understand why you are nervous. When I applied for my first job, I was more nervous than you are now."

* Comment on an accomplishment. "I note that you had a 3.7 GPA. That's commendable." Compliments inspire confidence.

Take Notes—But Not Too Many

One of my most embarrassing moments occurred in my first job as a personnel manager. I interviewed several candidates for a sales position. Two of the candidates had similar backgrounds but quite different personalities. You guessed it—I mixed them up and made the job offer over the telephone to the wrong person. Was I shocked when he walked in the following Monday morning!

It's difficult to remember every person you interview. It's advantageous to record the highlights of an interview and, of course, the decision you made. Taking detailed notes during an interview is neither possible nor desirable; doing so often makes an applicant "freeze up," and if you're busy writing, you can't fully listen.

Take brief notes during an interview. Write down enough information that you'll be able to remember who each applicant is, what makes one applicant different from another, and how each applicant measures up to the job specs for which that person has been interviewed.

In the case of investigations by federal or state EEO agencies, good records of an interview can be your most important defense tool. When records are unavailable or inadequate, the hearing officer bases judgment on the company's word against the word of an applicant. Complete and consistent records give your company solid evidence in case of an investigation.

As mentioned in Chapter 4, in the section "Five Tricks to Make You a Better Listener," take brief notes during an interview and write your report immediately afterward. If it helps, use the following sample interview summary sheet.

Interview Summary Sheet

Applicant: _____ Date: _____

Position applied for: _____ Interviewer: _____

Job factors[1]: _____

Applicant's background[2]: _____ Qualification rating[3] _____

Duties: _____

_____

_____

Responsibilities: _____

_____

_____

Skills required: _____

_____

_____

Education required[4]: _____

  Specific types: _____

  _____

  _____

  Educational achievement: _____

  _____

  _____

Other job factors: _____

_____

[1]Job factors should be listed from job specifications for position applicant applies for.

[2]Interviewer should note aspects of applicant's background that apply to each factor in this column.

[3]Rate applicant on a scale of 1 to 5 for how closely background fits specifications.

[4]Level of education means how much schooling completed; type represents subjects related to job taken; achievement represents grades or standing.

Personal factors	Comments	Qualification rating
Growth in career	_____	
Accomplishments	_____	

Intangibles

    Appearance _____

    Motivation _____

    Resourcefulness _____

    Stability _____

    Leadership _____

    Creativity _____

Mental alertness _____

Energy level _____

Communication skills _____

Self-confidence _____

Comments

Applicant's strengths: _____

Applicant's limitations: _____

[ ] Applicant should be hired.

    Recommendation for additional training: _____

[ ] Applicant should not be hired.

Reasons: _____

Additional comments: _____

_____

_____

Telling the Applicant About the Job

An important part of the interviewing process occurs when you tell applicants about your company and the job. An interviewer is often so ill at ease about asking questions that he or she spends most of an interview describing the duties of the job, the advantages of working in the company, and the benefits the company offers.

Power Principles

Don't give applicants a copy of the job description before an interview. Their responses to your questions will be influenced by what they have read.

There's a time during interviews to divulge this information—*after* you have obtained enough information about an applicant to determine whether he or she is a viable candidate.

At the beginning of an interview, briefly indicate the type of job you're seeking to fill. If you give away too many details about a job, a shrewd applicant will tailor the answers to your questions to fit what you have described.

The best way to give information about job duties is to ask questions about an applicant's qualifications in that area before you give information:

Interviewer: How much of your previous job involved copy writing?

Applicant: Most of it. I spent at least two thirds of my time writing copy.

Interviewer: Great, writing copy is a major part of this job.

Listening to and Evaluating the Applicant's Questions

Applicants usually have questions about your company and the job. Give them a chance to ask those questions. You should not only answer them, but also listen for the type of questions they ask.

Questions about job content, opportunities to use their own initiative, how your team operates, and what types of training and development are offered show positive qualities in an applicant. But if the questions concern primarily vacations, pay raises, or personal benefits, an applicant may not be as job oriented as you want.

Chapter 14

Making the Hiring Decision

Judges 7 recounts how God called Gideon to lead an army up against the Midianites, who had been oppressing the Israelites. But God wanted to trim down the Israelite troops to a lean fighting machine, so he instructed Gideon to call for a voluntary downsizing. Two thirds of the army left. (verse 3) In the next three verses, we read how God used rather unconventional methods to weed out the crowd until the army was reduced from 32,000 to 300. (verse 6)

While God's methods for selecting his team (as it were) may not be directly applicable to what you face in choosing an applicant, there is a fundamental premise here that is utterly relevant: Gideon relied upon God, and he communicated regularly with God throughout the entire process. Even when the outcome seemed beyond unreasonable, Gideon trusted God.

You may not hear the voice of God telling you to select an employee based upon how he or she drinks from the water cooler (see verse 5), but you are in a far better position than Gideon on one important factor: God's Holy Spirit is dwelling within you. So as you face the tough choices of choosing one person over another, prayerfully seek God's guidance. He'll make it clear in his good time.

Clearly, an interview is one of the primary tools for choosing new employees, but it's not the only one. An interview is subjective, after all. This chapter discusses several other approaches to learning as much as possible about applicants before making your hiring decision.

Two Heads Are Better Than One

Hiring an employee can be the most important decision you make as a manager. The people who comprise your team can make or break your endeavors. No matter how good you may be as an interviewer, it's a good idea to seek the reaction of others before making a final decision.

In larger companies, a member of the human resources (HR) department has preliminary interviews with applicants. Only people who meet basic job requirements are referred to you.

If you're the only person who has interviewed an applicant, it's a good idea to have the applicant interviewed by at least one other person. You may have missed important facts or been overly influenced by one factor or another.

The person (or persons) asked to be the other interviewer should have the appropriate type of job and level of responsibility. To interview for jobs of a technical or specialized nature, a person with expertise in that area is the best choice. If a new employee will work closely with another department, the opinion of the manager of that department will be meaningful. Many companies require finalists to be interviewed by the manager at the next higher level (your boss).

Because the team concept involves every member of a team, the process of choosing members for your team should be a team activity. however, it's not necessary for every team member to conduct a full interview. Each team member should concentrate on the part of an applicant's background in which she or he has the greatest knowledge.

How Good Are Employment Tests?

Except for performance tests (discussed later in this chapter), it's unlikely that you will have to administer tests. Nevertheless, the most frequently used tests in hiring are shown in this list:

- **Intelligence tests.** Like the IQ tests used in schools, these measure the ability to learn. They vary from brief, simple exercises (such as Wunderlich tests) that can be administered by people with little training to highly sophisticated tests that must be administered by someone who has a Ph.D. in psychology.

That's the Spirit

The Book of Proverbs states that there is wisdom in many counselors. Besides praying about candidates, ask others who work with you what they think about a particular job candidate.

That's the Spirit

The example in Acts 6:1–7 in which the early church selected seven caregivers illustrates not only delegation, but also the wisdom of involving all relevant parties in the selection process.

- **Aptitude tests.** These are designed to determine the potential of candidates in specific areas, such as mechanical ability, clerical skills, and sales potential. Such tests are helpful in screening inexperienced people to determine whether they have the aptitude in the type of work for which you plan to train them.

- **Performance tests.** These measure how well candidates can do the job for which they apply. Examples include operating a lathe, entering data into a computer, writing advertising copy, and proofreading manuscripts. When job performance cannot be tested directly, written or oral tests on job knowledge may be used. Keep in mind, though, that you must give the same test in the same manner to all applicants. In a word-processing test, for example, you must always use the same material, the same type of computer, and the same time frame.

- **Personality tests.** These are designed to identify personality characteristics. They vary from the *Reader's Digest* quickie questionnaires to highly sophisticated psychological evaluations. A great deal of controversy exists over the value of these types of tests.

"Wow! What a Background!" Is It True?

Applicants can tell you anything they want about their experiences. How do you know whether they're telling the truth? A reference check is one of the oldest approaches to verifying a background, but is it reliable? Former employers unfortunately don't always tell the whole truth about candidates. They may be reluctant to make negative statements, either because they don't want to prevent the person from working—as long it's not for them—or because they fear that they might be sued. Still, a reference check is virtually your only source of verification.

Unless your company policy requires that reference checks be made by the human resources department, it's better for you, the team leader, to do it. You have more insight into your team's needs and can ask follow-up questions that will help you determine whether the applicant's background fits your needs. Be careful to follow the same guidelines in asking questions of the reference as you do in interviewing applicants. Just as you can't ask an applicant whether she has young children, for example, you can't attempt to get this type of information from the reference.

Getting Useful Information from a Reference

Most reference checks are made by telephone. To make the best of a difficult situation, you must carefully plan the reference check and use diplomacy in conducting it.

The following list provides some tips for making a reference check:

- **Call an applicant's immediate supervisor.** Try to avoid speaking to the company's HR staff members. The only information they usually have is what's on file. An immediate supervisor can give you details about exactly how that person worked, in addition to his or her personality factors and other significant traits.

> **Avoiding Stumbling Blocks**
>
> Never tell an applicant that he or she is hired "subject to a reference check." If the references are good but you choose another candidate, an applicant will assume that you received a poor reference. Also, never tell a person that the reason for rejection is a poor reference. Reference information should be treated as confidential.

- **Begin your conversation with a friendly greeting.** Then ask whether the employer can verify some information about the applicant. Most people don't mind verifying data. Ask a few verification questions about date of employment, job title, and other items from the application.

- **Diplomatically shift to a question that requires a substantive answer,** but not one that calls for opinion. Respond with a comment about the answer, as in this example:

    You: Tell me about her duties in dealing with customers.

Supervisor: [Gives details of the applicant's work.]

You: That's very important in the job she is seeking because she'll be on the phone with customers much of the time.

By commenting about what you have learned, you make the interchange a conversation—not an interrogation. You're making telephone friends with the former supervisor. You're building up a relationship that will make him or her more likely to give opinions about an applicant's work performance, attitudes, and other valuable information.

"All I Can Tell You Is That She Worked Here"

If a former employer refuses outright to answer a question, don't push. Point out that you understand any reluctance. Make the comment, "I'm sure that you would want to have as much information as possible about a candidate if you were considering someone." Then ask another question (but don't repeat the same one). After the responses begin coming more freely, you can return to the original question, preferably using different words.

What happens if you believe that the person you're speaking to is holding something back? What if you sense from the person's voice that he or she is hesitating in providing answers or you detect a vagueness that says you're not getting the full story? Here's one way to handle this situation:

> "Mr. Controller, I appreciate your taking the time to talk to me about Alice Accountant. The job we have is very important to our firm, and we cannot afford to make a mistake. Are there any special problems we might face if we hire Alice?"

Here's another approach:

> "Ivan will need some special training for this job. Can you point out any areas to which we should give particular attention?"

From the answer you receive, you may pick up some information about Ivan's weaknesses.

Wise Counsel

One of the great paradoxes in reference checking is that companies want full information about prospective employees from former employers, but because of their fear of being sued for defamation, they give little more than basic information about former employees—usually dates of employment and job title.

Dealing with Poor References

Suppose that everything about Carlos seems fine, and in your judgment he's just right for the job. When you call his previous employer, however, you get a bad reference. What do you do?

If you have received good reports from Carlos' other references, it's likely that the poor reference was based on a personality conflict or some other factor unrelated to his work. Contact other people in the company who are familiar with his work and get their input.

Anna's previous boss might tell you that she was a sloppy worker. Check it out some more. Anna's ex-boss may have been a perfectionist who isn't satisfied with anyone.

When you contact Pierre's former supervisor, you hear a diatribe about how awful he was. But you notice that he had held that job for eight years. If he had been that bad, why did he work there for such a long time? Maybe his ex-boss resents his leaving and is taking revenge.

That's the Spirit

Good references say more at times than even solid performances. As Proverbs 22:1 says, "a good name is more desirable than great riches."

Knowing When to Check References

Check references after you believe that an applicant has a reasonable chance of being hired. If you have more than one finalist, check each one before making a final decision. A reference check may turn up information that suggests a need for additional inquiry. Arrange another interview to explore it.

It's Decision Time

The interviewing is over, and references have been checked. You now have to decide which candidate to hire. Before you make a decision, review the evaluations of all the people who interviewed applicants. Discuss the finalists with your team members and others who may have interviewed them.

One way you can help make a fair comparison of candidates is by making a comparison chart similar to the final selection worksheet that follows.

Final Selection Worksheet Job specifications				
	Education	Experience	Intangibles	Other
Applicant 1 Name:				
Applicant 2 Name:				
Applicant 3 Name:				
Applicant 4 Name:				

That's the Spirit

Beware of favoring a candidate simply because you believe he or she is a Christian. It is naïve to think that a person's faith will guarantee superior motivation and commitment. Sadly, being a Christian doesn't make one a good worker. Instead, keep your focus on comparing traits for traits and skills for skills, and consider potential faith as icing on an otherwise identical cake. God has placed you in a position of responsibility to the company, and showing favoritism even toward God's people is being a poor witness.

Avoiding Decision-Making Boo-Boos

In making a hiring decision, avoid letting irrelevant or insignificant factors influence you. These factors include the following:

- **Overemphasizing appearance.** Although neatness and grooming are good indicators of personal work habits, good looks are too often overemphasized in employment. This bias has resulted in companies rejecting well-qualified men and women in favor or their more physically attractive competitors.

- **Giving preference to people like you.** You may subconsciously favor people who attended the same school you did, who come from similar ethnic backgrounds, or who travel in the same circles as you.

- **Succumbing to the *"halo effect."*** Because one quality of an applicant is outstanding, you overlook that person's faults or attribute unwarranted assets to him or her. Because Sheila's test score in computer know-how is the highest you've ever seen, for example, you're so impressed that you offer her a job. Only later do you learn that she doesn't qualify in several other key aspects of the job.

> **def·i·ni·tion**
> **Interpret and Apply**
>
> When you assume that an applicant is outstanding in everything because of just one outstanding characteristic, you're applying the **halo effect** (you crown that person with a "halo"). The opposite is the "pitchfork effect," in which one trait is so poor that you assume that the person is all bad.

In making a final decision, carefully compare each candidate's background against the job specs and against other candidates' backgrounds. Look at the whole person—you have to live with your choice for a long time.

Making a Job Offer

You've made your decision, and now you're ready to offer the job to the lucky candidate. A few problems remain, however: negotiating salary, getting an applicant's acceptance, and arranging a starting date. In addition, you must notify the people you interviewed and didn't hire.

In most companies, the final offer, including salary, is handled by the HR department. Usually the HR representative discusses directly with the applicant the starting salary, benefits, and other facets of employment. If you're responsible for making the offer in your company, however, it's a good idea to check all the arrangements with your boss and the HR department to avoid misunderstandings.

Avoiding Stumbling Blocks

Don't let your anxiety over losing a desirable candidate tempt you to make an informal offer—for example, promising a higher salary or other condition of employment that hasn't been approved—with the hope that you can persuade management to agree to it. Failure to get this agreement will not only cause the applicant to reject the offer, but it can also lead to legal action against your company.

Finalizing the Salary Range

Most companies set starting salaries for a job category. You may have a narrow range of flexibility, depending on an applicant's background. But when jobs are difficult to fill and in many higher-level positions, starting salaries are negotiable.

In these types of jobs, an applicant is usually interviewed by several people, and you may have several interviews with finalists before making a decision. You should obtain a general idea of each person's salary demands early in this process so that you don't waste time even considering people whose salary requirements are way out of line.

Companies traditionally have used an applicant's salary history as the basis for their offer. Ten or 15 percent higher than a person's current salary is considered a reasonable offer. Because women usually have been paid less than men, however, basing the salary you offer on current earnings isn't always equitable. If the job had been offered to a man and you would have paid a higher rate based on his salary history, you should offer a woman the same rate, even though her earnings record has been lower.

In negotiating salary, keep in mind what you pay currently employed people for doing similar work. Offering a new person considerably more than that amount can cause serious morale problems.

There are exceptions to this rule, of course. Some applicants have capabilities that you believe would be of great value to your company, and to attract these people, you may have to pay considerably more than your current top rate. Some companies create special job categories to accommodate this situation. Others pay only what they must and hope that it won't lead to lower morale.

Some companies believe that they can avoid these types of problems by prohibiting their employees from discussing salary. This "code of silence" is virtually impossible to enforce. People talk—and discussion of who makes how much constitutes great gossip. Salary alone isn't a total compensation package. It includes vacations, benefits, frequency of salary reviews, and incentive programs. All these items should be clearly explained.

Even when the salary you offer is less than what an applicant wants, you may persuade that person to take your offer by pointing out how the job will enable him or her to use creativity, engage in work of special interest, and reach career goals.

Arranging for Medical Exams

Many companies require applicants to take a medical exam before they can be put on the payroll. You cannot reject an applicant on the basis of a medical exam, however, unless you can show that the reason for the rejection is job related. If a job calls for heavy lifting, for example, and the candidate has a heart condition that could be aggravated by that task, it's a legitimate reason for rejection. On the other hand, rejecting an applicant not because of the work, but because it will increase your insurance premiums isn't acceptable.

Most companies arrange for a medical exam close to a person's starting date. They tell applicants that they are hired subject to passing a physical exam. If this is your policy, caution applicants not to give notice to a current employer until after examination results have been received.

Congratulations—You Made an Offer!

Although most companies make job offers orally (no letter and no written agreement), an oral offer is just as binding as a written one. Some companies supplement an oral offer with a letter of confirmation so that there are no misunderstandings about the terms.

> **Wise Counsel**
>
> The Americans with Disabilities Act (ADA) requires that a medical exam be given only after the decision to hire is made. The exam cannot be used as a reason for rejection unless a person's physical condition is a job-related issue and your company cannot make accommodations for it.

> **Avoiding Stumbling Blocks**
>
> When you make a job offer, the salary should be stated by pay period, not on an annual basis. Rather than specifying $30,000 per year, specify $1,250 per half month. Why? Because some courts have ruled that if you quote a salary on an annual basis, you're guaranteeing the job for one year.

A job offer letter should contain these elements:

- Title of job (a copy of the job description should be attached)
- Starting date
- Salary, including an explanation of incentive programs
- Benefits (may be in the form of a brochure given to all new employees)
- Working hours, location of job, and other working conditions
- If pertinent, deadline for acceptance of offer

Employment Contracts—Yes or No?

In some situations, the employer and employee sign a formal contract. These contracts are often used with senior management people and key professional, sales, or technical personnel. Although it's rare, some organizations require all salaried employees to sign a contract—often little more than a formalized letter of agreement concerning conditions of employment. In many cases, they're designed for the benefit of the company, and the employee has little room for negotiation.

One of the most controversial areas covered in contracts is the so-called "restrictive covenant," which prohibits employees who leave the company from working for a competitor for a specified period of time. Although these types of contracts have been challenged, they're usually enforceable if they're limited in scope. Prohibiting a person from working for a competitor for a limited period of time, for example, is more likely to be upheld than prohibiting that type of employment forever.

Senior managers and other employees who hold critical positions in a company and applicants who have skills that are in great demand have the clout to negotiate personal contracts with the company. Any contract, whether it's generic or a negotiated special agreement, should be drawn up by a qualified attorney, not by HR or other managers.

When the Applicant Is Unsure About Accepting the Job

You've narrowed the field, and your first choice is Hillary. Early in the interview process, you explored her salary requirements, and your offer is in line. At least that's what you thought. Now Hillary demurs. "If I stay where I am, I'll get a raise in a few months that will bring me above that salary. You'll have to do better."

Power Principles

Don't notify unsuccessful applicants until shortly after your new employee starts work. If the chosen candidate changes his or her mind and doesn't start, you can go back to some of the others without having them feel that they were a second choice.

Having received approval of the hire at the salary offered, you have to either reject it, persuade her to take the job by selling her on other advantages, or go back to your boss for approval of the higher rate. What you do depends on many factors. Do you have other viable candidates for the job? If not, how urgent is it to fill the job? Determine whether you can legitimately offer other benefits, such as a salary review in six months, opportunity for special training in an area in which she is particularly interested, or other perks. Think over the situation carefully, and discuss it with your manager. *Caution:* Don't make commitments you don't have the authority to honor.

If you and your boss agree that Hillary should still be considered for the position, determine how much above your original offer you're willing to pay and what else you can offer. The meeting with Hillary should take place as soon as possible after you and your manager have determined the maximum deal you can offer. With this in mind, you can negotiate with her and try to reach an acceptable arrangement. If this new negotiation doesn't lead to agreement, discontinue the discussion and seek another candidate. Continuing to haggle over terms of employment is frustrating and keeps you from concentrating on your other duties. You're better off using your time and energy to find another candidate.

Countering a Counteroffer

You've knocked yourself out reading resumés, interviewing applicants, and comparing candidates. You make the decision that you'll hire Tom, and he accepts your offer. A week later, he calls to tell you that he has changed his mind: When he told his boss that he was leaving, his boss made him a counteroffer.

Frustrating? You bet. To minimize the possibility of a counteroffer, assume that any currently employed candidate will get one. At the time you make your offer, bring it up and make these points:

- You know that he has done a great job in his present company. You also realize that when he notifies his company that he's planning to leave, his company will undoubtedly make him a counteroffer. Why? Because they need him now.

- If his company truly appreciated his work, it wouldn't have waited until he got another job offer to give him a raise. You would have given it to him long ago.

- Many people who have accepted counteroffers from a current employer find out that, after the pressure is off the company, the company will train or hire someone else and let him go.

- He will always be looked on as a disloyal person who threatened to leave just to get more money.

- When the time for a raise comes around again, guess whose salary has already been "adjusted"?

When these arguments are used, the number of people who accept counteroffers decreases significantly.

Rejecting the Also-Rans

Some companies just assume that if applicants don't get an offer, they will realize that they were rejected. It's not only courteous but also good business practice to notify the men and women you have interviewed that the job has been filled.

You don't have to tell applicants why they didn't get the job. Explanations can lead to misunderstandings and even litigation. The most diplomatic approach is just to state that the background of another candidate was closer to your needs.

Part 5

Motivating Your Team for Peak Performance

Look at the word *motivation*. Two other words that begin with the same letters are *motion* and *motor*. We call the motors in our cars "internal combustion engines," and each of us has inside us a combusting engine that keeps us in motion.

As a team leader, your job is to provide your team members with the fuel that will start their "motors" and keep them going. Of course, not all motors take the same kind of fuel to keep them running; so it is with people. What motivates one person may not work for another. To help your team move forward, you have to know what kind of fuel to feed each of your members, how and when to use it, and what reaction you can expect. Tough job? Sure, but it's worth the effort.

As you read the five chapters in this part of the book, you'll pick up some ideas to help you fuel those motors. Remember to keep an open mind—some of the things you think are great motivators may not motivate anyone at all.

Chapter 15

Get a Move On!

Many Scripture passages call God's children to unity (for example, see Romans 15:5–6). Unless you are managing in the context of a formal ministry, these passages arguably don't apply directly to your circumstances. Nevertheless, there's a general principle that is universal: Effectiveness is multiplied many times over when individuals band together to accomplish a common goal. As team leader, regardless of the context, you should be seeking to meld your team members into a cohesive group and develop their motivation to accomplish the team's goals.

Successful team leaders develop such team spirit by getting to know their team members as individuals. Team members are humans, not robots; each has strengths and weaknesses, a personal agenda, and a style of working. Understanding each team member as an individual is the first step to building a team.

This chapter teaches you how to build a cohesive team and explores how functioning as a team leader differs from being a boss. And because many companies aren't organized on a team basis, the chapter also provides suggestions for applying several principles of team management to nonteam environments.

Different Strokes for Different Folks

Remember the rocket ship analogy in Chapter 1? You learned that to get a rocket ship off the ground, each of its components must be in A-1 shape and must then be coordinated to work interactively. Your team is the rocket ship, its members are the components, and you are the rocket engineer.

Your first job as team leader is to help your associates perform at top capacity. The best way to begin is to learn about each person as an individual.

> **That's the Spirit**
>
> The skill of empathy should be a natural fit for believers. If being a believer means having the mind of Christ (as in Philippians 2), then the evidence for such a mentality must be in placing others' interests above your own. Such humility is at the core of empathy—it's getting out of yourself and putting yourself in the shoes of another. That's how you truly get to know someone.

Maybe you think that all you have to know about your associates is the quality of their work. Wrong! Knowing the members of your team requires more than just knowing their job skills; that's an important part, but it's only a part of their total makeup. Learn what's important to your team members—their ambitions and goals, their families, their special concerns. In other words, learn what makes them tick.

> **Power Principles**
>
> Nothing stops the progress of an organization more quickly than leaders failing to listen. Like hardening of the arteries, hardening of the categories and a closed mind will destroy a leader's credibility.
>
> —Hans Finzel

Learning Each Team Member's M.O.

We all have M.O.s (*modus operandi,* or methods of operation) in the way we do our work and the way we live our lives. Study the way each of your team members operates, and you'll discover an M.O. You might notice that one team member always ponders a subject before commenting on it; another might reread everything she has worked on several times before starting new work.

Psychologists don't call them M.O.s; they call them "patterns of behavior." Whatever you call M.O.s, being aware of them helps you understand people and enables you to work with them more effectively.

That's the Spirit

Managers who are good listeners are rare but in great demand. As James 1:19 urges, "Be quick to listen, slow to speak and slow to become angry." Those are great words for people in leadership roles.

You don't want to be nosy? Okay, you don't have to *ask* personal questions directly. By observing and listening, you can learn a great deal about your colleagues. Listen when they speak to you: Listen to what they say, and listen to what they *don't* say. Listen when they speak to others. By listening, you can learn about the things that are important to each of them and the hot buttons that can turn them on or off. But you need help. The following Know Your Team worksheet can be an informal reminder of each of your team members' traits.

Know-Your-Team Worksheet

Member's name: _____

Position: _____ Date employed: _____

Spouse's name: _____

Children's names and ages: _____

_____

Hobbies: _____

_____

Other interests: _____

_____

Schools and colleges: _____

_____

Other pertinent information: _____

_____

_____

Behavioral traits: _____

Hot buttons: _____

Making Your Team Self-Motivating

When team members understand their new roles, you, as their team leader, must ensure that they begin to apply the team system to the job.

Let's look at how Denise did this. As sales manager, her primary role was to train, motivate, and lead her sales force. Denise discovered that, as in most companies, without the support of the office staff to obtain and maintain sales production, sales were lost and customers were dissatisfied.

The salespeople in Denise's company were paid on a commission basis. They worked long and hard to acquire and keep accounts. They were often frustrated, however, when the order department stalled deliveries or when indifferent customer service representatives antagonized customers.

Hot Buttons

Denise reorganized the department into five teams, each covering a different sales region. Each team was made up of salespeople, order clerks, and customer service personnel.

Denise followed the TEAM acrostic for successful team development:

Train: All sales and support people were brought in for a weekend training program in which the new system was explained. By using group discussions, case studies, and role playing, team members were trained to work together.

Enthusiasm: To make any team activity work, team members must not only accept an idea, but also greet it enthusiastically. Denise borrowed some sports techniques and had her teams choose names and colors. She announced contests between teams, with awards ranging from group dinners to cash bonuses.

Assurance: The teams were assured that they would not be left entirely on their own. Denise promised them that she and other company executives would give them as much informational and financial support as necessary, but she stressed that the team members' ideas and concepts were the keys to success.

Measurement: Specific goals were set for each team for the first period. After that, the teams were instructed to set their own goals. Each team would be measured by how close it came to achieving its goals; individuals would be evaluated not only by their own performance, but also by how they worked as a team.

The compensation system was changed so that instead of rewarding a salesperson alone for making a sale, bonuses and raises for all team members would be based on the team's productivity.

At the end of the first year, sales had increased significantly. Rather than stalling orders because of minor errors in an order form, order clerks went to the source and corrected the errors immediately. Secretaries and customer service reps went out of their way to help customers, and morale in the department grew immensely.

You, the team leader, must keep all members of your team aware of what is expected from them individually and from the team as a whole. Team members should be kept aware at all times of how the team is doing. In this way, they monitor their own activities (Chapter 19 discusses this subject in detail).

Power Principles

Andrew Carnegie once said, "It marks a big step in your development when you realize that other people can help you do a better job than you could do alone."

—John Maxwell

Watch Out for These Hurdles

So all you have to do is convert from traditional methods to team concepts, and all your troubles are over, right? Of course not. Teams aren't a cure-all for management problems. They have their share of problems.

One common problem occurs when team members don't carry their weight and other members have to work harder to maintain their team's productivity. Team members can often overcome this situation themselves by working with the weaker person to help him or her develop the necessary skills.

When Your Company Doesn't Use Teams

Your company may not be organized in teams. No matter what the organizational structure is, you can use any and all of the techniques in this chapter and in this book to improve your effectiveness as a manager. Just glean the suggested techniques and begin applying them today!

After José returned from an intensive management-development weekend at the university, he bubbled with enthusiasm about all the ideas he had learned. He wanted to take immediate action in restructuring his department into teams.

"Whoa," José's boss said. "Take it easy. We're not making any radical changes now." Rather than give up in frustration, José asked himself, "What can I do within the current structure to adapt what I've learned?"

Within the first few weeks, José made the following changes in his management style:

- He became more available to the people who reported to him. Rather than brush off their questions and suggestions, he took time to listen, evaluate, and respond to them.

- He overcame the temptation to make every decision. When asked for a decision, he threw the decision back to the person requesting it. "What do *you* think should be done?"

- Rather than plan the work himself when new assignments were received, he enlisted the participation of his entire team.

- He encouraged team members to acquire skills outside their usual work duties. He used cross-training and assigned them work that required interaction with others in the group with different types of work.

- He conferred with all team members to ensure that they understood what was expected of them on the job and how their performance would be evaluated. Most important, he learned more about their individual goals and aspirations.

- He periodically held exciting and productive department meetings.

- He visited suppliers and subcontractors, and invited them to visit the company and attend meetings.

That's the Spirit

Much about good management resembles discipleship. You're mentoring people so that they might grow into powerfully effective members of the body—the team.

The payoff didn't take long. Within a few months, productivity increased, quality improved, and cooperation and collaboration among the group members became a way of life. All this happened without changing the structure.

These changes in management style will go a long way in enhancing your Christian witness to your team because all of these points relate to the types of things Jesus would do on the job.

Money Talks, but Does It Talk Loud Enough?

Jesus was constantly engaging people over questions of money, especially in terms of how it controls lives. On one occasion, when challenged by someone in the crowd to settle a dispute over an inheritance, Jesus gave a foreboding caution and then an intriguing clarification: "Watch out! Be on your guard against all kinds of greed; a man's life does not consist in the abundance of his possessions." (Luke 12:15)

Jesus knew full well the powerful motivational force in money; yet he also insisted that money alone is not sufficient. A man's life consists of much more than mere financial gain. What's interesting is that most of your colleagues sense that, even if they're not believers. Humanity generally wants to believe that there has to be more to life.

While you may not be able to offer in your work context the level of meaning to life that Jesus was focusing upon (that is, a right relationship with God), the general principle still applies to how you manage people: Money is an important motivation, but don't fool yourself into believing it's all there is. After all, one's life does not consist in the mere abundance of his or her possessions.

Motivators vs. Satisfiers

Remember that the word *motivate* begins with the same three letters as *motion*. Motivation is the incentive to get into motion, or making things move.

Interpret and Apply

When managers **motivate,** they stimulate people to exert more effort, energy, and enthusiasm in whatever they're doing. The best motivation is self-motivation. Your job as a team leader is to provide a climate in which self-motivation flourishes.

A team of behavioral scientists led by Frederick Herzberg studied what people want from their jobs and classified the results in two categories:

- **Satisfiers (also called maintenance factors).** Factors that people require from a job to justify minimum effort. These factors include working conditions, money, and benefits. When employees are satisfied, however, just giving them more of the same factors doesn't motivate them to work harder. What most people consider motivators are really just satisfiers.

- **Motivators.** Factors that stimulate people to put out more energy, effort, and enthusiasm in their job.

To see how this concept works on the job, suppose that you work in a less-than-adequate facility in which lighting is poor, ventilation is inadequate, and space is tight. Productivity, of course, is low.

In a few months, your company moves to new quarters, with excellent lighting and air-conditioning and lots of space. Productivity shoots up.

The company CEO is elated. He says to the board of directors, "I've found the solution to high productivity: If you give people better working conditions, they'll produce more, so I'm going to make the working conditions even better." He hires an interior designer, has new carpet installed, hangs paintings on the walls, and places plants around the office. The employees are delighted. It's a pleasure to work in these surroundings—but productivity doesn't increase at all.

Why not? People seek a level of satisfaction in their job—in this case, reasonably good working conditions. When the working environment was made acceptable, employees were satisfied, and it showed up in their productivity. After the conditions met their level of satisfaction, however, adding enhancements didn't motivate them.

So What Does This Have to Do with Money?

Money, like working conditions, is a satisfier. You might assume that offering more money generates higher productivity. And you're probably right—for most people, but not for everyone. Incentive programs, in which people are given an opportunity to earn more money by producing more, are part of many company compensation plans. They work for some people, but not for others.

The sales department is a good example. Because salespeople usually work on a commission (or incentive) basis, they're in the enviable position of rarely having to ask for a raise. If salespeople want to earn more money, all they have to do is work harder or smarter and make as much money as they want. Therefore, all salespeople are very rich. Right? Wrong!

Why doesn't this logic work? Sales managers have complained about this problem from the beginning of time. They say, "We have an excellent incentive program, and the money is there for our sales staff. All they have to do is reach out—and they don't. Why not?"

You have to delve deep into the human psyche for an answer. We all set personal salary levels, consciously or subconsciously, at which we are satisfied. Until we reach that point, money does motivate us, but after that—no more. *This level varies significantly from person to person.*

Some people set this point very high, and money is a major motivator to them; others are content at lower levels. It doesn't mean that they don't want their annual raise or bonus, but if obtaining the extra money requires special effort or inconvenience, you can forget it.

The opportunity to earn money motivates everyone to the point that they are satisfied. Some people are content at lower levels. As long as they can meet their basic needs, other things are more important to them than money. To other people, this point is very high, and they "knock themselves out" to keep making more money.

Power Principles

Team leaders rarely have control over the basic satisfiers: working conditions, salary scale, employee benefits, and the like. These factors are set by company policy. But managers do have the opportunity to use the real motivators: job satisfaction, recognition, and the opportunity for team members to achieve successes.

By learning as much as you can about your associates, you learn about their interests, goals, and lifestyles, as well as the level of income at which they're satisfied. Offering the opportunity to make more money as an incentive to people who don't care about it is futile. You have to find other ways to motivate them.

Money as a Scorecard

When Barney was asked about his current quarter-of-a-million-dollar salary, he said, "I don't need the money. But my salary is the score that measures my success."

You don't have to be in the six-figure income bracket to consider your pay a scorecard. A merit raise given to a trainee or a production bonus paid to a factory worker is as much of a boost to that person's ego as is the money.

As discussed in the next several chapters, intangible motivators are extremely effective, and supplementing them with a reward in the form of a raise or bonus adds to their value. It's not only the money itself, but also the tangible acknowledgment of success.

When a person is promoted to a higher-level position, the increase in pay that goes with the promotion is a recognition of the person's new status. Being in a higher salary classification adds prestige both within and outside a company.

That's the Spirit

We Christians can sometimes be prone to look down upon rewards for good work. We like to think that there should be nobler motives than personal gain. And perhaps a valid argument can be made for a truly Christian motive being selfless, as was Christ's. Nevertheless, the good servants in the Parable of the Talents were rewarded, believers are ensured rewards in heaven for faithful works, and Christ himself has been raised up to sit at the right hand of God in all glory. Christlike motives are indeed selfless, but likewise a godly response to good work is one that lavishes rewards.

Benefits: Motivators or Satisfiers?

Benefits are important in today's companies. Most companies provide some form of health insurance, life insurance, pension, and other benefits to their employees. In fact, the benefits package is one of the factors that potential employees seek when they evaluate a job offer—but it isn't a motivator. (Have you ever known anyone who worked harder because the company introduced a dental insurance program?)

Benefits are satisfiers. Good benefits attract people to work for a company, and they also keep people from quitting. (Sometimes the people you wish would quit don't.)

Wise Counsel

A happy team is not necessarily a productive team. Permissiveness and indulgence lead to carelessness and poor work. A team leader's challenge is to develop, with team members, high performance standards that challenge and motivate people.

Raises, Cost of Living Increases, and Other Adjustments

In most companies, pay raises are given as part of the performance review system (see Chapter 19); they're rarely given out otherwise. Unless specified in a union or personal contract, companies have no legal obligation to give employees raises at all. The amount of an increase, and how and when it's given, depends on each company's policy.

When people don't get as high a raise as they expect—or when they get no raise at all—it leads to low morale. Encourage any dissatisfied team members to express their concerns. If the reason a member didn't get the raise is linked to poor performance, discuss it and pledge to help that person improve enough for a raise the next time around. If the reason is a company freeze on pay increases, explain it and point out that it's a temporary situation that should be alleviated soon. (Chapter 18 shows an example of how to handle this situation.)

Old and New Incentive Pay Programs

In an economy that is moving rapidly away from mass production and manufacturing-based businesses to custom-engineered production and service-type industries, pay per piece has little value. New types of incentive programs have had to be developed. This section looks at some old and new incentive-pay plans.

Piecework

Wages based solely on the number of units produced was the primary pay plan in some industries. The harder you worked, the more money you received. However, when workers mastered their work and produced more than quotas required, companies reduced the price paid per piece to keep their overall costs down. This practice led to reduced motivation; workers would do only a fixed amount of work, which defeated the purpose of the incentive program.

As work became more complex, paying by the piece was no longer practical. Because of pressure from unions and, later, minimum wage laws, hourly rates replaced piecework rates in most industries.

Quota Pay Plans

Industrial engineers in the age of scientific management (the 1920s and 1930s) introduced a variation of piecework. Quotas were established based on time and motion studies; people who exceeded quotas received extra pay. These types of programs still exist and, when properly designed and administered, succeed in motivating some people. Even the best of these programs, however, have problems.

I saw how this system worked during the summers of my college years, when I worked in a factory that used it. Because I was young and energetic and wanted to make money to pay my college expenses, I quickly mastered the work and soon exceeded my quota. One of my co-workers pulled me aside and said, "Hey, you're working too fast. You're making it bad for the rest of us." His implication was that if I didn't slow down, he would break my arm.

Incentive Programs for Salespeople

Most sales jobs are paid on an incentive basis. Salespeople earn a commission or bonus based on their personal sales. This system should motivate people to knock themselves out to make more sales, but, as mentioned, it doesn't always happen. Many salespeople set limits for themselves; when they reach that limit, they "take it easy."

Another adverse result of sales incentives is that they encourage salespeople to concentrate on getting new business, often at the expense of neglecting established customers.

Effective sales incentive programs present challenges to the sales reps. They may vary from one period to another. Depending on what the company wants to emphasize at any one time, the incentives may be based on one or more of the following:

- Number of new accounts opened
- Increase in volume of sales of current accounts
- Sales of specific items the company is pushing
- Introduction of new markets (for instance, the company has sold primarily to drug stores and now is promoting sales to food outlets)

Stock Options

Stock option programs provide opportunity for employees to benefit from an increase in the company's stock value. They are given "rights" to purchase the stock at a price that is lower than the market price. They do not pay for the "rights." Let's say that the stock is currently selling for $25 per share. The employees are given options to buy the stock at $22 per share. If they exercise the options immediately, they make a $3 per share profit. However, the incentive is to keep the options until the stock rises higher in value. A year later, the stock is selling at $40 per share. Employees can still purchase it at $22 and sell it immediately for a profit of $18.

The incentive is to help the company grow through employee efforts, which will result in higher stock prices.

The downside is that stock price does not necessarily reflect the company's profitability. Other market factors may influence it. If the stock falls below the option price, the rights are worthless.

Stock options usually are not offered to lower-level employees, but often they are a major part of executives' compensation packages.

Avoiding Stumbling Blocks

The benefits and incentive-pay area is complex and regulated by federal and state laws. Few companies have the expertise to institute effective programs without professional help. Some of the top consultants in this field are Towers Perrin (245 Park Avenue, New York, NY 10167), Hay Group (229 S. 18th Street, Philadelphia, PA 19103), and Hewitt Associates (40 Highland Avenue, Rowayton, CT 06853).

Hiring Bonuses

If you follow sports, you know all about signing bonuses. The sports pages are always reporting about fabulous amounts of money paid not only to top players, but also to promising rookies just out of high school or college.

To attract hard-to-find specialists, such as computer whizzes or financial geniuses, and sometimes just to get people who qualify for high-demand positions, companies have paid hundreds and sometime thousands of dollars in signing bonuses.

Incentive Plans That Work

In our tough, competitive economy, businesses need incentive plans. Even if money isn't the only, or even the best, way to motivate people, it can play an important role. Money combined with other types of motivation enhances the value of that approach. These programs may be based on exceeding predetermined expectations, rewarding special achievements, or sharing in the company's profits.

Management by Objective (MBO)

Management by objective is used in many companies as both a management tool and an incentive program. Although there are many variations, the basic idea is that managers and associates/team members determine together the objectives and results expected for that period. After a time period is agreed on, associates work with minimum supervision to achieve the specified goals. At the end of the period, the manager and the associates compare what has been accomplished with the objectives that have been set. In some organizations, bonuses are awarded for meeting or exceeding expectations.

Special Awards for Special Achievements

Xerox is an example of a company that adds financial reward to recognition. To encourage team participation, special bonuses are given to teams that contribute ideas leading to gains in production, quality, cost savings, or profits.

A company that has instituted a total quality management (TQM) program, in which it puts special emphasis on providing high-quality products or services to customers, often augments the program by offering financial rewards based on reduction of product rejects, measurable improvements in quality, and increased customer satisfaction.

Profit Sharing

Companies use many variations of profit-sharing plans—that is, plans that distribute a portion of the company's profits to the employees. Many of these plans are informal. The executive committee or board of directors sets aside at the end of the fiscal year a certain portion of profits to be distributed among employees. Other, more formal plans follow an established formula.

In many organizations, only managerial employees are included in a profit-sharing plan; in others, all employees who have been with the company for a certain number of years are also included. In still other companies, the entire workforce gets a piece of the profits. Some profit-sharing plans are mandated by union contracts.

A number of profit-sharing programs are based on employee stock ownership. Various types of stock ownership plans are used, including programs that give stock as a bonus, programs that give employees the option to buy company stock at below market rates, and employee stock ownership programs (ESOPs), in which employees own their company.

Another financial incentive approach is open-book management, which is revolutionizing the traditional compensation system. Its goal is to get everyone in a company to focus on helping to make money.

In the old approach, bosses ran a company and employees did what they were told (or what they could get away with). This system has been replaced by empowered teams that are given all the facts and figures necessary to make decisions; they're rewarded for their successes and accept the risks of failure.

In a June 1995 article in *INC.* magazine, John Case presents these essential differences between an open-book company and a traditional business. In open-book companies …

- Every employee has access to numbers that are critical to tracking the company's performance and is given the training and tools to understand them.

- Employees learn that, whatever else they do, they must never lose sight of the goal (to move those numbers in the right direction).

- Employees have a direct stake in their company's success. If the business is profitable, they share in the profits; if it isn't, there are no profits to share.

There are many variations of open-book management. In some companies, employees are given (or can purchase) shares in their company; in others, employees *do* own their company, through employee ownership plans (ESOPs). In still other plans, ownership remains with stockholders, but the books are open and profits are shared.

<table>
<tr><td>

Wise Counsel

According to the U.S. Chamber of Commerce, the fastest-growing areas of benefits over the past five years have been day care for working parents and flexible hours.

</td><td>

The resulting employee commitment is palpable. Rather than complain and gripe, employees pitch in to solve problems. Rather than evade assignments with the plaintive excuse "It's not my job," employees seek out areas in which they can contribute. They understand why raises are frozen, realize that some of their actions have curtailed productivity rather than enhanced it, and find out what steps they can take to save their company and their jobs.

</td></tr>
</table>

Perks: The Extras That Add Up

In many companies, employees are given "freebies"—those little extras that may not seem like much but that often are significant additions to the traditional compensation package. These include the following:

- **Subsidized lunch rooms.** I recently had lunch in the cafeteria of a large insurance company. My bill for a salad, entree, coffee, and dessert was less than half of what I normally pay at a restaurant. This is a great savings for employees.
- **Coffee and ....** Many companies provide a never-empty coffee pot for employees. Often the company offers free doughnuts, bagels, or sweet rolls at break time.
- **Child care.** With both parents working in many families, child care is a major problem. Some companies have child-care facilities right on the premises or arrange for child care at nearby facilities and subsidize the cost.
- **Transportation.** Vans or buses are made available to employees to bring them to and from work. It's cheaper for the employees to use the company's transportation than to take public transportation or drive themselves.

That's the Spirit

With all the legitimate opportunities for affirming and rewarding good work, be on the guard for those evil twin sins that pop up again and again throughout Scripture: covetousness and greed.

- **Tuition.** Companies often pick up the entire bill for courses taken by employees—even if not specific to their job training. If the company doesn't pay in full, it usually subsidizes the cost of education.

- **Scholarships.** Some companies set aside college money for children of employees.

In addition, some executives, salespeople, and specialized staff may be given perks, such as company cars, membership in country clubs, generous expense accounts, subscriptions to technical and professional journals, and membership in professional associations.

Chapter 17

Recognition and Praise: Motivators That Work

"Therefore, encourage one another and build each other up, just as, in fact, you are doing." (1 Thessalonians 5:11) This theme is constant throughout almost all of Paul's epistles to the church. Apparently the human tendency to withhold encouragement was as much a problem then as it is today. Be it in the church or in the workplace, humans desperately crave affirmation and yet are not offering it to one another.

If you are going to be about the business of being transformed into Christ's image, then you must appreciate that Christ was an encourager and affirmer. Whether it be in your church or in your office, you also have been called and equipped (by God's Holy Spirit) to affirm others. Indeed, there is probably no more potent witness to Christ than having a reputation as a positive affirmer.

As pointed out in Chapter 16, many things formerly considered motivators by conventional wisdom are now seen as *satisfiers*. Money, benefits, and working conditions are important in keeping employees satisfied, but they don't motivate people beyond a certain point. Some of the things that do motivate people are …

- Recognition of each team member's individuality.
- Praise for achievements, to stimulate continued achievements.
- Opportunity for growth.
- Challenge (remotivating when motivation has been lost).
- Job satisfaction—an ideal motivator.

This chapter discusses the first two items; Chapter 18 discusses the other three.

People Crave Recognition

Humans crave recognition. People like to know that others know who they are, what they want, and what they believe. Recognition begins when you learn and use people's names. Of course, you know the names of the men and women on your team, but you will be coordinating work with other teams, with internal and external suppliers, with subcontractors, and with customers. Everyone has a name. Learn them. Use them. It's your first step in recognizing each person's individuality.

> **Power Principles**
>
> The key to encouragement is in knowing what gives people courage, what spurs them on to action. Too many of us take pleasure in discouraging people by pointing out their mistakes and getting excited about their failures rather than focusing on their strengths and getting excited about their possibilities.
>
> —John Maxwell

> **That's the Spirit**
>
> "With the tongue we praise our Lord and Father, and with it we curse men, who have been made in God's likeness. ... My brothers, this should not be." (James 3:9, 11)

Providing Positive Reinforcement

An autocratic boss continually criticizes, condemns, complains, and never forgets negative performance. But he or she always takes good performance for granted. Team leaders today are more aware of the value of reinforcing the good things their associates do than of harping on their mistakes and inefficiencies.

When people hear continual criticism, they begin to feel stupid, inferior, and resentful. Even though someone may have done something that wasn't satisfactory, your objective is to correct the behavior, not to make the person feel bad.

Rather than bawl out an associate for doing something wrong, quietly tell the person, "You're making some progress in the work, but we still have a long way to go. Let me show you some ways to do it more rapidly." When the work does improve, make a big fuss over it.

Showing That You Care

Just as you have a life outside the company, so does every member of your team. A job is an important part of our lives, but many aspects of life may be of greater importance: health, family, and outside interests, for example. Show sincere interest in a team member's total person.

Virginia, the head teller of a savings and loan association in Wichita, Kansas, makes a point of welcoming back associates who have been on vacation or out for several days because of illness. She asks them about their vacation or the state of their health, and she brings them up-to-date on company news. She makes them feel that she missed them—and it comes across sincerely because she really did miss them.

Wise Counsel

"I find little resemblance between the people I work with and the Energizer Bunny. ... [Humans] need to have their emotional batteries charged often. I have seen in some quarters in my own organization an attitude that people are expected to work out of a sense of duty—so why bother with this thing called praise? ... I find that a pretty sad argument against lavishing your co-workers with affirmation and recognition for a job well done."

—Hans Finzel

Everyone Needs Praise, but What If They Don't Deserve It?

Humans thrive on praise. Although all of us require praise to help make us feel good about ourselves, you can't praise people indiscriminately: Praise should be reserved for accomplishments that are worthy of special acknowledgment. So how do you deal with people who never do anything particularly praiseworthy?

Maria faced this situation in her team of word processors. Several marginal operators had the attitude that, as long as they met their quotas, they were doing okay. So she gave one of the operators a special assignment for which no production quota had been set. When the job was completed, Maria praised the employee's fine work. She followed this practice with all new assignments and eventually had the opportunity to sincerely praise each of the word processors.

Looking for Praiseworthy Situations

Sometimes you tend to look for things to criticize rather than things to compliment. Douglas, a regional supervisor for a California supermarket chain, made regular visits to the eight stores under his jurisdiction. He reported that when he went into a store he looked for *problems*. He criticized store managers for the way products were displayed, for slow-moving checkout lines, and for anything else he noticed. "That's my job," he said, "to make sure that everything is being done correctly."

As you can guess, everyone working in the stores dreaded his visits. Douglas's boss acknowledged to him the importance of improving what was wrong but also pointed out that, because the store exceeded sales volume forecasts and kept costs down, the managers needed to hear compliments on their success.

Although it wasn't easy, Douglas followed his boss's advice. Within a few months, store managers looked forward to his visits. They began to share new ideas and seek his counsel about store issues. Clerks and other store staffers soon overcame their fear of the "big boss" and welcomed his comments and suggestions.

> **That's the Spirit**
>
> No matter how faithless and slow to learn the disciples were at times, Jesus was always finding occasion to praise and encourage. When we'd be inclined to roll our eyes and say, "It's about time," Jesus was praising God for the work he was accomplishing in them.

Five Tips for Effective Praise

As important as praise is in motivating people, it doesn't always work. Some supervisors praise every minor activity, diminishing the value of praise for real accomplishments. Others deliver praise in such a way that it seems phony. To make your praise more meaningful, follow these suggestions:

1. **Don't overdo it.** Praise is sweet. Candy is sweet, too, but the more you eat, the less sweet each piece becomes—and you may get a stomachache. Too much

praise reduces the benefit that's derived from each bit of praise; if it's overdone, it loses its value altogether.

2. **Be sincere.** You can't fake sincerity. You must truly believe that what you're praising your associate for is actually commendable. If you don't believe it yourself, neither will your associate.

3. **Be specific about the reason for your praise.** Rather than saying, "Great job!" it's much better to say, "The report you submitted on the XYZ matter helped me to clearly understand the complexities of the issue."

4. **Ask for your team members' advice.** Nothing is more flattering than to be asked for advice about how to handle a situation. This approach can backfire, though, if you don't *take* the advice. If you have to reject advice, ask people questions about their inadequate answers until *they* see the error of their ways; then reissue good advice (refer to Chapter 5).

Wise Counsel

> When I must criticize somebody, I do it orally; when I praise somebody, I put it in writing.
>
> —Lee Iacocca

5. **Publicize praise.** Just as a reprimand should always be given in private, praising should be done (whenever possible) in public. Sometimes the matter for which praise is given is a private issue, but it's more often appropriate to let your entire team in on the praise. If other team members are aware of the praise you give a colleague, it spurs them to work for similar recognition.

In some cases, praise for significant accomplishments is extremely public, such as when it's given at meetings or company events.

Give Them Something They Can Keep

Telling people that you appreciate what they've done is a great idea, but writing it is even more effective. The aura of oral praise fades away; a letter or even a brief note endures.

You don't have to spend much money, and it doesn't take much time. This section looks at how writing the praise has worked for some team leaders.

Writing Thank-You Cards

At the A&G Merchandising Company in Wilmington, Delaware, team leaders are given packets of "thank-you" cards on which the words *Thank You* are printed in beautiful script on the front flap and the inside of the card is left blank. Whenever someone does something worthy of special recognition, that person's team leader writes a note on one of the cards detailing the special accomplishment and congratulating the employee for achieving it. The recipients cherish the cards and show them to friends and family.

Something to Hang on the Wall

No matter what type of award you give employees—large or small (cash, merchandise, tickets to a show or sports event, or a trip to a resort)—it's worth spending a few more dollars to include a certificate or plaque. Employees love to hang these mementos in their cubicles or offices, over their workbenches, or in their homes. The cash gets spent, the merchandise wears out, and the trip becomes a long-past memory, but a certificate or plaque is a permanent reminder of the recognition.

Success Files—the Scorecard

Hillary, the sales manager of a large real estate office in Florida, makes a practice of sending letters of appreciation to sales staffers who do something special—selling a property that has been difficult to move, obtaining sales rights to a profitable building, or taking creative steps to make a sale.

With the first of these letters that Hillary sends to a salesperson, she encloses a file folder labeled Success File with this suggestion: "File the enclosed letter in this folder. Add to it any other commendatory letters you receive from me, from other managers, from clients, or from anyone else. As time goes on, you may experience failures or disappointments. There may be times when you don't feel good about yourself. When this happens, reread these letters. They're the proof that you're a success, that you have capability, that you are a special person. You did it before; you can do it again!"

Creating Recognition Programs That Work

Any form of sincere recognition can be effective—some for short periods of time and others for much longer. Recognition programs that affect the entire organization are usually developed and administered by the human resources department. You participate in implementing the programs in your team. But even if there's no company-wide program, with a little imagination and initiative, you can create a variation just for your own team. This section discusses a few of these techniques.

Employee of the Month

Choosing an associate every month for special recognition is probably the most popular form of formal recognition. The method of choosing employees and deciding which rewards and recognition to offer varies from company to company. This list shows some of the methods used to run an employee-of-the-month program:

- **Selection.** In most companies, each team leader or department head nominates candidates for an award. A committee weighs the contributions of each candidate and chooses the winner. In some organizations, peers make nominations in each department; increasingly, all employees are encouraged to make a nomination by writing a note or filling out a form. The committee makes its choice by comparing the nominees against a list of criteria and against each other.

- **Award.** Awards vary from company to company. The most frequently awarded prizes are cash, a day off with pay, and merchandise.

- **Recognition.** Almost all companies with employee-of-the-month programs have a permanent, prominently displayed plaque on which the winner's name is engraved. In some companies, a photo of the winner is also displayed during the month. In addition, individual certificates or plaques are given to monthly winners.

That's the Spirit

The Apostle Paul was seeking the right kind of recognition and awards as his ultimate goal. "I am focusing all my energies on this one thing …. I strain to reach the end of the race and receive the prize for which God through Christ Jesus, is calling us up to heaven." (Philippians 3:13, 14) As a godly manager, spouse, or parent, this should be your ultimate purpose as well.

Awards often are presented at luncheons to which all nominees for that month are invited. The winner is interviewed for an article in the company newsletter, and press releases are sent to local newspapers, radio, and TV stations.

As with anything else, there are drawbacks to the employee-of-the-month program. Here are a few:

- **Resentment.** Envy is difficult to overcome, but there will always be unhappy losers.

- **Overexposure.** After a while, any monthly program can become overdone— it's difficult to maintain excitement and enthusiasm month after month.

- **Lack of team recognition.** When people work in teams, individual efforts are subordinate to team efforts. When recognition belongs to a team, no single member of that team should be singled out for recognition.

Team Recognition

When individual commendation is undesirable, companies institute team-recognition programs. In Xerox's successful program, individuals receive awards for special achievement, but, to encourage teamwork, recognition is also given to teams. These awards include honors to teams that perform outstanding work and special recognition to teams for "Excellence in Customer Satisfaction."

Another way Xerox recognizes teams is by holding an annual Teamwork Day. On the first Teamwork Day, held in 1983 in a company cafeteria in Webster, New York, the objective was to teach managers the results of planning quality-circle activities and fostering a truly competitive team spirit. Today, Teamwork Day is now a highly anticipated and well-attended annual event.

> **def·i·ni·tion**
> **Interpret and Apply**
>
> An **internal customer** is a member of your team or another team to whom you provide materials, information, or services. An **internal supplier** is another person in your organization who provides you with materials, information, or services. You may be a customer in some aspects of your work and a supplier in others.

Peer Recognition

In the total quality management movement (TQM), the commitment to work toward continuing improvement of quality has made every member of a team more aware

of the importance of customer satisfaction. One way companies increase this awareness is by considering other employees with whom they interact as *internal customers*
or *internal suppliers.*

Encourage your associates to recognize any special achievements of their internal
suppliers and customers who enabled them to work with you more effectively.

Supervisors, managers, and team leaders aren't the only people who see the special efforts their associates make. All team members and co-workers are exposed
daily to each other's efforts. Enabling them to recognize the work of peers not only
brings to the forefront any accomplishments that may not have been recognized by
managers, but it also makes both the nominator and the nominee feel that they are
part of an integrated, interrelated, and caring organization.

Special Awards for Special Achievements

In some organizations, special awards are given not as part of a formal program, but
on a manager's initiative. During the pre-Thanksgiving rush at Stew Leonard's food
market in Norwalk, Connecticut, several office personnel noticed the long, creeping
lines at checkout counters and—with no prompting from management—left their
regular work duties to help cashiers bag the groceries, which helped speed up the
lines.

That's the Spirit

As a manager, put
the limelight on others
rather than yourself. Paul
tells the Philippians, "Don't
be selfish; don't live to
make a good impression
on others. Be humble, thinking of others as better than
yourself." (Philippians 2:3)

Stew, the owner of the market, resolved to do something special for the employees who helped out. After
the holiday rush was over, he bought for each of the
employees a beautifully knitted shirt with the embroi-
dered inscription "Stew Leonard ABCD Award." The
inscription stands for "*a*bove and *b*eyond the *c*all of
*d*uty." By giving special recognition to associates who do
more than their jobs require, he not only gave credit
where credit was due, but he also let everyone—the associates and their co-workers and supervisors, in addition
to customers—know that he appreciated the extra effort.

Motivating Off-Site Employees

Motivating telecommuters, independent subcontractors, and others who do most of their work away from the central facility, while keeping them from feeling like outsiders, is a challenge for managers. Here are a few suggestions:

- Schedule meetings either monthly or every other month with all employees working on a project. If the people are scattered all over the country, regional meetings at a convenient location are more feasible. This enables them to get to know each other and to discuss ideas face to face. It also gives people a feeling of community and a closer relationship to the company. They don't feel left out.

- Encourage managers to telephone off-site people—frequent but brief calls to touch base and occasional conference calls to the entire project team.

- People working off-site should be invited periodically to come to the home office to meet with staff. The personal contacts between on-site and off-site employees build up feelings of belonging.

- Managers should make periodic visits to the locations where off-site people work.

- Send a weekly newsletter to all off-site people, telling them about the latest developments in the company. Make it newsy and include human interest stories about employees.

  In addition to, or instead of, a newsletter, provide a website, updated daily to keep everybody current on company activities. Add some humor. Make it a site they'd want to read every day.

Chapter 18

Keep 'Em Moving

In the preface of his best-selling classic *Be a Motivational Leader*, Leroy Eims explains a connection between "motivation" and "animation." He notes the dictionary definition of *animation:*

> "The wind animated the flags." Can't you just see it? There droop the flags. And then the wind picks up and the flags begin to flutter and fly. And much of what God can use to inspire people to action is motivation. One of the prime jobs of the leader is to help people get fired up about the right stuff and keep them fired up.

When you work with a team, it's essential that you, as the team leader, identify how each person on the team reacts to various types of motivation. It's easy to fall into the trap of assuming that what motivates you, or what has been successful in motivating other people in the past, will work for everyone.

This chapter looks at some other motivators that work—for some people, not all. It also explores problems that develop in motivating a team when companies downsize, freeze wages, or change policies.

Opportunity—for What?

You're ambitious. You knock yourself out to get ahead, so you assume that everyone is ambitious. Not so!

> **That's the Spirit**
>
> Pray daily for each of your staff members. Ask God specifically to show you how to utilize each team member's special skills and how you might gain recognition for them by the company. God's Holy Spirit will guide you, and you will see results that you never dreamed of.

During the years I've been in the business world, I've seen plenty of people refuse a promotion, insisting that they are perfectly content to just "have a job." They do what they have to do and no more. Their real interests lie somewhere outside their work. Before you decide to offer a promotion to a team member, learn that person's real goals.

Alicia was desolate. When her boss was transferred, she expected to be promoted to his job, but the company promoted someone else. She complained, "I've been in the department longer than anyone else and have never missed a day's work. My performance reviews are always good. I should have gotten the promotion."

Why was Alicia passed over? Seniority, good attendance, and satisfactory work are important, but they're not the only reasons—or even the primary ones—for promotion. Management knew that Alicia was perfectly happy to do her work, but not one bit more. To her, it seemed, advancement was something to which she was entitled, not something toward which she had to work.

Encouraging People to Aim for Advancement

Suppose your organization has excellent opportunities for advancement. You believe that some of your team members have the potential to move up to those jobs, but they seem perfectly content to do no more than what they have to do. You don't want all that talent to be wasted. Here are some guidelines for motivating these folks to change their attitude:

> **Avoiding Stumbling Blocks**
>
> Don't project your ambitions on others; their desires may be much different from yours. To motivate an individual, you must know that person's goals and what he or she seeks from a job.

- Find out what really turns them on. They may be satisfying their needs outside of work.

- Show how working toward advancement might help them meet their outside goals. For example, Christine is a winter skier and summer surfer. To pursue these sports, she needs money, and higher-level jobs pay higher salaries. Or what about Ken, whose life centers on his children? Working toward a higher-level job will let him afford the type of education he wants to provide his kids.

- Some people are status conscious. Point out how advancement increases prestige not only in the company, but also in the community.

- Creative people can be encouraged to work for advancement by showing how higher-level positions give them the chance to use their own initiative and institute some of their creative ideas.

Dealing With People Who Want to Advance When There's No Opportunity

When ambitious people are frustrated by lack of opportunity for career advancement, it's tough to keep them motivated. They often quit or request a transfer to a department that offers better opportunities. If it's unlikely that advancement will occur in a reasonable period, you have to expect that ambitious people won't be content. Do your best to motivate them in other ways:

- Make special assignments to enable them to stretch their minds.

- Get them deeply involved in team projects so that their satisfaction in seeing the team's achievements replaces their personal desires.

- If you can, set up a compensation system that rewards them financially.

Some companies use a two-track compensation program so that people can be given financial reward and status without being promoted. One track is in management (the traditional promotional ladder); employees on the other track receive the equivalent pay and rank but are nonmanagerial. A technical company's tracks may look like this:

Managerial	Technical
Section leader	Engineering leader
Department chief	Principal engineer
Project manager	Project engineer
Engineering manager	Chief engineer

Motivating the Unmotivated

You have to accept that some people just can't be motivated (short of putting a stick of dynamite under their chairs). With the right approach, many men and women who seem to be complacent and unmovable might be spurred toward improved performance.

Some employees have been with their organization for many years. They've gone as far as they can go—and they know it. They also know that it's unlikely they'll ever be fired as long as they meet minimum performance standards because most companies don't fire long-term employees except under dire circumstances. People with the attitude of "I'll do as little as I can get away with" are called coasters.

It's difficult to motivate people who really don't want to be motivated, and many managers and team leaders don't even try. They just look at these people as crosses they have to bear.

One often successful approach to motivating coasters is giving them challenges—assignments or projects they can really "sink their teeth into."

Realistically, not everyone gets excited by challenges. When faced with a challenge, some people turn away from it—it's too much trouble. But for those who enjoy a challenging assignment, it can be a powerful motivator. Here are some guidelines:

- **Make the coaster a mentor to a new team member.** Many "old-timers" are flattered when asked to pass on their know-how and experience to the next generation. To ensure that they train newcomers properly, they hone their own skills and brush up on the latest developments in their field. Serious mentors do more than just train—they set good examples for their new associates.

- **Assign special projects.** Before the Associated Merchandise Company introduces a new product, it conducts a test market in key cities, a task it usually subcontracts to a market research firm. In testing its latest product, Associated tried a new approach: Rather than subcontract the job, it chose six men and women who had good marketing backgrounds but were now coasting. The six employees were relieved from their regular duties for four weeks. After a week of special training, each was sent to a test site to run the project. The challenge of a special assignment, enhanced by the success of the test, gave the coasters new enthusiasm that carried over into their regular work.

* **Plan future projects.** Coasters often feel left out. "I'll be retiring in a few years, so why worry about what the company will do then?" Their attitude is exacerbated by the fact that their managers have already given up on them. By bringing coasters into the process of planning projects along with younger employees, you let them know that they are valued team members and that they can bring to the group the value of their experience. An added benefit is that the coasters will learn from other members.

Using the Best Motivator of All

Although many new jobs being created in growth industries have the ingredients that lead to enjoyment and satisfaction, a large number of people have jobs that are routine, dull, and sometimes tedious. One way to make dull jobs more "worker-friendly" is to redesign these jobs. Rather than look at a job as a series of tasks that must be performed, study it as a total process. Make the job less routine by enlarging the scope of the job. This section presents some examples.

Enriching the Job

When Jennifer was hired to head the claims-processing department at Liability Insurance Company, she inherited a department with low morale, high turnover, and disgruntled employees. The claims-processing operation was an "assembly line" in which each clerk checked a section of the form and sent it to other clerks, who each checked another section. If errors were found, the form was sent to a specialist for handling. Efficient? Maybe, but it made the work dull and not very challenging.

Jennifer reorganized the process. She eliminated the assembly line and retrained each clerk to check the entire form, correct any errors, and personally deal with problems. Although operations slowed down during the break-in period, it paid off in a highly motivated team of workers who found gratification in working through the entire process and seeing it completed satisfactorily.

When team members are trained to perform all aspects of the jobs their team handles, you can not only assign any part of the work to any member (which gives a team leader much more flexibility), but you can also break the boredom of routine because members do different work at different times.

Involving Everyone in Planning

Production quotas are established for many types of work. Have your team members participate in setting quotas for their own jobs. You might think that they'll set low quotas that are easy to meet, and it may happen. That's why the process is *participatory*—you haven't stepped out of the picture completely. You're one of the participants. Your role is to ensure that realistic goals are set. In most cases, however, team members do set reasonable quotas—and because it's *their* goal, they accept it and work to achieve it.

> ### That's the Spirit
>
> Christian humility is not just about how we act, but it's also about how we think. And thinking humbly about your team members means putting their needs above our own, even when it amounts to your letting them think that the innovative ideas are theirs or that their buy-in is important. But if you try to put on a mask and pretend at humility, they'll see through it: You can't hide the quick, slight roll of the eye or the sarcastic twitch at the corner of your mouth. You're not even aware of such, but the holes in the mask reveal all—you don't mean it!

Another example of participation in planning is the experience of Ford Motor Company in its development of the Taurus. Ford didn't follow the usual industry practice of having a group of specialists design the car. Workers representing every type of job that would be involved in building the car were brought in to work with designers during the planning stage. The suggestions culled from workers' experience on the production line brought forth ideas that might never have occurred to the specialists. When the Taurus was brought to the factory floor, workers looked on it as *their* car. The result: The Taurus became the most trouble-free and profitable car Ford has introduced in recent years—because the company's workers were involved.

Some Motivators to Remember

This section lists some of the best techniques (in my experience) for motivating people to commit themselves to superior performance:

- Encourage participation by setting goals and determining how to reach them.
- Keep team members aware of how their job relates to others.
- Provide the tools and training necessary to succeed.
- Pay at least the going rate for jobs that are performed.
- Provide good, safe working conditions.
- Give clear directions that are easily understood and accepted.
- Know people's abilities, and give them assignments based on their ability to handle those assignments.
- Allow team members to make decisions related to their jobs.
- Be accessible. Listen actively and empathetically.
- Give credit and praise for a job well done.
- Give prompt and direct answers to questions.
- Treat team members fairly and with respect and consideration.
- Help with work problems.
- Encourage employees to acquire additional knowledge and skills.
- Show interest and concern for people as individuals.
- Learn employees' M.O.s, and deal with them accordingly.
- Make each person an integral part of the team.
- Keep people challenged and excited by their work.
- Consider your team members' ideas and suggestions.
- Keep people informed about how they're doing on the job.
- Encourage team members to do their best, and then support their efforts.

Avoiding Negative Motivation

Chapter 2 debunked the myth that to get people to work you have to give them a kick.

Threatening to fire people if they don't work is sometimes effective, at least temporarily. When jobs are scarce and people know that they won't have a job if they get fired, they *do* work. But how much work do they do? Some folks work just enough to keep from getting fired, and not one bit more. This fear isn't real motivation; *real* motivation spurs people to produce more than just what's necessary to keep their jobs.

Fear of being fired becomes less of a motivator as the job market again expands. If comparable jobs are available in more amenable environments, why work for a martinet? Some people do respond to negative motivation. Good leaders must recognize each person's individualities and adapt to them.

Motivating People Under Unfavorable Circumstances

Things don't always go well. Businesses go into slumps. Companies downsize and eliminate jobs. Large companies swallow smaller ones. How can morale be maintained and staff members be motivated when they see their economic world toppling around them? It's not easy, but as you'll learn in this section, there are ways to do it.

When the Company Downsizes

When business is slow, companies reduce costs by laying off employees. Layoffs have always been an element of the job world, particularly among blue-collar industries. When business picks up, workers are likely to be rehired.

Wise Counsel

> John Maxwell agrees that care must be taken for the employees who have not suffered the loss of their jobs: "Consider the effect on those who are close to the person. How might you help those who may be hurt or offended in this change. Do you need to be involved in some emotional healing?"

Downsizing differs from traditional layoffs in that total job categories are eliminated: There's little chance that people who have held these jobs will ever be rehired. Downsized positions are increasingly white-collar and managerial jobs.

Elliot left his boss's office in shock. He had been told that the company was downsizing and that he would have to cut his team from 20 people to 15. He had worked hard to build a highly motivated team. Not only would he lose five good members, but the remaining employees also would feel insecure, stressed, and unmotivated.

After the trauma of the layoffs subsided, Elliot took these steps to begin the rebuilding process:

* Reassured team members that management had completed the downsizing process and that their jobs were secure

* Set up a series of meetings to restructure the team so that all work would be covered

* Assigned projects to subteams to implement the new structure with minimum loss of productivity in ongoing activities

* Personally counseled team members who showed signs of unusual stress

Within a short time, Elliot's team again functioned at optimum capacity.

When Your Company Is Merged or Acquired

It seems that every time you pick up a newspaper, you read about another merger or acquisition. Chase Manhattan's acquisition of Chemical Bank is the largest bank merger ever, but it resulted in the loss of thousands of jobs. Disney bought Capitol City/ABC, and more jobs were lost as the offices of its headquarters were consolidated. Your company could be next.

The people most likely to survive an acquisition are those who work for the acquiring company, but even that's not a sure thing. Federated Department Stores bought Macy's and closed several of its own stores.

Whenever a merger or acquisition occurs, employees of both groups are certain to be insecure and concerned. As a team leader, little ol' you can do nothing until the dust settles, which often takes months or even years.

> **That's the Spirit**
>
> To work well in a team, you have to respect and accept each other's contributions. You have to see the synergy factor in diversity. Romans 15:7 advises us, "Accept one another, then, just as Christ accepted you, in order to bring praise to God."

The following suggestions can give your team a better chance of survival:

* **Work harder, work smarter.** When Associated Finance acquired Guardian Loan, all of Guardian's employees were concerned. They were sure that the larger company would eliminate their jobs. Alberta, Guardian's credit manager, thought differently. She told her team, "Our credit people are the best in the business. One reason they bought us was our excellent record in this area. They

need us. It will take at least six months before Associated can make any changes here. Let's show them that we are essential to their success." And they did. When the reorganization finally took place, Associated merged several departments with its own, but the credit department was left intact.

- **Be prepared to do things differently.** Companies that acquire others install their own systems and procedures. Accept them without complaints. Neither you nor your associates should ever say, "We never used to do it that way." Work their way. If it requires you to learn new technology, learn it as soon as possible.

- **Be patient.** After you master the new company's methods and win the confidence of the new management team, they will listen to your ideas for improvements and innovations.

When the Pressure Is On

Regardless of whether a company has downsized or reorganized because of an acquisition or another reason, you usually wind up with fewer people having to accomplish more work.

> **Wise Counsel**
>
> A 1995 survey of managerial and professional personnel by the U.S. Chamber of Commerce showed that the 40-hour work week is dead. Most respondents said that they work nine-hour days, another hour or more at home, and at least two hours on weekends.

How to motivate people who work longer hours and under constant pressure is the primary challenge managers face, and there are no easy answers. Some managers counter complaints by telling team members that they're lucky to have a job. This answer isn't a good one, though. As mentioned, negative motivation has limited value.

By encouraging your team to find shortcuts to better production, to eliminate unnecessary paperwork, and to come up with creative innovations, you can help reduce some of the added burden.

When Wages Freeze

Suppose your company hasn't raised anyone's wages for three years. Your team members are unhappy and resist all your efforts to get them to produce more. You repeatedly hear the complaint, "Why should I knock myself out when they won't pay me more?"

Sanjay, a chief engineer at a chemical company, was tired of hearing this complaint. At one of his team meetings he addressed the issue: "I know you haven't had a raise in three years. Neither have I, nor has my boss. You all know that business has been down during this time. Let's get to work so that we can do our part to make this a profitable company again."

This technique is one way to help team members understand the problem—that it's one that can and will be overcome. (Of course, it doesn't help if people read in the newspaper that the company CEO has just taken a $1 million bonus.)

Part 6

Dealing With Employee Problems on the Job

You have a good team in place, and all its members are carrying their weight—well, maybe not everyone. You know that some of your co-workers can do better. They're meeting their performance standards, but just barely. Performance review time is approaching, so here's your chance to shape them up. There's Burt, who seems to be on the verge of burnout; Ellen, who is so sensitive you're afraid to correct her errors; Stacey, who's always finding something to gripe about; and that new programmer, whom you suspect has a drinking problem. To keep your team functioning effectively, you need to counsel and help them.

So, you shape up your team, but your company decides to outsource some of your team's work to consultants and subcontractors. Now you're concerned about melding the scattered members of your team into the total operation.

This part of the book provides tips and techniques to help you overcome the challenges of maintaining a top-performing team.

Evaluating Team Members' Performance

We can be prone to think of evaluation as a negative thing—as a necessary evil. But God himself evaluates performance. To be sure, our quality of work in this world is not a condition of salvation—that's a free gift granted to those who will accept it. Nevertheless, Jesus assured us that a time will come when God will, in essence, sit down with us and review our performance.

In Matthew 25:14–30, Jesus illustrated this principle of accountability with the Parable of the Talents. His conclusion? To those who had worked at what the master had given them, he declared, "Well done, good and faithful servant," and he rewarded them. But to the servant who did nothing with what he'd been given, the master declared, "You wicked, lazy man!"

The work that Jesus was illustrating has a deeper spiritual meaning than our tasks at the office, but the value God places upon evaluation is still very relevant. Our goal, whatever the circumstances, should be to hear "Well done, good and faithful servant."

This chapter discusses how to set performance standards that are meaningful to team members and describes some of the techniques for measuring performance. You'll also learn how to conduct a formal appraisal interview.

Setting Performance Standards

All employees should know just what's expected of them on the job. Many companies develop and incorporate *performance standards* at the time they create a job description. In other companies, a job evolves as standards are established.

In routine jobs, the key factors of performance standards involve quantity (how much should be produced per hour or per day) and quality (what level of quality is acceptable). As jobs become more complex, these standards aren't an adequate way to measure performance. Ideas and innovations that are conceived in creative jobs cannot be quantified, and quality may be difficult to measure. This situation doesn't mean that you can't have performance standards for these jobs, but it does require a different approach, such as the results-oriented evaluation system described later in this chapter.

Establishing Criteria for Performance Standards

Performance standards are usually based on the experiences of satisfactory workers who have done that type of work over a length of time. Whether the standards cover quality or quantity of the work, or other aspects of the job, they should meet these criteria:

- **Specific.** Every person doing a job should know exactly what he or she is expected to do.

- **Measurable.** The company should have a touchstone against which performance can be measured. When a numerical measurement isn't feasible, some of the criteria may include timely completion of assignments, introduction of new concepts, or contribution to team activities.

- **Realistic.** Unless standards are attainable, people consider them unfair and resist working toward them.

Let Them Evaluate Their Own Performance

When all team members know what's expected of them and against which standards they'll be measured, self-evaluation becomes almost automatic. Members don't have to wait for their team leader to tell them that they're below standard or behind schedule—they see that for themselves and can take corrective action immediately.

Self-evaluation makes a team leader's job easier. Like a good coach, he helps keep the team aware of the standards and provides support and encouragement to stay on target.

Conducting Formal Performance Appraisals

Even if team members know the performance standards and can measure their own performance, and if team leaders reinforce this process with ongoing discussions about performance, there's still a need for formal appraisals. Most formal appraisals are conducted annually. Many team leaders add an informal appraisal semiannually or quarterly as a means of making team members aware of their progress.

This list describes some of the reasons that formal appraisals are important:

- They provide a framework for discussing a team member's overall work record. The team leader can use this meeting to recognize an employee for past successes and provide suggestions for even greater contributions.

- They become more objective and enable team leaders to compare all members of the team against the same criteria.

- They provide helpful data for determining what type of additional training team members need.

- In many companies, they're the primary factor in determining salary increases and bonuses.

- Their formality causes them to be taken more seriously than informal comments about performance.

- They can be used as a vehicle for goal setting, career planning, and personal growth.

Power Principles

When you rate your team members, don't be overly influenced by their most recent behavior. Employees know that it's rating time, and they'll be as good as a kid just before Christmas. Keep a running log of their behavior during the entire year.

Examining the Downside of Formal Appraisals

Formal appraisals have some inherent problems, a few of which are listed here:

- They can be stressful for both leaders and team members.

- They make some team leaders so uncomfortable about making associates unhappy that the leaders overrate their performance.

- Many are inadequate, cumbersome, or poorly designed, which creates more problems than solutions.
- In some appraisals, good workers are underrated because their team leaders are afraid that team members might become competitors.

> **That's the Spirit**
>
> If ever there was occasion for seeking God's guidance (what occasion wouldn't be?), evaluation time is it. Spend a long period in prayer ahead of time, pleading for God's wisdom and discernment on your behalf, and the softening of hearts and opening of ears on the evaluatee's behalf.

A properly managed performance appraisal can be a highly stimulating experience for both team member and team leader. To make it most effective, don't treat it as a confrontation.

Choosing the Best System for You

Your company may have in place an appraisal system that you are obligated to use. It may be helpful, however, to use aspects of other appraisal methods in addition to the method formally requested by your company. In addition, many companies use an appraisal system that combines aspects of all the methods described here, so these aren't "pure" types.

Check the Box: The Trait-Based System

You've been rated by them. You've used them to rate others. The most common evaluation system is the "trait" format, in which a series of traits are listed in the left margin and each is measured against a scale from unsatisfactory to excellent (see the following figure):

Trait-Based Appraisal Worksheet					
	Excellent (5 points)	Very Good (4 points)	Average (3 points)	Needs Improvement (2 points)	Unsatisfactory (1 point)
Quantity of work					
Job knowledge					
Dependability					
Ability to take instruction					
Initiative					
Creativity					
Cooperation					

This system seems on the surface to be simple to administer and easy to understand, but it's loaded with problems:

- **A central tendency.** Rather than carefully evaluating each trait, it's much easier to rate a trait as average or close to average (the central rating).

- **The "halo effect."** Some managers believe that one trait is so impressive they rate all traits highly. Its opposite is the "pitchfork effect" (see Chapter 14).

- **Personal biases.** Managers are human, and humans have personal biases for and against other people. These biases can influence any type of rating, but the trait system is particularly vulnerable.

- **Latest behavior.** It's easy to remember what employees have done during the past few months, but managers tend to forget what they did in the first part of a rating period.

Some companies encourage the use of the bell curve in rating employees. The trouble with the use of the bell curve in employee evaluations is that small groups are unlikely to have this type of distribution—and it may work unfairly against top- and bottom-level workers.

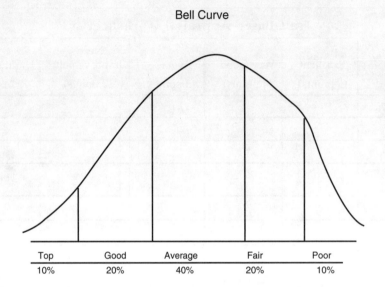

Bell Curve

Top	Good	Average	Fair	Poor
10%	20%	40%	20%	10%

The best way to overcome deficiencies in the trait system is to replace them with a results-oriented system (described later in this chapter). If your company does use the trait method, here are some suggestions to help make it more equitable:

- Clarify standards. Every manager and team leader should be carefully informed about the meaning of each category and the definition of each trait. Understanding quantity and quality is relatively easy. But what is dependability? How do you measure initiative, creativity, and other intangibles?

  By using discussions, role playing, and case studies, you can develop standards that everyone understands and uses.

- Establish criteria for ratings. It's easy to identify superior and unsatisfactory employees, but it's tougher to differentiate among people in the middle three categories.

- Keep a running log of member performance throughout the year. You don't have to record average performance, but do note anything special that each member has accomplished or failed to accomplish.

- Make an effort to be aware of your personal biases and to overcome them.

- Have specific examples of exceptional and unsatisfactory performance and behavior to back up your evaluation.

Measuring Results: A More Meaningful System

Rather than rate team members on the basis of an opinion about their various traits, in this appraisal system the people who do the rating focus on the attainment of specific results. Results-based ratings can be used in any situation in which results are measurable. The expectations are agreed on at the beginning of a period and are measured at the end of that period. At that time, new goals are developed to be measured at the end of the following period.

Here's how this system works:

- For every job, the team leader and the people doing the job agree on the key results areas (KRAs) for that job. Employees must accomplish results in these areas to meet the team's goals.

- The team leader and the team member establish the results that are expected from the team member in each of the KRAs.

- During a formal review, the results that an employee attained in each of the KRAs are measured against what was expected.

- A numerical scale is used in some organizations to rate employees on how closely they come to reaching their goals. In others, no grades are given. Instead, a narrative report is compiled to summarize what has been accomplished and to comment on its significance.

- Some companies request that team members submit monthly progress reports compiled in the same format as the annual review. This technique enables both the team member and the leader to monitor progress. By studying the monthly reports, the annual review is more easily compiled and discussed.

Following is a sample form for a results-oriented evaluation.

Results-Oriented Evaluation

Team member: _____

Job: <u>Tax accountant</u>   **Date:** _____

Results expected   **Results achieved**

Key Results Area 1   Prepare federal, state, and local tax
                                       returns on a timely basis.

_____   _____

_____   _____

_____   _____

Key Results Area 2   Advise management of changes in,
                                       and administrative changes of tax laws.

_____   _____

_____   _____

_____   _____

Key Results Area 3   Study management policies and report
                                       on their tax ramifications.

_____   _____

_____   _____

_____   _____

Although results-oriented evaluations can be more meaningful than trait systems, they're not free of problems:

- **Set reasonable goals.** Unless you and the team member take an objective view of what he or she should accomplish, you may set unrealistic expectations. The danger is that you may set standards so low that employees attain them with little effort, or that you set them so high that employees have little chance of attaining them.

- **Not all goals are equal in importance.** You should consider the value of the expectation in comparison to the overall goals of the team and the company.
- **Intangible goals are more difficult to measure.** Even intangible factors, however, have tangible phases that can be identified. For example, rather than indicate that a goal is "Improve employee morale," specify it in terms that are measurable, such as "Reduce turnover by X percent" or "Decrease the number of grievances by Y percent." Rather than state a goal as "Develop a new health insurance plan," break it into phases, such as "Complete study of proposed plans by October 31" or "Submit recommendations by December 15."

Collaborative Evaluation

To make the results-oriented format even more meaningful, use the joint leader/ associate model. If performance evaluations are based on the arbitrary opinion of a supervisor, they serve only part of the real value that reviews can provide. Such a model provides a formal evaluation for the purpose of raises or promotions, and it enables you to tell employees how to improve performance—but it doesn't involve team members in the process.

Avoiding Stumbling Blocks

If a team member gives himself or herself a significantly higher rating than you do, be particularly sensitive in the discussion so that it doesn't degenerate into a confrontation. Use specific examples rather than statements of opinion to make your points.

A joint review can do this more effectively. The joint leader/associate review is particularly useful for evaluating creative jobs such as research and development positions or jobs in the arts. Team members and their leaders collaborate on the standards that are expected, build in the flexibility to accommodate the special circumstances under which they are working, and agree on the criteria that will be used in evaluating the work.

The team member and team leader then complete the evaluation form. The KRAs and the "results expected" items are agreed on in advance (usually during the preceding review). The team member and the leader independently indicate the "results achieved."

Many companies that don't use joint evaluations ask employees to evaluate their own performance before meeting with their team leader. The employee completes a copy of the appraisal form. At the meeting, similarities and differences in the ratings are discussed. If the employee still disagrees with the evaluation after the discussion, in some companies a rebuttal may be written, which is filed along with the team leader's report.

At the appraisal interview (described later in this chapter), the team leader and the team member discuss the comments on the form. During this session, the appraisal begins to move from a report card to a plan of action for growth and team-work.

A collaborative review of performance has the following advantages:

- Gives team members the opportunity to make a formal appraisal of their own work in a systematic manner
- Allows for a thorough discussion between the team leader and the team member about their different perceptions of expectations and results achieved
- Enables a team leader to see areas in which he or she may have failed in developing a team member's potential
- Helps the team member and the team leader identify problem areas that might easily be overlooked on a day-to-day basis
- Pinpoints areas in which employees need improvement and in which they need additional training
- Gives an opportunity to discuss areas in which a team member can become even more valuable to the team
- Provides a base on which realistic goals for the next period can be discussed and mutually agreed on
- Helps team members measure performance and progress against their own career goals, and serves as a guide in determining the appropriate steps to move forward

The Nuts and Bolts of the Appraisal Interview

Regardless of whether you have evaluated employees by the trait method or the results method, and whether they have made a self-evaluation, the most important facet of the appraisal process is the face-to-face discussion of the evaluation.

To make this interview most valuable, you should carefully plan it and systematically carry it out.

Prepare and Plan Your Approach

Before sitting down with a team member to discuss a performance appraisal, study the evaluation. Make a list of all aspects you want to discuss—not just those that need improvement, but also those in which the employee did good work. Study previous appraisals, and note improvements that have been made since the preceding one. Prepare the questions you want to ask about past actions, steps to be taken for improvement, and future goals and how the team member plans to reach them.

That's the Spirit

When Jesus spoke of correcting someone who was sinning in the body (Matthew 18), or when Paul similarly called for sin to be dealt with (2 Corinthians 2 and Galatians 6, to cite just a few), the purpose was always clear: not to punish for the sake of punishment, but rather to restore. Similarly, when we are confronting inadequacies in performance, we must always keep in sight the goal: to restore, not to tear down.

Discussing Performance with a Team Member

After you have made a team member feel at ease, point out the reasons for the appraisal meeting. Say something like this: "As you know, each year we review what has been accomplished during the preceding year and discuss what we can do together in the following year."

Point out the areas of the job in which team members have met standards, and particularly the areas in which they have excelled. By giving specific examples of these achievements, you let team members know you're aware of their positive qualities.

Because salary adjustment is usually based on overall performance, team members should be made aware that your praise of one or a few accomplishments isn't a guarantee of a raise. You might say, "The way you handled the *XYZ* account shows that you're making great progress. Keep up the good work." By saying it this way, you show that you're aware of the progress but that there's still a ways to go. Rather

Interpret and Apply

The word **interview** is derived from **inter** (which means "between") and **view** (which means "look"). An interview is a "look" at a situation "between" the parties involved—it's a two-way discussion about performance.

than interpret the praise as, "Wow, I'm good—this means a big raise," the reaction is, "I'm doing fine, but I'm not there yet."

Encourage team members to comment. Listen attentively, and then discuss the aspects of performance or behavior that didn't meet standards. Be specific. Ask what team members plan to do to meet standards and what help they want you to provide.

If employees' problems aren't related to performance, but rather to behavior, provide examples. Try to obtain a commitment and a plan of action to overcome this fault.

Making Criticism Constructive

Many managers find it difficult to give criticism. Here are some guidelines to help deal with this sensitive area:

Power Principles

Most people are uneasy about appraisal interviews. Allay these fears by making some positive comments when you schedule an interview. You can say, "I've scheduled your appraisal interview for 2:30 on Wednesday. I want to talk about your accomplishments this year and discuss our plans for next year."

- Begin with a positive approach by asking the team member to assess the successes achieved and the steps taken to achieve those successes.

- Encourage the team member to talk about projects that didn't succeed and what caused the failure.

- Ask what might have been done to avoid the mistakes made.

- Contribute your suggestions about how the matter could have been done more effectively.

- Ask what training or help you can provide.

- Agree on the steps that the associate will take to ensure better performance on future assignments.

Soliciting Team Members' Comments

Throughout interviews, encourage team members to comment on or make suggestions about every aspect of the review. Of course, they may have excuses or alibis. Listen empathetically—you may learn about some factors that have inhibited optimum performance. There may be factors within the company that keep an employee from performing adequately. By giving the person the opportunity to express his or her reasons or arguments, you can take steps to correct the situation.

Even if a team member's excuses are superficial and self-serving, allowing them to be voiced clears the air. Then you both can be prepared to face real situations and come up with viable ideas.

Reviewing Last Year's Goals and Setting Next Year's

If the preceding year's goals were met, congratulate the team member. Talk about the steps that were taken to meet goals and what was learned from this experience. If not all the goals were met, discuss any problems and the steps that might now be taken to overcome them.

An appraisal interview isn't just a review of the past—it's also a plan for the future. Ask the question, "What do you want to accomplish during the next 12 months?" The answer might include production goals, quality improvement, behavioral changes, and plans for advancement. In addition to goals directly related to work, team members' future plans may include personal career-development plans.

Have team members write down each of their goals, and indicate next to them what they plan to do to achieve them. Give one copy to the team member and keep one with the performance appraisal form. You can use it as part of the appraisal interview the following year.

Conclude with a Summary and an Action Plan

At the end of an interview, ask the team member to summarize the discussion. Make sure that the person fully understands the positive and negative aspects of performance and behavior, plans and goals for the next review period, and any other pertinent matters. Keep a written record of these points.

In many companies, team members who disagree with an evaluation are given the opportunity to write a rebuttal to be attached to the appraisal. When salary adjustments are based on ratings, some organizations provide a procedure for appealing a review.

End the interview on a positive note, by saying, "Overall, you've made good progress this year. I'm confident that you'll continue to do good work."

Recording the Review

In most companies, the appraisal form is sent to the human resources department to be placed in the employee's personnel file. Some companies require that a copy be sent to the next level of management—the person to whom the team leader reports.

Even if it's not a formal practice in your company, it's a good idea to give a copy of the appraisal to the team member. It serves as a reminder of what was discussed at the appraisal interview and can be referred to during the year. And, as mentioned, if it includes goals that the employee and you have agreed on for the year, the employee can reread it from time to time to keep motivated.

Ten Points to Remember When Reviewing Performance

1. Know exactly what you want to achieve. Let your employees know what is expected of them.

2. Keep a record of employee performance from which to cite specific examples.

3. Discuss the written evaluation with the team member.

4. Listen to the team member's comments and then ask questions to stimulate thought.

5. Focus on the individual. Do not compare him or her with other members of the team.

6. Show that you care about the employee's performance and career.

7. Reinforce good behavior. Be specific in your criticism. Give examples from the team member's performance record. Ask how the person can do even better. Add your own suggestions.

> **Power Principles**
>
> In the evaluation interview, concentrate on the work, not on the person. Never say, "You were no good." Say instead, "Your work didn't meet standards."

8. Focus on the behavior, not on the person.

9. Don't be afraid to give honest criticism. Most employees want to know where they stand and how to improve.

10. Help the team member to set personal goals that are congruent with the goals of the team—and the company—and to develop a plan of action to reach those goals.

The 360° Assessment

Multilevel assessments have become an increasingly popular approach, used to identify how a manager is viewed by bosses, peers, subordinates, and even outsiders (for example, vendors and customers). Usually referred to as 360° assessments, such reviews have been adopted by companies such as AT&T, IBM, and other Fortune 500 corporations.

Despite the advantages of multilevel assessments, there are also potential drawbacks. Feedback can hurt. Evaluators aren't always nice or positive. Some people see their role as assessor as an opportunity to criticize others' behavior on the job.

Another flaw concerns conflicting opinions. Who decides who is right? Or what if an appraisal is biased? If the evaluator does not like the person being evaluated, the responses might be skewed negatively; if the assessee is a friend, the evaluation might be skewed positively. Often people rating senior executives fear that it is dangerous to be completely truthful.

In order to ensure that the 360° assessment has a better chance of producing a change, it is recommended that …

- The appraisal be anonymous and confidential.
- To have sufficient knowledge of the person being rated, the appraisers should have worked with the appraisee for at least six months.
- Appraisers should give written comments as well as numerical ratings. This enables their evaluations to be more specific and meaningful.
- To avoid "survey fatigue," 360° assessments should not be used on too many employees at one time.
- Appraisers should avoid the temptation to allow personal likes and dislikes to influence performance reviews. The Scriptures say that God shows no favoritism.

Turning the Tables: When Your Boss Reviews Your Performance

Performance reviews aren't limited to you assessing your staff. Your own performance is also evaluated by your boss. Now it's you sitting in the hot seat.

Even though you may have undergone many such reviews in your career, it's always a bit disquieting to be in that spot. It is human nature to fear such an important meeting. So much depends on it: your immediate future, whether or not you'll get a raise, and the opinion your boss has of your potential. And for sure, the boss will have something negative to say.

Here are some tips to help you handle this situation:

- **Review your own performance.** Whether or not your company requires employees to make self-evaluations, do it. Make a blank copy of the review form in this chapter and fill it out. This will allow you to think about your performance in the same way your boss does.

- **List your accomplishments.** Specify all the special things you did over the past year to contribute to the success of the department.

- **Consider your deficiencies.** None of us is perfect. You probably did some things that did not work out, and you probably have can do better in some areas. Your supervisor is likely to bring this up at the review. Instead of thinking up excuses, point out what you have already done or what you plan to do to improve your skills in those areas.

- **At the interview, listen attentively.** Do not interrupt except to ask clarifying questions. Under no circumstances should you disagree or try to rebut a point. Let the supervisor finish before you make any comments.

- **Be constructive.** Now is the chance to make your rebuttal. If you have carefully prepared a list of accomplishments and are cognizant of your deficiencies, you are ready to make your points. Start by thanking your supervisor for his or her support over the past year, and then say: "I understand what you have told me and I appreciate your frankness. However, there are certain accomplishments of which I am particularly proud and for which you complimented me at the time, which you may not have taken into consideration in the review." Then enumerate the items. If the supervisor focused on some of your deficiencies, don't make excuses for them. Instead, talk about what you are doing to overcome them. Suggest that these be considered before the evaluation is made final.

- **Set goals for the future.** If you had set goals for this year at last year's review, discuss how close you came to reaching them. If they changed during the year, discuss the circumstances. Now discuss your goals for the ensuing year. Get your boss's agreement that these are worthwhile goals, and then commit yourself to attain them.

This process is similar to your times of prayer, in which you review your own performance with God. You're honest and transparent, rejoicing in your progress in holiness and repenting of sinful behavior at the same time.

Chapter 20

Dealing With Problem Employees

In Paul's first epistle to the church of Corinth, he expressed his concern for their unity in Christ, using the analogy of a body. (Corinthians 12:12–26) "Many parts with many unique attributes make up a body, yet they are all one in Christ."

We can draw our own analogy from this passage and apply some principles, as long as we understand the one key factor that is missing: The unifying force in the church is Christ. Obviously, when you are working with nonbelievers, there cannot be comparable unity. Nevertheless, the principle of valuing and supporting the unique strengths and weaknesses of team members is still relevant. So when problems arise in the team-body, it doesn't make sense to say to a hand, "Why can't you be more like the eye?" (v. 21). After all, you don't want a team that is one big eyeball (v. 17).

To be sure, problems will arise. The question is, how will you deal with them honestly while also maintaining team unity? One of the great challenges of being a leader lies in recognizing and dealing with these types of problems so that your department will run smoothly.

Some of the more common problems that leaders must deal with are discussed in this chapter. Among them are helping to build up team members' self-confidence so that they'll become better contributors to your team's efforts, overcoming negative thinking, and dealing with sensitive and temperamental people.

You'll also learn how to cope with members who are under stress and those who burn out. In addition, this chapter explores what can be done if team members have AIDS or are facing alcohol and drug abuse.

Building Up Low Self-Esteem

Consider the phrase "developing self-esteem." Many people who have had a low opinion of themselves have been able to overcome it by making a commitment to make a change. Sometimes they seek professional help, but often they do it through self-determination: They rewrite the script on which they base their life. As a team leader, you're in a position to help such people develop self-esteem.

That's the Spirit

True self-esteem comes from knowing our worth to God. We are beings created in his image, beings so unfathomably valuable that he would give his only begotten son that we might be saved—even though many of us won't accept the gift. This goes for your unsaved colleagues and team members, too: They are created in God's image, and God the Son died for them as well. However, they perceive their own value, they are humans and are worthy of your highest esteem.

As a manager, you can help by focusing on successes, not on failures. Most people don't loathe themselves, but they may have temporary self-esteem slumps and need bolstering. If they don't deal with those slumps, more serious consequences can occur.

Focusing on Success, Not on Failure

Loss of self-esteem stems from failure. All of us have failures and successes in our jobs and in our lives. By focusing on failure, self-esteem deteriorates. Concentrate instead on the successes you have achieved.

One technique involves keeping a success log (see Chapter 17). Enter in this log any accomplishments you're especially proud of—things for which you've been commended. These things prove that you've succeeded in the past and serve as your assurance that you can succeed again.

Esteem-Building Suggestions

In addition to maintaining success logs, you can help team members build self-esteem in other ways:

- Give them positive reinforcement for every achievement, and praise them for progress made in their work or for coming up with a good idea.

- Give them assignments that you know they can handle, and provide added training, coaching, and support to ensure that they'll succeed.

- Suggest that they take courses designed to build self-confidence. Provide them with inspirational tapes or books.

- If appropriate, you can also tell the person that the source of your self-esteem is Jesus Christ and share what he has done for you.

> **Power Principles**
>
> Keep a success log for your team. Enter in it the special achievements of each of your team members and of your team as a whole. Encourage each team member to keep a personal success log. When things don't go well or when you and your team members are feeling low, have everyone reread the log.

If, despite these efforts, a person doesn't become more self-confident, professional help may be necessary. Suggest that the person see a counselor in your employee-assistance program (see Chapter 21).

Dealing With Sensitive Sam, Temperamental Terry, Negative Nell, and Others

You undoubtedly have some of these people on your team. Every team leader does. They can make your life miserable or make it an ever-changing challenge. You can't ignore these folks—you have to deal with them. This section gives you some suggestions.

Sensing the Overly Sensitive

No one likes to be criticized, but most people can accept constructive criticism. Some people resent any criticism, though. Whenever you make even the slightest criticism

Avoiding Stumbling Blocks

Don't praise sensitive people *only* as a prelude to criticism. They may have low self-esteem and, therefore, need a great deal of positive reinforcement.

of their work, they pout and get defensive and accuse you of picking on them.

Be gentle with them. Be diplomatic. Begin by praising the parts of assignments that they have done well. Then make some suggestions about how they can do better in unsatisfactory areas.

If members of your team operate too slowly because of oversensitivity, follow these guidelines to help them overcome their fears:

- Assure them that, because of their excellent knowledge in their field, their work is usually correct the first time and doesn't have to be checked repeatedly.

- Point out that occasional errors are normal and that they can be caught and corrected later without reflecting on the ability of the person who made the errors.

- If you agree that team members need more information before making a decision, guide them toward resources to help them obtain it. If you feel that they have adequate information, insist that they make prompt decisions.

- If team members ask you what to do, tell them that it's their decision and to make it quickly.

In most cases, overly sensitive people have the expertise and do make good decisions. They may need your reassurance to help convert their thinking into action.

Tampering with Temper Tantrums

Terry is a good worker, but from time to time he loses his temper and hollers and screams at his co-workers and even at you. He calms down quickly, but his behavior affects the work of your entire team, and it takes a while to get back to normal performance. You've spoken to Terry about his temper several times, but it hasn't helped.

It isn't easy to work in an environment in which people holler and scream, particularly if you're the target. Because the victims of a tirade may be unable to work at full capacity for several hours afterward, this situation cannot be tolerated.

Here are some suggestions for dealing with someone who has temper tantrums:

- After the person calms down, have a heart-to-heart talk. Point out that you understand that it's not always easy for someone to control his or her temper, but stress that such tantrums aren't acceptable in the workplace.

- If another outburst occurs, send the person out of the room until he or she can calm down. Let the person know that the next offense will lead to disciplinary action.

- Recommend the old adage "Count to 10 before opening your mouth."

- If you have an employee-assistance program (see Chapter 21), suggest that the team member see one of its counselors.

Power Principles

If the person you're criticizing begins to cry or throw a tantrum, walk out! Say that you'll return after he or she calms down. Wait 10 minutes and then try again. Assure the person that this isn't a personal attack, but a means of correcting a situation. *Note:* Don't conduct these types of meetings in your office. It's not a good idea to leave an upset person alone in your office—use a conference room instead.

Negating Negativity

Almost every organization has a Negative Nell and Ned. Whenever you're for something, that person is against it. He or she always has a reason why what you want to accomplish just can't be done. Such a negative person can tear down your team with pessimism.

The reasons for a team member's negativity vary. The negative outlook may stem from some real or perceived past mistreatment by your company. If that's the case, look into the matter. If the person has justifiable reasons for being negative, try to persuade him or her that the past is past and to look to the future. If misconceptions are involved, try to clear them up.

Negativity is often rooted in long-term personality factors that are beyond the ability of any team leader to overcome. In that case, professional help is necessary.

Let's look at some of the problems negative people cause:

- **Resistance to change.** Even people with a positive attitude are reluctant to change. It's comfortable to keep doing things the way they've always done them. Positive-thinking people can be persuaded to change by presenting logical arguments. Negative people resist change just for the sake of resisting.

- **Impact on team morale.** Just as one rotten apple can spoil a whole barrel, one negative person can destroy the entire team's morale. Because the negativism spreads from one person to another, it's tough to maintain team spirit under these circumstances.

When you present new ideas to negative people, get them to express their objections openly. Tell them, "You bring up some good points, and I appreciate them. As we move into this new program, let's carefully watch for those problems. We must give this new concept a try. Work with me on it, and together we'll iron out the kinks."

Negative Personalities

Negative people often don't realize how disruptive they are to others. They probably act this way in their personal lives as well as on the job. They're the type of people who don't get along with their families, have few friends, and are forever the dissenters. Have a heart-to-heart talk with these people to let them know how their attitude affects your team's morale. You might suggest that they enroll in a personal improvement program.

Playing "Gotcha"

Have you ever worked with an associate whose greatest joy in life is to catch other people—especially you—making an error?

People who play this game are trying to show their superiority. Because they usually have no original ideas or constructive suggestions, they get their kicks from catching other people's errors, particularly their boss's. They try to embarrass you and make you uncomfortable. Don't give them that satisfaction. Make a joke about it ("What a blooper!"), or smile and say "Thanks for calling it to my attention before it caused real problems." If Gotchamongers see that you're not riled by their game, they'll stop and try to get their kicks elsewhere.

Working With Unhappy People

There's likely to be at least one unhappy person on your team. We all experience periods when things go wrong at home or on the job—and it affects the way we do our work and how we interact with other team members. Team leaders should be alert to this likelihood and take the time to chat with the person. Giving a person the opportunity to talk about a problem often alleviates the tension. Even if the problem isn't solved, it clears the air and enables the team member to function normally.

> **That's the Spirit**
>
> A Christian, of all people, should appreciate how implausible it must be to make people think and feel differently than they want to. God in all of his sovereignty won't do it. Why should you think you can improve on him?

Some people, however, will always be unhappy about something. They often aren't satisfied with work assignments. Even when you comply with their requests and accommodate their complaints, they're not satisfied. You can never make everyone happy. Rebuilding the morale of people who believe that they've been treated unfairly takes tact and patience. Team leaders can avoid some unfair situations by explaining the reasons behind the decision at the time a decision is made.

If this technique doesn't satisfy your team member, have a heart-to-heart talk with the person. Point out how constant griping and a negative attitude affect other team members. Make reassurances that the person is a valuable member of your team and that it's not always possible to get everything we want. Encourage the person to be mature—to accept disappointments and go on with life.

Addressing Stress and Burnout

All jobs have their share of stress. If they didn't, they would quickly become boring. It's when *stress* becomes *distress* that problems occur. The stress may show up in the way employees' behavior has changed. People who had always been patient become impatient. Calm people may become tense. Team members who have always been cooperative rebel. All these signs show up when people are under stress. Team members under stress may show physical symptoms or complain that they have trouble falling asleep or sleeping through the night. They're often tired all the time—even if they do get a good rest. They may have stomach pains, a fast heartbeat, or frequent headaches.

"I'm So Tired I Can't Think Straight!"

Physical fatigue can be cured by rest, but most people are more likely to be mentally, not physically, fatigued on the job. If your team members work with computers or in other mentally strenuous jobs, remind them that physical exercise can alleviate fatigue and stress. People who have a regular regimen are less likely to become mentally fatigued.

Burnout

People are not light bulbs. A light bulb shines brightly and suddenly—poof! It burns out. People burn out slowly and often imperceptibly. Although some burnouts result in physical breakdowns such as a heart attack or ulcers, most are psychological. Team members lose enthusiasm, energy, and motivation, and it shows up in many ways. They hate their job, can't stand co-workers, distrust the team leader, and dread coming to work each morning.

Often the only means of helping someone recover from burnout is to suggest professional help (see Chapter 21). There are some things you can do, however, to help put a burned-out team member on the road to recovery:

> **That's the Spirit**
>
> Consider it pure joy, my brothers, whenever you face trials of many kinds, because you know that the testing of your faith develops perseverance. Perseverance must finish its work so that you may be mature and complete, not lacking anything.
>
> (James 1:2–4)

- **Be a supportive person.** Demonstrate your sincere interest by encouraging the person to talk about and assess any concerns, and put them into perspective.
- **Consider changing job functions.** Assigning different activities and responsibilities or transferring the person to another team changes the climate in which that person works and provides new outlets that may stimulate motivation.
- **Give the team member an opportunity to acquire new skills.** This not only helps the person focus on learning rather than on the matters that led to the burnout, but it also makes him or her more valuable to your company.

If, despite your efforts, the person doesn't progress, strongly suggest professional counseling.

Plowing into Pressure

When pressure on a job becomes so great that you feel like you're going to break down, follow these suggestions:

- **Take a break.** If possible, get away from your workplace—get out of the building and take a walk. In 10 or 15 minutes, you'll feel the stress dissolve and will be able to face your job with renewed energy.

- **Exercise.** If you work in a crowded office, it's obviously not expedient to get up in the middle of the room and do jumping jacks or push-ups, but you can choose from several relaxation exercises without being obtrusive.

- **Change your pace.** Most people work on more than one project at a time. If the pressures are too great on your current project, stop for a while and work on another one. When you return to your original assignment, it will go much more smoothly.

When There's Too Darn Much Work to Do

Your team has survived downsizing and reorganization. You now have fewer members, and each of them is working longer and harder. Your boss is piling more work on you, and your team just can't handle it. Because there's a limit to any group's time and energy, you decide that you have to speak to your boss.

Power Principles

Learn to say "no." When you're asked to take on a special assignment that won't help you meet your goals, decline diplomatically.

Before you approach your manager, thoroughly analyze the jobs your team is doing. Indicate how much time team members devote to each project, and determine each project's importance to the accomplishment of your team's goals. Re-examine your boss's priorities. Decide with your team what all members can do to work smarter rather than harder.

If you still feel after this analysis that your team has more work than it can handle effectively, meet with your boss to review its results and try to reorder your team's priorities. Your boss may agree to defer certain time-consuming jobs because others are more important, reassign some jobs to other groups, or authorize the hiring of additional personnel.

Don't let other teams push your team around. Sometimes pressure comes from other teams or departments with which you're collaborating. If you can't agree with the other team's leader, take it up with the supervisor in a spirit of godly humility.

Managing Stress

Although some physicians treat stress with tranquilizers and other medication, unless you're under extreme pressure, you can take other steps to help manage your own stress:

- Keep in tiptop shape. Watch your diet, and engage in a regular exercise program.

- Learn to relax. Quiet time in meditation and prayer can bring remarkable peace in the midst of heavy storms. Be sure to reserve time to spend alone.

- Learn to love yourself. People who have a right relationship with God know that he doesn't value them for what they do, but for who they are.

- Be Still and Know He Is God. Take time to read God's word and pray. Often stress can be a tool God uses to draw you closer to him.

- Keep learning. The experience of ongoing learning keeps you alert, open-minded, and stimulated.

- Develop a support team. Avoid major stress by having friends and family members available to back you up when things don't go well.

- Accept only commitments that are important to you. Politely turn down other projects that drain your time and energy.

- Seek new ways of using your creativity. By rethinking the way you perform routine tasks, you make them less boring and stressful.

- Welcome changes. Consider them new challenges rather than threats to the status quo.

- Replace negative images in your mind with positive ones.

Some Jobs Are Boring—Most Can Become Boring

Some jobs are basically boring, but any job can become boring when you do it over and over again, day after day, year after year. In many companies, jobs are enriched to minimize boredom. By adding new functions and combining several simple tasks into a more challenging total activity, jobs can be made less boring.

To prevent your team members' jobs from becoming boring you might

- Re-examine all routine work that your team performs. Encourage all people who perform the work to suggest ways of making it more interesting.

- People performing routine work often get into a rut. They start out every day performing aspect 1, then go to aspect 2 and 3, and so on. Unless it's essential that work be done in a predetermined order, suggest that they change the pattern

- Cross-train team members to do a variety of jobs so that they can move from one type of work to another and be less likely to become bored.

Dealing With Alcohol and Drug Problems

Suppose that one of your team members seems to have an alcohol problem. You've never seen the person drink or come to work drunk, but you often smell alcohol on the person's breath. This person is frequently absent, especially on Mondays.

You can't ignore this situation. Speak to the team member about it, and prepare to hear all sorts of denials: "Me, drink? Only socially." Or, "Alcohol breath? It's cough medicine."

Rather than talk about a drinking problem, talk about job performance, absence from work, and other job-related matters. Inform the person that if the situation continues, you'll have to take disciplinary action.

If your team member continues this behavior pattern, bring up your concern about the drinking and suggest—or insist on—counseling.

Discussing Alcohol Problems

It isn't easy to discuss with a team member such a sensitive and personal matter as an alcohol problem. The U.S. Department of Health and Human Services suggests the following approach in its pamphlet "Supervisor's Guide on Alcohol Abuse":

- Don't apologize for discussing the matter. Make it clear that job performance is involved.

- Encourage your team member to explain why work performance, behavior, or attendance is deteriorating. This approach may provide an opportunity to discuss the use of alcohol.

- Don't discuss a person's right to drink or make a moral issue of it. Alcoholism is a disease that, left untreated, can lead to many more serious illnesses. Beyond being a disease, it's another form of sin. Pray that this person can be set free from the bondage.

- Don't suggest that your team member use moderation or change drinking habits. According to Alcoholics Anonymous, alcoholics cannot change their drinking habits without help. It's up to them to make the decision to stop drinking and take steps to get that help.

> **Power Principles**
>
> To prevent any misunderstandings or ambiguities, every company should have a formal policy prohibiting drinking on company premises or during working hours. This policy should be in writing and should be reviewed periodically with all employees. Restrictions should specifically include beer and wine in addition to "hard" liquor.

- Don't be distracted by excuses for drinking. The problem as far as you're concerned is the drinking itself—and how it affects work, behavior, and attendance on the job.

- Remember that alcoholics, like any other sick people, should be given the opportunity for treatment and rehabilitation.

- Emphasize that your primary concern is the team member's work performance. Point out that if the person's behavior doesn't improve, you'll have to take disciplinary action, including suspension or discharge.

- Point out that the decision to seek assistance is the team member's responsibility.

If your company has an employee-assistance program (see Chapter 21), describe it and strongly recommend that it be used.

Preventing Drinking and Drug Use on the Job

In most companies, showing up at work drunk or drinking on the job is a punishable offense. But it's not always easy to prove that a person is drunk. Appearing to be drunk isn't enough. Even a police officer cannot arrest a suspect for driving while intoxicated unless the officer substantiates the claim with a breath or blood test.

If one of your employees seems to be drunk, your safest course is to send the person to your medical department for testing. If that's not possible, don't allow the person to work—send the person home, but don't let him or her drive. If the employee gets into an accident, you or your company may share liability. Don't ask another employee to drive the person home, either; call a taxi. The next day, discuss the situation and point out that if it occurs again, you'll take disciplinary action. Also, be sure to suggest counseling.

Although drug use on the job has increased, it isn't nearly as common as drinking. Treat drug users in the same way that you deal with drinkers. Because drug use (and particularly the sale of drugs) is illegal, however, you should consult your attorney about the best ways to handle this situation. Testing for the use of drugs is becoming an increasingly routine practice in many companies, although most of them test employees only when they suspect drug use.

The Americans with Disabilities Act includes alcoholism and drug addiction as disabilities (see Chapter 10).

HIV/AIDS in the Workplace

Despite all the articles and TV programs that make clear it that HIV is spread primarily through semen and blood, many people still have an unreasonable fear of even casual contact with a person who has the virus.

Wise Counsel

You can obtain literature about HIV/AIDS and information about awareness programs from your local health department or from the CDC National AIDS Clearing House at 1-800-458-5231.

When it becomes known that an employee of a company has HIV or AIDS, many co-workers refuse to work with that person. If the person with AIDS is on your team or works in conjunction with it, this attitude can disrupt your team's activities.

To avoid these situations, companies have instituted programs to inform employees of the true facts about the virus and the disease. HIV/AIDS–awareness programs include videos, pamphlets, articles in the company newspaper, and talks to employees by doctors.

"It's Not My Staff—It's My Peers"

You get along fine with your boss. You and your team members have a great relationship. But you keep running into conflicts and problems with one or more of your peers—other team leaders or staff managers. Why?

There could be dozens of reasons. First, look into yourself. Is it you or them who cause the problem? It's not easy to be introspective, but try to be honest with yourself. If you don't get along with many people, something that you are doing or thinking may be causing it. You may be stubborn and insist on doing things your way. You may come across as arrogant or domineering. So evaluate yourself. Ask friends or associates to help you with this. But must of all, ask God to show you your faults, and seek his grace to overcome them.

On the other hand, if you get along fine with most people but have problems with one or a few, the difficulties are more likely their fault. Look for the cause, if you can. Maybe they're the kind of people who can't get along with anyone. Maybe their goals and agenda differ from yours. Here are a couple of explanations:

- **Competition.** The other person may look upon you as a competitor for advancement in the company and may consciously or subconsciously fear cooperating with you.

- **Jealousy.** The other person may resent your position or accomplishments.

There is not much you can do about your peers' personality problems. These people need professional help. They rarely succeed in their jobs—and unless they are experts in a hard-to-replace technical job, they won't be around for long.

As for problems stemming from competition or jealousy, you can deal with them diplomatically. Remember, you need to gain the cooperation of even competitive or jealous people to accomplish any project in which both of you are collaborating.

Follow the principles of good salesmanship when you deal with peers who are reluctant to cooperate:

1. **Gain their attention.** When presenting an idea these people may resist, make a comment that will get them to sit up and take notice. Everybody likes compliments. So compliment them on something they accomplished that you truly admired. You now have their attention.

2. **Ask questions.** Find out what excites the other person about the situation that is involved. Instead of presenting your idea, ask questions. Listen to that person's responses. Most people are so anxious to "sell" their ideas that they do not fully listen to what the "buyer" really wants. Do not presuppose that this person's interests are identical to yours.

3. **Present evidence.** Develop considerable evidence to back up the ideas you want to sell. Once you learn what the other person really wants, you can tailor your evidence to that person's desires.

4. **Be prepared to deal with objections.** If you have had previous dealings with that person, you may anticipate what objections may be raised and be ready to counter them. Your questions will uncover others. Learning the objections is the best way to know where the real problems lie.

5. **Close the sale.** Get the other person to agree to a plan of action that you both feel will get the job done. Ask the person to summarize it so that you are sure that there is a clear understanding.

Dealing With the Boss's Relatives

Have you ever worked for a company in which the boss placed his relatives in key positions? Well, sometimes these men and women are real contributors, but often they are incompetent or worse. Smart managers place them in positions where they can do minimal harm.

In one company, the boss's daughter held a variety of jobs. She not only messed up the jobs, but she cried on her daddy's shoulder if her supervisors criticized her. Rather than lose some of his top producers, the boss transferred her to another department—where, of course, the same thing occurred.

What can you do when faced with this nepotism? Here are some suggestions:

- **Make an honest effort to smooth the relationship.** Be diplomatic. Be patient. Try to persuade the relative to see things your way. Let the person think that what you want is really his or her idea.

- **If that fails, have a heart-to-heart talk with the boss.** Let the boss know what the specific problems are, and suggest solutions that are in the best interest of the company.

- **Find ways to bypass the relative.** For example, in dealing with the penny-pinching brother, sell the boss on the value of your idea before you even bring it up to the brother.

- **Be prepared to defend your stand.** The boss may favor relatives, but the success of the business comes first. Have the pertinent facts and figures to back you up.

- **Last resort: Draw the line.** This is not to be used unless you are confident that you'll win. Point out that unless the relative ceases to interfere, you cannot do the job you have been assigned to do. This may be interpreted as an ultimatum, and it may force you to quit if it's not accepted. But if the boss is objective about it, you may win your point.

Workplace Violence—A Growing Menace

Workplace violence is the second leading cause of death in the workplace. Three people in America are murdered on the job every working day. Although the rate of homicides has decreased in recent years, the rate of violent assaults has increased. Reasons that workplace violence occurs include these:

- **Economic.** Corporate downsizing and layoffs cause unrest in the company.
- **Societal.** These include drugs, alcohol, availability of guns, fractured families.
- **Psychological.** Serious problems in people's lives can cause personal breakdowns.
- **Organizational culture.** These include an overstressed workforce and the pressure of the job.
- **Workplace climate.** Some workplace environments have the seeds of violence built into them, just waiting for a chance to explode. Some of these are as follows:
  - Authoritarian management style
  - Unpredictable supervisory methods
  - Undervalued work and dignity of people
  - High degree of secrecy (not sharing information)
  - Disproportionate discipline
  - Bias against and favoritism toward some employees
  - Strained labor/management relations

In recent years, post offices have drawn much public scrutiny for seeming to breed workplace violence. The actual incidence of such violent acts at post offices, however, is well below average. As a matter of fact, the U.S. Postal Service has taken special steps to provide a safe working environment for its employees.

A six-step procedure, emulated by many private sector companies, has been established to strategize prevention of violence in the postal service:

- **Selection.** Hire the right people for the right job in the first place. By carefully selecting and placing new employees, you greatly minimize the risk of their ever becoming discontent.

- **Security.** Ensure appropriate safeguards for people and property.

- **Communication of policy.** The policies of appropriate behavior on the job should be clearly established and communicated to all employees at all levels of the organization. Employees should fully understand what constitutes acceptable and unacceptable behavior. And management should reinforce its policy: All employees should be aware of the penalties of violation.

- **Environment and culture.** Create a work environment and maintain a climate that is perceived as fair and free of unlawful and inappropriate behaviors.

- **Establishment of resources.** Ensure that managers, supervisors, and employees are aware of the available resources to assist them in dealing with the problems of work and daily living. Employee-assistance programs should be set up and should be easily accessible to all employees.

- **Separation.** When separation is necessary, the process should be handled professionally. Managers should assess the possibility of inappropriate behavior or potential violence and confer with specially trained people to figure out how to handle the situation.

Power Principles

Prevent trouble by rapid redress of disputes:

Resolve

Employment

Disputes

Reach

Equitable

Solutions

Swiftly

Before a worker is ever handed a pink slip, the service makes sure that the employee receives a threat assessment interview to assess any inappropriate behavior or potentially violent circumstances. A union representative is called in to outline the reasons termination is necessary. Often that representative agrees and explains to the worker why he or she will not represent that person in a protest of the firing.

In addition, company-paid career-counseling sessions can go a long way in creating goodwill and a peaceful parting. Follow-up security by an outside firm can also be helpful.

To implement this strategy, workplace violence-awareness programs have been instituted for Postal Service managers, supervisors, and union leaders. In these programs, people are taught to use the skills and techniques that foster professional interactions with employees.

Chapter

21

The Manager as a Counselor

You can learn a lot from a shepherd, especially when your concern is for a biblical model of leadership. In his classic book *Be a Motivational Leader*, Leroy Eims emphasizes shepherding traits that are instructional for leaders—especially in ministry, but similarly in secular settings:

> A leader must watch out for his people and tend to their needs. Solomon said, "Be sure you know the condition of your flocks, give careful attention to your herds." (Proverbs 27:23) God has called us to be shepherds. Our Master's words to Peter should be enough motivation for us: 'Jesus said ... Do you truly love me? ... Take care of my sheep.' (John 21:16)

As shepherd of the team, you must identify problems in their early stages and correct a situation before it mushrooms into a major problem. Your tool: counseling.

Counseling is a means of helping troubled associates overcome barriers to good performance. Through careful listening, open discussion, and sound advice, a counselor helps identify problems, clarify misunderstandings, and plan solutions.

When a team leader "counsels" an associate, it's more analogous to a coach of an athletic team counseling a player than to a psychotherapist counseling a patient. Professional counseling should be done by trained specialists; as you will learn in this chapter, sometimes referrals to these specialists are necessary.

Interpret and Apply

A **gripe** is an informal complaint. A **grievance** is a formal complaint, usually based on the violation of a union contract or formal company policy.

Avoiding Stumbling Blocks

As tempting as it may be to threaten to fire uncooperative team members, don't do it unless you really can carry it out. Most union contracts make the process for firing employees complex. Sometimes company policies, EEO implications, or other factors restrict these actions.

Handling Gripes and Grievances

Sometimes you see a problem. Sometimes you don't— you find out only when someone complains. A complaint may be your first hint of an impending problem, a reminder of an ongoing situation that hasn't been attended to, or just be one of your associates letting off steam. But you don't know until you check it out. This section addresses how you can best work through *gripes* and *grievances* with your team members.

Dealing with Chronic Complainers

You know your team members. Some of them are always complaining. They seem to get their kicks from complaining. Sometimes they do have legitimate complaints, of course, so you can't just automatically ignore them. You have to listen, and that can be time-consuming and annoying.

One way to minimize this kind of griping is to pay more attention to the people who complain. The reason for the complaints is often their desire to be the center of attention. By talking to them, asking their opinions, and praising their good work, you satisfy their need for attention and give them less reason to gripe.

Checking Out Complaints

Most complaints are signals to you that shouldn't be ignored. Even if a complaint seems to have no validity, check it out anyway. You don't always have all the information, and you may discover facets of the situation you weren't aware of.

Follow these steps to find out what's going on:

1. **Listen.** Even if a complaint seems to be unfounded, in the mind of the complainant it's a serious matter.

2. **Investigate.** Take nothing for granted. Look at the record, and talk to others who know about the situation.

3. **Report back.** If the gripe is unfounded, explain your reasoning to the complainant. If it *is* substantiated, explain what you will do to correct it.

4. **Take action.** Do what must be done to correct the problem. If your investigation verifies that the complaint is justified, but you can't do anything about it, find out who can. Bring the situation to the attention of your boss or whoever can adjust it.

Filing Formal Grievances

When a company has a union contract, the procedures for handling grievances are clearly outlined. Companies that don't have union agreements often set up their own procedures for dealing with employee grievances.

Here's a typical four-step approach:

1. The person making the complaint discusses it with his or her immediate supervisor or team leader. Every attempt to resolve the problem should be made at this level.

2. If no settlement is reached, the individual should be given an opportunity to bring the problem to the next level of management without fear of reprisal.

3. If the complaint is still unresolved, it may go to the general manager or a specially appointed manager (often the human resources director). An agreement is usually reached during this stage.

4. Although arbitration is rare in a nonunion environment, management in some companies provides for a mutually agreed upon third party to be available if the company and the aggrieved person cannot work out their problem.

As the immediate supervisor or team leader, you play the key role in this process. You should make every effort to resolve grievances without having to go beyond step 1. Grievance procedures take time and energy that would be better spent doing your team's primary work. To help you deal with a grievance systematically, use the following sample grievance worksheet.

Grievance Worksheet

Complainant: _____ Date: _____

Team leader: _____

Grievance: _____

_____

_____

_____

Report of investigation: _____

_____

_____

_____

If justified, action taken: _____

_____

_____

_____

If not justified, reason: _____

_____

_____

_____

Date reported to complainant: _____

Complainant's comments: _____

_____

_____

Team leader's comments: _____

_____

_____

That's the Spirit

Jesus' call for forgiveness is a foreign concept to the world. Turning the other cheek seems, at best, laughable or, at worst, suicide. So, you may not see from an employee the level of forgiveness that you would expect in Christian fellowship. One thing's for certain, though: Forgiveness can't happen as long as the wrong is not understood. Always begin by listening to grievances.

Preventing Grievances

Dealing with grievances is time-consuming and takes you away from more productive work. This section provides some suggestions for preventing grievances from developing on your team:

- Regularly let all team members know how they're doing. People want feedback on not only their failures, but also on their successes.

- Encourage team members to participate in all aspects of planning and performing the team's work.

- Listen to team members' ideas.

- Make only promises that you know you can keep.

- Be alert to minor irritations and trivial problems so that you can correct them before they become serious dissatisfactions.

- Resolve problems as soon as possible.

Interpret and Apply

definition

In **arbitration**, both parties present their side of a problem and an arbitrator decides what should be done. In **mediation**, both parties present their side of a problem and a mediator works with them to reach a mutually satisfactory solution.

Resolving Conflicts Within Your Team

Two types of conflicts occur when people work together. One is tangible (a disagreement about a project, for example), and the other is intangible (two people just don't like each other, for example, and can't get along). In this section, you'll learn some techniques for managing both types of conflicts.

Suppose you give an assignment to two of your team members, Ken and Barbie. They discuss the project and cannot agree about how it should be pursued. They both come back to you, their team leader, to resolve the problem.

You can use one of two approaches: *arbitrate* or *mediate*.

Mediating Disagreements

Mediation is the preferred approach because it's more likely to result in a win-win compromise. The most negative effect of using mediation is that it's time-consuming (and you often don't have much time to solve a problem).

Suppose you have chosen to mediate a disagreement between two team members. The first person recounts how she views the situation. You might think that the next step is for the second person to state his side, but it isn't. Instead, he is asked to recount her view as he understands it. The reason for this step is that when the first party explains her view to the other party, the other person typically only partly listens. That person may be thinking about what she plans to say and how to rebut the argument. By being aware of having to repeat the first person's views, that person becomes aware of having to listen carefully.

By having the second person repeat the first person's side of the story, any areas of misunderstanding can be clarified before the second person presents her views. It's amazing how often conflicts are caused by these types of misunderstandings. The same process is then followed with the second person stating her views.

During this discussion, you (as the mediator) take notes. After each person presents his or her views, you review your notes with the participants. Most disputes have many more areas of agreement than disagreement. By identifying these areas, you can focus on matters that must be resolved and tackle them one at a time.

Because you don't have an unlimited amount of time, you must set a time limit on these meetings. Suppose you've set aside two hours for the first meeting. At the end of the specified time, you still have several more items to discuss. Set up another meeting for that purpose. Suggest that the participants meet in the interim without you to work on some of the problems. Often, after a climate of compromise is established, a large number of issues can be resolved without your presence.

Now the next meeting is scheduled for one hour, and more problems are resolved. If the project must get underway, this may be all the time you have. If some unresolved problems still exist, you have to change your role from mediator to arbitrator and make the decisions.

Time to Arbitrate

The following five steps can help you arbitrate a conflict, if you choose to deal with it in that way:

1. Get the facts. Listen carefully to both sides. Investigate on your own to get additional information. Don't limit yourself to "hard facts." Learn about underlying feelings and emotions.

2. Evaluate the facts.

3. Study the alternatives. Are the solutions suggested by the two parties the only possible choices? Can compromises be made? Is a different resolution possible?

4. Make a decision.

5. Notify the two parties of your decision. Make sure that they fully understand it. If necessary, "sell" it to them so that they will agree and be committed to implementing it.

Power Principles

It's childish to say, "I'm the boss, and this is what I've decided." Let team members know the reason behind decisions, and clarify misunderstandings before implementing a decision.

When Team Members Can't Get Along

If two people on your team dislike each other so much that it affects their work, you have to do something about it. First find out why the two people dislike each other. This type of animosity often stems from a past bitter conflict.

If at all possible, transfer one or both parties to different departments that have little contact with each other. That option isn't always feasible; because there may not be any other departments in which they can use their skills, you have to take steps to overcome this situation.

Speak to each person. If your attempts to persuade them to cooperate fail, lay down the law: "If this team is to succeed, all its members must work together. What happened in the past is past. Write it off. I'm not asking you to like each other. I don't care if you never associate with each other off the job. I'm demanding that you work together to meet our goals." If necessary, follow up this directive with disciplinary action.

Often the reason for the dislike isn't based on any specific factor. It happens to all of us: You meet a person, and something about him or her turns you off and you immediately dislike that person.

> **That's the Spirit**
>
> Don't give advice about serious personal matters. You're not a trained psychologist, nor are you a pastor or Christian counselor (at least, that is our assumption in this book). Listen! Help put the problem into perspective. Provide or suggest sources for additional information. Help associates clarify a situation and come to their own conclusions. And if opportunity seems to be arising to communicate how Christ is the relevant solution, be sensitive to what might be a more appropriate time and place: Consider meeting after and away from the office. (Always trust in God's Spirit to lead someone; don't push your own agenda for fear of a missed opportunity. God's Spirit will make it happen, not your cleverness or opportunism.)

Psychologists say that this reaction occurs because something about this person subconsciously reminds the other of some unpleasant past experience. Something about Jack (his haircut, the manner in which he speaks, a mole on his left cheek) reminds Rachel of a third-grade bully who made life miserable for her that year, and she hates him. These factors, called minimal cues, trigger long-forgotten subconscious memories that still influence our reactions to people.

When you notice that team members have an unexplainable dislike for other members, tell them about minimal cues. Help them understand that their reactions are normal but that it's important not to let these reactions influence their attitudes toward other people. Awareness of the psychology underlying this feeling will help overcome a person's irrational attitude.

"I'm Not Ann Landers"

Another area in which supervisors counsel their associates concerns personal matters that may affect employees' work. All of us have personal problems. We worry about our health, about our families, and about money. We always have something to worry about. People carry their worries with them into the workplace, and worries do affect their work.

You may be reluctant to pry into an associate's personal life—and many people resent prying. Sometimes, however, it's necessary. It's much easier if you and your team members have good personal relationships and if you've always shown interest in the members as individuals. Counseling is a natural follow-through on your usual interest.

If you have this type of relationship, begin the discussion by commenting about job-related matters. Ask a question about the project that's involved, for example. It may lead into a discussion of the problems the person is having with the project, which may be caused by personal matters.

Be an empathetic listener. Your role as counselor is to give team members an opportunity to unload their problems. Encourage them by asking questions. Don't criticize, argue a point, or make a judgment. Act as a sounding board to help release the pressures that are causing the problem. Help the person clarify the situation so that the solution will be easier to reach.

Power Principles

John Maxwell advises that when you have to work with a difficult person, practice these five principles:

1. Love them unconditionally.
2. Ask God for wisdom in working with them.
3. Stay emotionally healthy yourself.
4. Do not elevate people to positions of leadership in order to rescue them.
5. Be honest with God, yourself, and them.

Counseling isn't a cure-all. In many areas you just can't help. When a problem is one that you can help by just talking it out, your intervention can be useful. Don't lose patience or give up too easily. Often more than one session is necessary to build a sense of trust and to get a team member to open up. Although you're not a counselor, you should have some related experience as a Christian. You are called to admonish, rebuke, instruct, and encourage other Christians in righteous living. Try to transfer some of these skills to the workplace.

Knowing What to Do When Talking Doesn't Help

You may be reluctant or even embarrassed to suggest that a team member see a professional counselor. Many people take umbrage at this suggestion: "Do you think

Avoiding Stumbling Blocks

When you refer someone for professional help, avoid using the terms *psychiatrist, psychologist,* or *therapist*—they have negative connotations to most people. Tell a troubled person that he or she might benefit from seeing a counselor who specializes in a particular area. Back up your advice by explaining how counseling has helped other people.

I'm nuts?" Point out that going to a professional counselor is now as accepted as going to a medical doctor. Young people are exposed to counseling beginning in elementary school. The most frequently given advice offered by Ann Landers, Dear Abby, and other advice columnists is to seek counseling when faced with serious problems.

Not all problems that require professional assistance are psychological. They may be caused by a medical condition or serious financial troubles. Often they're marital or family situations.

If your company has an employee-assistance program, making a referral to it immediately relieves you of the burden of suggesting specific counseling (see the following section). If not, your human resources department may help provide referrals. You may find it helpful to research the available sources of help in your community:

- **Medical doctors.** If a company doesn't have its own medical department or an employee doesn't have a primary-care physician, local hospitals or medical societies can provide a list of qualified physicians.

- **Psychiatrists.** These MDs deal with serious psychological disorders.

- **Psychologists or psychotherapists.** These specialists usually have a degree in psychology or social work, and handle most of the usual emotional problems people face.

- **Marriage counselors and family therapists.** These professionals deal with marital problems, difficulties with children, and related matters.

- **Financial counselors.** These people help others work out payment plans with creditors, develop budgets, and live within their income. Your bank or credit union can provide referrals.

- **Pastors and Christian counselors.** If your team member is a church-goer or acknowledged Christian, spiritual direction can help in the psychological, emotional, and physical dimensions.

Employee Assistance Programs (EAPs)

An employee-assistance program, or EAP, is a company-sponsored counseling service. Many companies have instituted these programs to help employees deal with personal problems that interfere with productivity. The counselors aren't company employees, but are outside experts retained on an as-needed basis. Initiating the use of the EAP can be done in two ways, which are discussed in this section.

Sometimes an employee takes the initiative in contacting the company's EAP. The company informs its employees about the program through e-mail, bulletins, announcements in the company newspaper, meetings, and letters to their homes. Often a hotline telephone number is provided.

Another way to start the process is by having a supervisor take the initiative to contact the EAP. Suppose the work performance of one of your top performers has recently declined. You often see him sitting idly at his desk, his thoughts obviously far from his job. You ask him what's going on, but he shrugs off your question by saying, "I'm okay—just tired."

After several conversations, he finally tells you about a family problem, and you suggest that he contact your company's EAP.

Even though you've made the referral and the employee has followed through, don't expect progress reports. From now on, the matter is handled confidentially. Your feedback comes from seeing improvement in the employee's work as the counseling helps with the problem.

Employee-assistance programs are expensive to maintain, but organizations that have used them for several years report that they pay off. EAPs salvage skilled and experienced workers who, without help, may leave a company.

Doling Out Discipline

"My son, do not make light of the Lord's discipline, and do not lose heart when he rebukes you, because the Lord disciplines those he loves, and he punishes everyone he accepts as a son" (Heb. 12:5–6).

When you hear or see the word *discipline*, the first thing that usually pops into your mind is punishment. Look at that word again. Notice that by dropping just two letters, it turns into *disciple*, a synonym for "student" and a concept very familiar to followers of Christ.

Both words are derived from the Latin word meaning "to learn." If you look at discipline, not as punishment, but as a means of learning, both you and your associates get much more out of it. You are the *coach*, and your associates are the *learners*.

Unfortunately, people don't always learn what they are taught. Despite your best efforts, some of your team members may not perform satisfactorily. If infractions still occur, even after you've clearly explained the rules, you must take steps to get things back on track.

Regardless of the cause, discipline begins when you work to correct the problem. When you've made every effort to help your associates learn and when all else fails, only then does discipline take the form of punishment.

This part of the book looks at the steps involved in progressive discipline and explores the dos and don'ts of punishment and termination.

Spare the Rod and Spoil the Employee

"Flog a mocker, and the simple will learn prudence; rebuke a discerning man, and he will gain knowledge." (Proverbs 19:25) It's probably a good thing that the first option (flogging) is not a plausible one today. But there's a principle of wisdom here that gives important perspective on the purpose of discipline—to learn, to gain knowledge.

Some people are admittedly slow to learn, and they may require more drastic intervention—granted, not the inflicting of pain, but perhaps discomfort in the form of loss of benefits or privileges. What we want is the second scenario, though. We hope that our team members are discerning men and women who will take a rebuke for what it is intended: opportunity to gain knowledge.

This chapter looks at the system of progressive discipline used by most organizations today and examines how it can be used effectively by team leaders. This chapter also explores some alternative approaches to progressive discipline.

Keep in mind that the contents of this chapter are based on general practices that are used in many organizations. Your company's policies may differ. You may get some good ideas from this chapter that you can't use now, but you can suggest them to your company's management. Until your company incorporates these ideas into its policies, however, follow your company's current practices.

Progressive Discipline

In most organizations, it's important for every member of a team to be at his or her workstation at starting time. If one person comes to work late, it can hold up an entire team.

Suppose that an employee was late three times in his first month on the job. You spoke to him about it, and for several months he kept his promise to be on time. He was late one day last week, and this morning he was late again. His reason for the tardiness is vague. Your informal chats with him about the matter haven't done any good, so now you're ready to apply progressive discipline.

The Reprimand: An Informal Warning

The chats you've had with the team member weren't part of the progressive discipline system; instead, they were a friendly reminder of his responsibility to your team.

The first official step in the progressive discipline system is often called the oral, or verbal, warning: You take the team member aside and remind him that the two of you have discussed his lateness and that, because he continues to come to work late, you must put him on notice. Inform him of the next steps you'll take if the behavior continues.

You may be exasperated about a team member's failure to keep a promise to be on time. It's normal to be annoyed if your team's work is delayed, but don't lose your cool. Consider this positive example of a confrontation:

You: You know how important it is for you to be here when the workday begins. The entire team depends on all of us being on time.

Employee: I'm sorry. I ran into unusual traffic this morning.

You: We all face traffic in the morning. What can you do to make sure that you'll be on time in the future?

Employee: I've tried alternative routes, but it doesn't help. I guess I'll have to leave earlier every day so that, if I do run into traffic, I'll at least have a head start.

You: That sounds good to me. You're a valuable member of our team, and being on time will help all of us.

When you're preparing to reprimand someone, to ensure that you conduct the reprimand in the most effective manner, reread the following guidelines for reprimanding.

Guidelines for Reprimanding

Time the reprimand properly. As soon as possible after the offense has been committed, call the employee aside and discuss the matter in private.

Never reprimand when you're angry. Wait until you have calmed down.

Emphasize the *what*, not the *who*. Base the reprimand on the action that was wrong, not on the person.

Begin by stating the problem and then ask a question. Don't begin with an accusation: "You're always' late!" Say instead, "You know how important it is for all of us to be on the job promptly. What can you do to get here on time from now on?"

Listen! Attentive, open-minded listening is one of the most important factors of true leadership. Ask questions to elicit as much information about the situation as you can. Respond to the associate's comments, but don't convert the interview into a confrontation.

Encourage your team member to make suggestions for solving the problem. When a person participates in reaching a solution, there's a much greater chance that it will be accepted and accomplished.

Provide constructive criticism. Give your team member specific suggestions, when possible, about how to correct a situation.

Never use sarcasm. Sarcasm never corrects a situation; it only makes the other person feel inadequate and put upon.

End your reprimand on a positive note. Comment on some of the good things the person has accomplished so that he or she know that you are not focusing only on the reason for this reprimand, but instead on total performance. Reassure the person that you look on him or her as a valuable member of your team.

> **Avoiding Stumbling Blocks**
>
> Never reprimand people when you're angry, when they're angry, or in the presence of other people. Reprimands should be a private matter between two calm people working together to solve a problem.

They Always Have an Excuse

If you've been in management for any length of time, you've probably heard some wild excuses. No matter how silly, ridiculous, or improbable the excuse may be, listen—and listen carefully—for these reasons:

- Until you listen to the entire story, you cannot know whether it has validity. In most companies, there are acceptable reasons for not following a company rule or procedure. Under extenuating circumstances, it's sensible to be flexible when you enforce the rules.

- Even if an excuse is unacceptable, let your team member get it out of her system (a process called catharsis). When people have something on their mind, they won't listen to a word you say until they get their story out. Afterward, you can say, "I understand what you're saying, but the important thing is to be here on time."

Asking for a Plan of Action

When you deliver a verbal warning, throw the problem back to your team member. Rather than say, "This is what you should do," ask "What do you think you can do to correct this situation?" Get people to come up with their own plans of action. In more complex situations, a plan may take longer to develop.

Documenting a Reprimand

Even informal reprimands shouldn't be strictly oral. You should keep a record of the reprimand. Legal implications mandate that you document any action that could lead to serious disciplinary action.

Some team leaders document an informal warning by simply noting it on their calendars or entering it in a team log. Others write a detailed memo for their files. You should use the technique your company prefers.

Conducting a Disciplinary Interview

If an employee repeats an offense after receiving a verbal warning, the next step is the disciplinary interview.

This interview differs from a reprimand in that it is more formal. A verbal warning is usually a relatively brief session, often conducted in a quiet corner of the room. A disciplinary interview is longer and is conducted in an office or conference room.

A disciplinary interview should always be carefully prepared and should result in a mutually agreed upon plan of action. Whereas a plan of action after a verbal warning is usually oral, the resulting plan in a disciplinary interview should be put in writing. It not only reminds both the leader and the team member of what has been agreed on, but it also serves as documentation.

To ensure that a disciplinary interview is carried out systematically, use the following discipline worksheet.

> **That's the Spirit**
>
> When you sense problems are developing, prayerfully seek God's guidance as to how it might be addressed before it explodes. With God's Spirit of merciful discernment, you can actively keep an eye out for problems, even before they develop.

Discipline Worksheet

Part I (Complete before interview begins)

Team member: _____ Date: _____

Offense: _____

_____

_____

Policy and procedures provision: _____

Date of occurrence: _____

Previous similar offenses: _____

_____

What I want to accomplish: _____

_____

continues

continued

Special considerations: _____

_____

Questions to ask at beginning of interview: _____

_____

_____

Part II (Keep in front of you during interview)

- Keep calm and collected   .
- Listen actively.
- Emphasize the *what*, not the who.
- Give *team member* the opportunity to solve the problem.

- Get the whole story.
- Don't interrupt.
- Avoid sarcasm.

Part III (Fill out near end of interview)

Suggestions made by team member: _____

_____

_____

Agreed-on solution: _____

_____

_____

Part IV (Action taken: Fill in when interview is finished)

Documentation completed: _____

_____

Writing Up Warnings

The next step in progressive discipline is to give the offender a written warning—a letter or form that will be placed in the employee's personnel file. Written warnings often are taken more seriously than the first two steps. Employees don't want negative reports in their personnel files, and even the possibility that they'll be "written up" serves as a deterrent to poor behavior.

If the written warning concerns poor performance, specify the performance standards and indicate in what way the employee's performance fell short of the standards. Also state what was done to help the employee meet the standards. This will protect you against potential claims that you made no effort to bring the performance up to standard.

If the warning concerns infraction of a company rule, specify the nature of the offense and what disciplinary steps were taken before writing the warning (see the following two sample letters).

To protect your company from potential legal problems, check any form letters concerning discipline with your legal advisors before sending them to be printed.

Although it's always advantageous from a legal standpoint to have employees sign *all* disciplinary documents, it becomes imperative when the warning itself is in writing.

You can't force anyone to sign anything. If an employee refuses to sign a disciplinary document, call in a witness—a person who isn't directly involved in the situation—and repeat your request. If he still refuses, have the witness attest to that response on the document.

To avoid misunderstandings, give copies of all disciplinary documents to the employee. In addition, you should send a copy to the human resources department to include in the person's personnel file.

The preceding sample Memo for Poor Conduct and following Memo for Poor Performance can help you prepare written warnings. Refer to them for ideas about how to phrase a written warning.

Putting Employees on Probation

Until now, all your attempts to correct a team member's performance or behavior have been positive, and you've provided advice and counsel. If nothing has worked, your next step is to put the team member on probation. Set a deadline for adjusting the situation.

What you're doing is giving your associate one more chance to shape up before you invoke some form of punishment. Most people take probation seriously—they know that you mean business. If that doesn't help, additional disciplinary steps won't help. If you can transfer the person to a more suitable job, do so; if not, you have no other choice than to terminate him or her.

Company practices for administering probation vary considerably. They're governed by union contracts, company policy manuals, or sometimes unwritten (but previously followed) practices. Usually the notification of probation is in the form of a written statement, signed by the team leader or a higher-ranking manager and acknowledged by the employee. The employee keeps one copy, the team leader gets another copy, and the human resources department keeps a copy in its files.

Probationary periods vary from as few as 10 days to the more customary 30 days and sometimes even longer. If an employee makes significant progress, lift the probation. If he or she repeats the offense after the probation is lifted, you can either reinstate the probation or invoke the next step.

When an offense violates company rules (tardiness, absenteeism, or other misconduct), proceed to the next step, which is usually suspension.

Suspension: The First Real Punishment

You're severely limited in the ways you can punish employees. Ever since flogging was abolished, only a few types of punishment can be legally administered. The most commonly used method, short of termination, is suspension without pay. Of course, the downside of suspension is that you lose that person's contribution to the team for a period.

That's the Spirit

Often in disciplinary scenarios you can find yourself in the difficult position of having to maintain integrity and keep the matter confidential, even though the disciplined is freely sharing his or her skewed version of the story. Proverbs 10:19 touches on this: "When words are many, sin is not absent, but he who holds his tongue is wise." Trust God to bring about justice, and hold your tongue.

The mechanics of issuing a suspension are similar to those of probation. Union contracts often mandate consultation with a union representative before suspending an employee. Most companies aren't unionized and require approval for suspensions by both the manager to whom the team leader reports and the human resources department. Appropriate documentation specifying the reason for the suspension and the exact period of time involved should be made, signed by the appropriate manager and acknowledged by the suspended employee.

If an employee returns from a suspension and continues to break the rules, your next step may be a longer suspension or even termination.

Termination: The Final Step

The chief purpose of progressive discipline is to give the offending employee an opportunity to change his or her behavior and become a productive, cooperative team member. If the employee fails to improve, however, the termination should take place.

The practical and legal facets of terminating employees are discussed in detail in Chapter 23.

Affirmative Discipline: A New Approach

Some companies have done away with punishment, based on this logic: Team members are adults, adults take responsibility for their own actions, and punishment is therefore childish.

> **That's the Spirit**
>
> To the wise rather than the foolish person, affirmative discipline should be more effective. Proverbs 16:21–22 explains this well: "The wise in heart are called discerning, and pleasant words promote instruction. Understanding is a fountain of life to those who have it, but folly brings punishment to fools."

Here's how affirmative discipline works:

1. When a person is hired, the team leader and the new team member thoroughly discuss company rules and policies. The new employee is asked to make a commitment to comply with the rules.

2. If a rule is violated, the team leader points out the infraction and reminds the person of the agreement to comply with the rules. Both parties sign a memo to document the meeting.

3. If a violation occurs again, a second conference is held. The team member is asked to sign a special affirmation statement to show that the company takes the rules seriously and expects all employees to do the same.

4. If a member violates a minor rule for the third time or a major rule even one time, the leader asks the team member whether he really wants to continue working for the company. If the answer is yes, the team member is asked to sign a document acknowledging the violation and indicating that he understands that additional violations will lead to termination.

5. In some organizations, the employee is then asked to take a day off—with pay—to consider seriously whether she can live up to the commitment. Why is it a paid day off? By paying an employee under these circumstances, the company is expressing confidence in the person and in the system: It puts its money where its mouth is, not by punishing that person, but by treating him or her as an adult.

> **Avoiding Stumbling Blocks**
>
> It's not a good idea to extend a probationary period more than once. Continuous probation is bad for morale and rarely solves the problem.

Companies that use affirmative discipline report that although terminations do occur occasionally, discipline problems significantly decrease.

In most organizations, senior management makes the decision to convert to an affirmative discipline system and ensures that it's applied throughout the company. With the increasing autonomy some companies grant to teams, the team itself may have the authority to implement affirmative discipline within the team.

Letting Team Members Monitor Their Team

When you have a highly motivated team, the need for discipline becomes superfluous. Each member of the team becomes a support person and a motivator to other members. The team leader often doesn't have to reprimand or engage in formal disciplinary measures.

If everyone on a team is committed to meeting the team's goals and is given the tools to measure their own and the team's progress, they become self-controllers. The need for formal discipline fades into the background and is used only rarely, when all other means have been exhausted.

Chapter 23

"You're Fired!"

John Maxwell cautions, "Being released from one's responsibilities can have a devastating effect on a person. It is not an action to be taken on a whim, but only after careful, prayerful consideration." It's never pleasant to fire people. Even if you're glad to get rid of someone, firing is a disagreeable task that most people do reluctantly. Terminating employees is a serious matter that always needs careful consideration. In most companies, before a supervisor or team leader can terminate anyone, approval must be obtained from both the person to whom the leader reports and the human resources department. This chapter examines the importance of this process.

The End of the Line in Progressive Discipline

Employees who have experienced the steps of progressive discipline (see Chapter 22) should never be surprised when they get fired. Presumably, at every step along the way they were told what the next step would be. When you suspend an employee—the next-to-the-last stage in the disciplinary process—you must make clear that, if he doesn't improve in the areas that are suggested, the next step is termination.

Careful: What You Say and How You Say It Are Important

Because the issue of firing employees is such a sensitive one, you must do it diplomatically and be fully aware of any legal implications. Ask your human resources department for advice about dealing with this situation.

That's the Spirit

The following advice is paraphrased from John Maxwell's book *Be a People Person:*

- **Do it personally.** A letter or memo is cruel and impersonal.
- **Do it gently.** The person may become angry or defensive, but that is the time for a "soft answer."
- **Do it without bitterness or malice.** Emotional outbursts or attacks on the person's character do not characterize one who is under the Holy Spirit's control.
- **Close off responsibilities quickly.** The longer a lame duck has to drag on, the lower the productivity is and the greater the depression is.
- **Be discriminating.** "All the facts" do not need to be divulged to those whose interest is to slander or gossip.
- **Anticipate the person's reactions.** Be prepared with your answer.

Power Principles

"A gentle answer turns away wrath." (Proverbs 15:1) If an employee raises his voice, lower yours. Most people respond to a raised voice by raising their own. By responding in a soft voice, you disarm the other person. It has a calming effect.

Some team leaders get more upset about having to fire someone than the person who is being fired. Here are some suggestions to help you prepare:

- Review all documents so that you're fully aware of all the reasons and implications involved in the decision to terminate the team member.
- Review all that you know about the team member's personality:
  - What problems have you had with the person?
  - How did the team member respond to the preceding disciplinary steps?

That's the Spirit

When you fire someone, you may feel the guilt of ruining someone's life. Yet God not only allows, but also causes this event to discipline that individual for his own good and to provide something better if he or she responds to that discipline.

- How did you and this person get along on the job?
- How did this person relate to other team members?
- What personal problems does the person have that you're aware of?

• Review any problems you've had in firing other employees, and map out a plan to avoid those problems.

• Check your company's policy manual, or discuss with the human resources department any company rules that apply.

• Relax before the meeting. Do whatever helps you clear your mind and calm your emotions. If you've done your job correctly, you've made every effort to help the team member succeed. The progressive discipline system has given the person several chances to change, so you don't have to feel guilty about the firing.

It's Show Time!

You've stalled as long as you can. Now you're ready to sit down with the employee and make clear that this is the end of the line.

Find a private place to conduct the meeting. Your office is an obvious spot, but it may not be the best one. A conference room is better because, if the fired employees breaks down or becomes belligerent, you can walk out.

Most people who are fired expect it and don't cause problems. They may beg for another chance, but this isn't the time to change your mind. Progressive discipline gives people several "other chances" before they reach this point. Don't let the termination meeting degenerate into a confrontation.

If the employee gives you a hard time, keep cool. Don't lose your temper or get into an argument.

It's a good idea to have another person in the room at a termination meeting. A person being fired may say or do inappropriate things. Also, you may become upset and say something that's best left unsaid. The presence of a third person keeps both you and the employee from losing your temper and from saying or doing something that can lead to additional complications.

The best "third person" in a termination meeting is a representative from the human resources department. If this person isn't available, call in another manager or team leader. If the employee belongs to a union, the union contract usually stipulates the presence of a union delegate.

> **Wise Counsel**
>
> Most people are fired at the end of the workday on Friday afternoon. Some companies prefer to terminate employees in the middle of the week, however, so that people have a chance to begin looking for a new job the next day and not brood about the firing over the weekend.

Having a third person in the room when you terminate an employee also provides a witness if an employee later sues your company. Even though the claim is false, you'll have to spend time, energy, and money to defend against it—and it's your word against the other person's.

If you request that a third person attend termination meetings, former employees will be less likely to file false claims because they know that they'll be refuted by a witness.

In most organizations, when a termination meeting ends, the employee is sent to the human resources department for outprocessing or handling the administrative details for completing the separation procedure. If your company assigns a team leader to handle this chore, follow the company's procedures carefully.

Use the following termination checklist to ensure that you take the necessary steps in terminating an employee.

Termination Checklist

Name of employee: _____ Date: _____

Part I: If discharged for poor performance, steps taken to improve performance:

Date   Action

_____

_____

_____

Comments: _____

_____

_____

If discharged for poor conduct, list progressive disciplinary steps taken:

Date   Action

_____   Informal warning

_____   Written warning

_____   Disciplinary interview

_____   Suspension

_____   Other (specify)_____

_____

Comments: _____

_____

_____

Part II

Have you reviewed all pertinent documents?   _____

Have you treated this case in the same way as similar cases in the past?   _____

Has this action been reviewed by your immediate superior?   _____

By the human resources department?   _____

Does the employee have any claim pending against the company?   _____

Any worker's compensation claims?   _____

Other (specify): _____

_____

Part III: Termination interview

Conducted by: _____

Date: _____ Place: _____

Witness: _____

continues

continued

Comments: _____

_____

_____

Final actions: _____

ID and keys returned?: _____

Company property returned?: _____

Final paycheck issued?: _____

Additional comments: _____

_____

_____

Spontaneous Termination: When You Fire Someone Without Progressive Discipline

Occasionally, termination without warning is permitted. These occasions are rare and usually limited to a few serious infractions that are clearly delineated in company policies. Serious offenses include drinking on the job, fighting, stealing, and insubordination. Because these charges aren't always easy to prove, be very careful before you make the decision to fire someone without progressive discipline. You must have solid evidence that can stand up in court.

Insubordination, which is one of the most frequent causes of spontaneous termination, isn't always easy to prove. If an employee simply fails to carry out an order, it's not grounds for termination. Unless a failure to obey instructions can lead to serious consequences, it's better to use progressive discipline. On the other hand, if a team member becomes unruly in his refusal (if he hollers and screams or spits in your face, for example), spontaneous discharge may be appropriate.

When you fire someone after progressive discipline procedures fail, you have an entire series of documents to back you up. In spontaneous termination, however, you have no documents.

Immediately after a termination, write a detailed report describing the circumstances that led up to it. Get written statements from witnesses. If you can, get the employee to sign a statement presenting her side of the story. If this discharge is challenged, having the terminated employee's immediate comments will protect you in case she presents a different version of what happened. This is time for the Christian manager to remember the biblical injunction to love one's enemies and pray for those who abuse you, if indeed this is the case.

💡 **Power Principles**

A termination is a business decision, not a personal one. Don't use the termination meeting to tell off the person.

📖 **Interpret and Apply**

When an employee quits because of intentional unfair treatment on the job, it is "constructed" by the courts to be equivalent to being fired and is referred to as **constructive discharge.**

You Can't Fire Me—I Quit!

If you give someone the option of resigning, be sure to inform the person about loss of unemployment insurance and any other negative factors.

Now suppose that you think you'll be shrewd in getting rid of the person: "If I fire him, he'll give me problems. I'll just make his life so miserable that he'll quit." Over the next few weeks, you give him as many unpleasant assignments as you can. You time his returns from breaks and even how long he spends in the restroom. You chastise him for every minor violation of company rules. After a few weeks, the team member quits.

Don't be shocked when the person sues your company for unlawful discharge! When you tell the court, "I didn't fire him—he quit," the judge will respond, "Not so. This is a *constructive discharge*—your treatment forced him to quit." You must then pay the person back wages, rehire him, or make a satisfactory financial settlement.

oyment at Will" Really Means

al contract with your employer or are a member of a union,
bers are "employees at will."

verned employment since colonial times. Bosses always had
employees, and employees could always quit. Only recently has this
en challenged. For example, some laws prohibit a company from firing
using to hire someone for union activity, race, religion, national origin, gender,
disability, and age. Your right under common law to hire or fire at will, therefore, is
restricted in these circumstances.

This principle also means that you can agree to waive employment at will by
mutual consent. You can sign a contract with your company in which you agree not
to quit and it agrees not to fire you for the duration of the contract. Or, your company
and a union can agree that no union member will be fired except under the terms of
the contract. In both cases, the company has given up its right to employment at will.

Avoiding Stumbling Blocks

You cannot waive a legislated right by signing a contract. An employee cannot agree to work for less than the minimum wage, for example.

Power Principles

To avoid legal problems, be sure to have all the facts before you fire someone. Investigate: Get witnesses, and get legal advice. Don't discuss the case with people who don't have a need to know.

Employment Rights When No Contract Exists

During the past several years, a number of cases have extended employees' rights that are not covered by specific legislation. Courts in several states have ruled that, although a company's policies and procedures manual isn't a formal contract, it can be considered to have the same effect as a contract.

To avoid this type of problem, attorneys advise their clients to specify clearly in their company policy manuals that they are "at will" employers and to include a statement to that effect on their employment-application forms.

Oral Commitments

Suppose that, during an interview, you told Stella that her job would be permanent after a six-month probationary period. A year later, your company downsizes and Stella is laid off. She sues. She says, "I left my former job to take

this one because the team leader assured me that it was a permanent job." You
respond, "I made that comment in good faith. Our company had never had a lay
off." Your reply won't be good enough—the court will award Stella a large settlement.

An Ounce of Prevention

To avoid these types of these complications, follow these guidelines:

- All managers and team leaders should be trained in procedures concerning
  termination and should adhere to them.

- Team leaders or anyone who represents management should never make
  commitments concerning tenure or other employment conditions orally or
  in writing.

- Make written job offers only after consulting with legal specialists.

- Never use the term "permanent employee." *No one* is a permanent employee.
  If your company must differentiate between temporary and part-time staff
  members, refer to the full-time people as "regular employees."

- On all documents and records relating to employment conditions, state that
  the company has a policy of employment at will.

Chapter 24

Separations, Layoffs, and Downsizing

Ecclesiastes 3 assures us that there is a time for everything: a time to be born and a time to die, a time to plant and a time to uproot, a time to weep and a time to laugh, a time to keep and a time to throw away …. Perhaps an appropriate addition to that list might be "a time to hire, and a time to fire … or separate." Ecclesiastes is a good study in this context because it reminds us of how little control we have over anything.

Occasions will come when people move on—sometimes under difficult circumstances, sometimes under joyful circumstances. You're happy for their good fortune but sad for your loss of a good employee.

Every time an employee leaves a company, whether it's voluntary or involuntary, it costs the company a great deal of money. The investment involved in hiring, training, and supervising that person, in addition to the enormous administrative expenses that are incurred, are lost forever. The company loses production output until a replacement is hired and trained, and the interaction among team members is disrupted every time there's a change in the makeup of the group. Team leaders must make every effort to keep turnover down. This chapter explores those issues.

Learning Why Good People Quit

People may leave a job for any number of reasons. Sometimes it's personal: A spouse has to relocate for a job, or someone decides to return to school to pursue a different career. There's not much a team leader can do to reduce turnover based on personal factors.

Often the reason is job-related. Employees may feel that they aren't making the progress they had hoped for, that their salary is too low, that working conditions are unsatisfactory, or that the job has become boring. In these cases, it's sometimes possible to reduce turnover by identifying recurring problems and correcting them so that other team members don't leave for the same reasons.

Conducting a Separation Interview

A separation interview, sometimes called an exit interview, is designed to help team leaders or supervisors determine the real reasons people leave a job and to obtain information about the company or the job that may have caused discontent.

One reason you may be able to get more information during a separation interview is that people often feel freer to open up when they have nothing to lose.

Here are some guidelines for conducting an effective separation interview:

Avoiding Stumbling Blocks

An unbiased, objective separation interview shouldn't be conducted by the team leader or supervisor of the employee who is leaving. The interview should be conducted by a member of the human resources (HR) department, the leader of another team, or another management-level person.

- To avoid getting superficial or even misleading reasons from a departing employee, don't ask, "Why are you leaving?" You can develop better information by asking good questions. Ask questions about the job itself:

    "What did you like most about the job? Least?"

    "How do you feel about the progress you've made in this company?"

    "How do you feel about compensation, benefits, and working conditions?"

    From the patterns of answers you get from people who are leaving your company, you can gain insight into facets of the job you hadn't realized.

- Ask questions about supervision, such as, "How would you describe your team leader's style of leading the team, and how did you react to it?" and "What do you feel were your team leader's strengths and weaknesses?" It's important to explore the area of employee-supervisor relations because it causes problems in many companies.

- Ask questions that might give you insight into other problem areas: "If you could discuss with top management exactly how you feel about this company, what would you tell them?" This open-ended question often elicits interesting responses. Let employees speak freely.

- If an employee has accepted a job with another company, ask, "What does your new job offer you that you're not getting here?"

Knowing What to Do When Employees Give Notice

Some supervisors and team leaders take an employee's resignation as a personal affront. Take care to make the transition smooth. The following suggestions help reduce the confusion that often results when a team member leaves your company:

- Don't blow up. I once worked for a manager who considered anyone who quit to be disloyal. If someone gave him the courtesy of two weeks' notice, he ordered the person to leave immediately. He then bad-mouthed the employee to everyone in the company. The result was that employees quit without giving notice, which caused serious production problems.

- Agree on a mutually satisfactory departure date. You may need time to readjust your plans.

- Request a status report on the team member's projects so that you can arrange for others to handle them. Develop a list of vendors, customers, or other people outside your department that the member interacts with so that you can notify them of the change.

- Contact your personnel department to arrange for either an internal transfer or hiring from outside.

- Let other team members know as soon as you're notified. Tell them how it will affect their work until someone else is hired.

Wise Counsel

> No law requires employees to give notice when they leave a company. The customary two-week notice is a courtesy that gives team leaders the opportunity to plan for a smooth transition. If you feel that the continued presence of this person may be disruptive to the team, you don't have to accept the notice, and you can then arrange for immediate separation.

Furloughs: Short-Term Layoffs

If you work in an industry in which work is done seasonally, you're accustomed to temporary layoffs or furloughs. Workers in these fields expect to be laid off at certain times of the year and plan their lives accordingly. They're usually covered by unemployment insurance or, in some union contracts, additional payments. When the new season begins, most of them are rehired.

Some layoffs are unexpected, however, even though they're temporary. Business may slow down or a company may cut its payroll, for example. Laid-off workers have a reasonable chance of being rehired when business picks up, but they have no guarantee.

Although some people will wait for a recall, many choose to look for other jobs. This situation poses a problem for the company because many experienced workers won't be available when they're needed.

Alternatives to Layoffs

When team members know that a layoff is for a specified period and that the company has a history of calling back the entire team after a furlough, they're less likely to seek other jobs. If a layoff is indefinite but you know that you will be rehiring sooner or later, take steps to keep available as many people as you can so that, when the recall comes, your team will be intact and ready to function.

When you're part of a smoothly running, highly productive team, a layoff can be devastating. The loss of some workers means that the surviving members will have to do more work to pick up the slack. Team interaction that had been developed over time is lost and must be rebuilt. Morale suffers, and productivity is most likely reduced. The best way to rebuild morale is to find alternatives to a layoff.

That's the Spirit

God expects you as a Christian manager to show mercy in these difficult situations. Perhaps it will simply amount to words you speak—or perhaps words you don't speak; perhaps it will mean sacrifice on your own part. However it may be accomplished, though, it must be personal, it must be authentic, and it may very well hurt you a great deal. But in all you do, be merciful. "Blessed are the merciful, for they will be shown mercy." (Matthew 5:7)

This list describes some ways companies have avoided layoffs:

- **Pay cuts.** The main reason for most layoffs is to reduce payroll. When companies institute a general pay reduction for all employees (including management), the entire workforce shares the burden.

  It's easier to reduce the payroll in a unionized organization. Because a union speaks for its entire bargaining unit, it can negotiate this technique as a means of saving its members' jobs.

  Where no union exists, a company can arbitrarily cut its payroll. No one wants to take a pay cut, of course, but some people aren't willing to suffer a small personal loss to save even a close colleague's job. Unless management can "sell" it to employees by appealing to their nobler motives, a pay cut causes more problems than it solves.

- **Work sharing.** All team members share the work that remains after jobs are eliminated. The standard work week is reduced by working fewer hours each day or fewer days each week; another alternative involves working full weeks but fewer weeks each month. With this strategy, hourly pay remains the same, but reduced hours decrease the payroll.

  Work sharing enables companies to keep skilled employees during slow periods and enables teams to stay together. Employees earn less total pay but retain their benefits. Some states have amended their unemployment-insurance laws so that employees can collect some unemployment benefits during work-sharing periods.

- **Early retirement.** One way to minimize the number of employees who are laid off during an indefinite layoff is by encouraging older workers to retire earlier than they had planned. Under the Age Discrimination in Employment Act (see

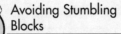

Avoiding Stumbling Blocks

As much as you may want to keep laid-off team members available for recall, don't mislead them with false hopes. It not only isn't fair to someone who may turn down another job, but it also can have legal repercussions. Former employees have sued companies because of implied promises to rehire that didn't materialize.

Chapter 11), companies cannot compel employees to retire. They can offer incentives, however, to make it worth their while. When more highly paid senior employees leave a company, the payroll is reduced significantly.

Usually, an entire team isn't laid off. Unless you have a union contract or rigid policy that mandates that layoffs happen on a seniority basis, keep your best team members—those who can form the cadre of a new team if some of the laid-off members don't return when they're recalled.

Keep in touch with laid-off team members. Phone them and send them the company newsletter. Let them know that you still consider them part of your team and that you're looking forward to the recall so that you can work together again.

Rehiring Furloughed Workers

Seniority in most companies is the basis of both layoffs and recalls. The most senior employees are the last to be let go and the first to be rehired. But this approach isn't always the most desirable one. If you have no contractual obligation to do so, it may be more advantageous to rehire people according to the skills you need as the work expands.

Power Principles

Even if you know that a laid-off team member has accepted another job, offer the person the opportunity to return to your team. He may not be satisfied with the new job and may prefer to rejoin your team.

Downsizing: The Permanent Layoff

As defined earlier, downsizing involves the elimination of a job. An entire facility may be closed, an entire unit or department may be eliminated, or an organization may be restructured by doing away with certain jobs or entire job categories.

"WARN": The Law on Downsizing

To ease the burden on laid-off workers, Congress passed the Worker Adjustment and Retraining Notification Act (WARN). This law applies to companies that have 100 or more employees when they have mass layoffs or plant closings. The law exempts companies with fewer than 100 employees. Companies that are covered aren't required to comply with the law when they lay off small numbers of workers; it affects only mass layoffs.

Wise Counsel

When a company closes a facility or lays off a large number of people, you may need certain employees for continuing production. Offer them financial incentives so that they'll stay to the end after they've been given notice. At this point, you need them more than they need you.

A mass layoff is a layoff or reduction in hours at a single site that affects 500 or more full-time employees, or 50 or more if they constitute at least 33 percent of an active, full-time workforce. A reduction in hours means cutting hours worked by 50 percent or more each month for a six-month period or longer. A company must give notice to employees who will be laid off at least 60 days before their final day of work. There are some exceptions to this rule, so check with your legal department to determine how it affects you.

Dealing with Downsizing and the EEO Laws

If seniority is the policy followed during downsizing, minorities and women—who often have relatively low seniority—are often the first to have to leave. This practice can have an adverse effect on a company's affirmative action endeavors.

The Civil Rights Act of 1964 specifically exempts companies that have established a seniority system for layoffs and rehiring from being charged with discrimination if seniority is the basis for their actions. There is, however, an exception: If a member of a protected group can show that she personally experienced discrimination that resulted in lower seniority than if there had been no discrimination, that person may claim protection.

Providing Continuing Benefits

Under the federal law known as COBRA (Consolidated Omnibus Budget Reconciliation Act), employees of companies with 20 or more employees are entitled to maintain their health insurance coverage for 18 months after they leave a company (disabled people can maintain it for 29 months). The company isn't expected to pay their premiums, however. Former employees who enroll in COBRA must pay the full premium at the same rate the company had been paying (usually considerably less than if they had to purchase individual insurance) plus a small administrative charge. COBRA also provides for continuing health insurance coverage for survivors of employees who die.

Processing Out Laid-Off Employees

The administrative details of the separation processing is usually done by the human resources department. In smaller companies or at branch facilities that have no HR department, a team leader usually handles the process.

Inform the people who are to be laid off at an appropriate time. If your company is covered by WARN, you must provide written notice 60 days in advance. If it's not covered by WARN, there's no required time, but it's only fair to give adequate notice about when they will be laid off. For temporary layoffs, two weeks is typical; for permanent layoffs, 30 days is sufficient.

At the time of the separation, follow these guidelines. Using a checklist will ensure that everything is covered.

- Discuss the continuation of benefits under COBRA, as discussed earlier in this chapter.
- Discuss severance pay. No law requires severance pay, but some union contracts do mandate it. Many companies voluntarily give severance pay to laid-off workers.
- If appropriate, discuss the callback procedure.
- If an employee isn't receiving a final paycheck at the same time that person is leaving the company, specify when it's expected.
- If provisions have been made to help laid-off employees seek other jobs, refer the person to whomever is responsible for that function.
- Retrieve company property: keys, credit cards, ID cards, tools, company computers used at home, computer logon IDs, or computer passwords, for example.
- If an employee has incurred expenses for the company, such as travel and entertainment that have not yet been reimbursed, arrange for prompt attention to this matter.

- Answer any questions the employee has.
- Arrange for the employee to clean out his or her desk, office, or locker.
- Arrange for forwarding of any mail and messages that are received at the company after the employee leaves.
- Express your good wishes.

That's the Spirit

How do you as a manager respond if any of these adverse circumstances arrive in your life? What if you have to quit, are fired, or are the victim of a layoff or separation? Remember the classic verse Romans 8:28: "And we know that in all things God works for the good of those who love him, who have been called according to his purpose."

Appendix A

Glossary

affirmative action A written plan to commit to hiring women and minorities in proportion to their representation in the community where the firm is located. Required of companies that have government contracts in excess of $50,000 and more than 50 employees.

affirmative discipline A technique in which, instead of being punished, employees are counseled and asked to make commitments to comply with company rules.

Age Discrimination in Employment Act (ADEA) As amended, prohibits discrimination against individuals 40 years of age or older. Some state laws cover all persons over the age of 18.

Americans with Disabilities Act (ADA) Prohibits discrimination against people who are physically or mentally challenged.

aptitude test A test designed to determine the potential of candidates in specific areas, such as mechanical ability, clerical skills, or sales potential. The tests are helpful for screening inexperienced people to determine whether they have an aptitude for the type of work in which a company plans to train them. Most aptitude tests can be administered and scored by following a simple instruction sheet.

arbitration A process in which two parties present their sides of a problem and an arbitrator decides how the problem should be resolved. *See also* mediation.

behavioral science The study of how and why people behave the way they do.

benchmarking A process of seeking organizations that have achieved success in an area and learning about their techniques and methods.

body language A method people use to communicate—not only by what they say, but also by their gestures, facial expressions, and movements.

bona fide occupational qualifications (BFOQ)   Positions for which a company is permitted to specify only a man or only a woman for a job. There must be clear-cut reasons, however, for why a person of only that gender can perform the job.

brainstorming   A technique for generating ideas in which participants are encouraged to voice any idea, no matter how "dumb" or useless it may be. By allowing participants to think freely and express ideas without fear of criticism, the people can stretch their minds and make suggestions that may seem worthless but that may trigger an idea that has value in the mind of another participant.

buzzword   A bit of jargon—a phrase or term—that comes to popular use throughout society for a short period of time.

case study   A description of a real or simulated situation presented to trainees for analysis, discussion, and solution; used in graduate schools, seminars, and training programs to enable trainees to work on the types of problems they're most likely to meet on the job. Case studies are often drawn from the experiences of real companies.

channel of communication   The path information takes through the organization. If you want to give information to (or get it from) a person in another department, you first go to your boss, who goes to the supervisor of the other department, who, in turn, goes to the person with the information, who gets it and conveys it back through the same channels. By the time you get the information, it may have been distorted by a variety of interpretations.

charisma   The special charm some people have that secures for them the support and allegiance of other people.

Civil Rights Act of 1964   Title VII, as amended, prohibits discrimination in employment on the basis of race, color, sex, religion, and national origin.

coasters   Long-term employees (not likely to be fired because of their tenure) who have gone as far as they can and "coast along" until their retirement.

COBRA   An acronym for the Consolidated Omnibus Budget Reconciliation Act, in which employees of companies with 20 or more employees are entitled to maintain their health insurance coverage for 18 months after they leave the company (29 months for people who are disabled at the time they leave). The company isn't expected to pay their premiums. Former employees must pay the full premium at the same rate the company had been paying (usually considerably less than if they had to purchase individual insurance) plus a small administrative charge.

communication   The process by which information, ideas, and concepts are transmitted between persons and groups.

constructive discharge   When an employee quits because of purposeful unfair treatment on the job, it is "constructed" by the courts to be an involuntary termination.

control point   A point in a project at which you stop, examine what has been completed, and correct any errors that have been made (before they blow up into catastrophes).

counseling   A means of helping troubled associates overcome barriers to good performance. With careful listening, open discussion, and sound advice, a counselor helps identify problems, clarify misunderstandings, and plan solutions.

cross-training   A method of training team members to perform the jobs of other people on the team so that every member is capable of doing all aspects of the team's work.

decentralization   Shifting the focus of a business from one central facility where all decisions are made and most of the work is done to localized facilities where, within guidelines, decisions are made and work is performed autonomously.

delegation   A process that enables you to position the right work at the right responsibility level, helping both you and the team members to whom you delegate to expand skills and contributions while ensuring that all work gets done in a timely manner by the right person with the right experience or interest in the right topic.

documentation   A written description of all disciplinary actions taken by a company to protect it in case of legal actions. ("If it ain't written down, it ain't never happened.")

downsize   To lay off employees, primarily when business is slow, so that a company can reduce costs. Downsizing differs from traditional layoffs in that total job categories are eliminated—people who held these jobs have little chance of being rehired. *See also* layoff.

employee assistance program (EAP)   A company-sponsored counseling service. Many companies have instituted these types of programs to help their employees deal with personal problems that interfere with productivity. The counselors aren't company employees; they're outside experts who are retained on an as-needed basis.

employee stock-ownership program (ESOP) A program in which a major portion of a company's stock is given or sold to employees so that they actually own the company.

employment at will A legal concept under which an employee is hired and can be fired at the will of the employer. Unless restricted by law or contract, the employer has the right to refuse to hire an applicant or to terminate an employee for any reason—or for no reason at all.

empowerment Sharing your managerial power with the people over whom you have that power.

Equal Pay Act of 1963 An act that requires that the gender of an employee not be considered in determining salary (equal pay for equal work).

goals/objectives Interchangeable terms to describe an organization or individual's desired long-term results.

going rate An amount paid to employees to keep them from leaving a company.

grievance A formal complaint, usually based on the violation of a union contract or formal company policy.

gripe An informal complaint about working conditions or other aspects of an employee/company relationship.

halo effect The assumption that, because of one outstanding characteristic, all of an applicant's characteristics are outstanding (that person then "wears a halo"). The opposite is the pitchfork effect, or the symbol of the devil: You assume that because one trait is so poor, the person is entirely bad.

hot button The one thing in a person's makeup that really gets him excited—positively or negatively. (To really reach someone, find that person's hot button.)

"I" meeting An idea-generating meeting at which each participant presents at least one idea for solving the problem being considered.

intelligence test Like the IQ test administered in schools, this test measures the ability to learn. It varies from brief, simple exercises that can be administered by people with little training to highly sophisticated tests that must be administered by a person with a Ph.D. in psychology.

job analysis The process of determining the duties, functions, and responsibilities of a job (the job description) and the requirements for the successful performance of a job (the job specifications).

job bank   A computerized list of the capabilities of all employees in an organization.

job description   A listing of the duties, responsibilities, and results a job requires.

job enrichment   Redesigning jobs to provide diversity, challenge, and commitment (and to alleviate boredom).

job-instruction training (JIT)   A systematic approach to training that has four steps: preparation, presentation, performance, and follow-up.

job posting   A listing on company bulletin boards of the specifications for an available position. Any employee who is interested can apply. After preliminary screening by the human resources department, employees who meet the basic requirements are interviewed.

job specifications   The requirements an applicant should possess to successfully perform a job.

joint leader/associate evaluations   Using the same evaluation format, associates evaluate their own performance. The leader also evaluates the performance. The final report results from a collaborative discussion between leader and associate.

just-in-time delivery   Rather than store large inventories of supplies, companies today arrange with suppliers to deliver supplies as needed. The project manager or team leader must interface with the suppliers to schedule and ensure that supplies are delivered at the exact time they're needed.

KRA (key results area)   An aspect of a job in which employees must concentrate time and attention to ensure that they achieve the goals for that job.

lateral thinking   Looking at a problem from different angles that may give new insights into its solutions (instead of approaching it by logical thinking).

layoff   Termination of employees permanently or for a specific period of time due to lack of work or restructuring of an organization.

leadership   The art of guiding people in a manner that commands their respect, confidence, and wholehearted cooperation.

management   The process of achieving specific results by effectively using an organization's available resources (money, materials, equipment, information, and employees).

mediation   A process in which two parties present their sides and a mediator works with them to reach a mutually satisfactory solution. *See also* arbitration.

mentor   A team member assigned to act as counselor, trainer, and "big brother" or "big sister" to a new member.

M.O. (method, or mode, of operation)   The patterns of behavior a person habitually follows in performing work.

motivators   Factors that stimulate a person to expend more energy, effort, and enthusiasm in a job. *See also* satisfiers.

negative personality   A person's outlook in which any suggestion is taken as a personal affront, any new assignment is accepted with reluctance, and relations with co-workers and leaders are usually considered confrontational.

network   To make contacts with managers in other companies to whom you can turn for suggestions and ideas.

objective   *See* goals/objectives.

open-book management   A management style in which employees are considered full partners in the operation of a business. One characteristic of this management style is that employees have a direct stake in their company's success (if the business is profitable, they share in the profits—if not, there are no profits to share). Another characteristic is that every employee has access to numbers that are critical to tracking the company's performance and is given the training and tools to understand them.

opportunity   The combination of being in the right place at the right time and having the ability and desire to take advantage of it.

outsourcing   Contracting to outside sources any work that previously had been done in-house. As companies become "leaner and meaner," they outsource activities that can be done more effectively by outside specialists. Some examples are payroll, traffic, training, computer programming, advertising, and certain manufacturing activities.

ownership   A feeling that you're a full partner in the development and implementation of a project, committed to its successful achievement.

performance standards   The results expected from persons performing a job. For performance standards to be meaningful, every person doing that job should know and accept these standards.

performance test   A test that measures how well candidates can do the job for which they apply (for example, operating a lathe, entering data into a computer, writing advertising copy, or proofreading manuscripts). When job performance cannot be tested directly, a company may use written or oral tests about job knowledge.

personality test A test designed to identify personality characteristics that varies from *Readers Digest*–type quickie questionnaires to highly sophisticated psychological evaluations.

piece work A system of compensation in which earnings are based solely on the number of units produced.

pitchfork effect *See* halo effect.

platinum rule "Do unto others as they would have you do unto them."

prioritize To rank tasks by determining their degree of importance, to accomplish your goals on the job or in your life and to take action accordingly—putting first things first.

profession An occupation requiring special training or advanced study in a specialized field. Physicians, lawyers, psychologists, and engineers all have to take advanced education and pass examinations to qualify for certification in their professions.

progressive discipline A systematic approach to correcting infractions of rules. A typical program has six steps, the first of which is an informal warning. If this step isn't successful, it's followed by (as necessary) a disciplinary interview, a written warning, probation, suspension, and possibly termination.

project manager A team leader assigned to head up a specific project, such as the design and manufacture of an electronic system or the development and marketing of a new product.

quality circles Groups of workers who voluntarily meet on a regular basis to discuss ideas about improving the quality of a product or service they produce.

real time What's going on here and now. The actual time in which a process occurs (for example, a computer can report real-time data or information about the status of a situation as of the time it's provided).

recruit To seek candidates to be considered for employment, usually done by personnel or human resources departments.

re-engineer To radically restructure the design of business processes (not just tinker with methods and procedures). When companies re-engineer their processes, its managers must rethink everything they're doing in order to take advantage of the changes that will be made.

religious practices Practices that include, according to the EEOC, not only traditional religious beliefs, but also moral and ethical beliefs and any beliefs that an individual holds "with the strength of a traditional religious view."

results-oriented evaluation system A system in which performance expectations are agreed on at the beginning of a period and measured at the end of that period. At that time, new goals are developed, which are to be measured at the end of the next period.

role playing A variation of case studies in which participants act out the parts of the characters involved. Used chiefly in studying problems in which interaction between characters is a major aspect.

satisfiers Also called maintenance factors. The factors—including working conditions, money, and benefits—that employees must get from a job in order to expend even minimum effort in performing their work. After employees are satisfied with these factors, however, just giving them more of the same factor doesn't motivate them to work harder. *See* motivators.

selection A process of screening applicants to determine their suitability for a position. Preliminary screening is usually done by the human resources department; subsequent screening is done by supervisors or team leaders.

self-directed team A team with no permanent team leader; team members are self-managed. Some teams have permanent administrative leaders to deal with the paperwork, but members rotate as project leaders. Team members schedule work, hire and train new members, budget funds, and monitor their own performance.

self-esteem The way you feel about yourself. If you think of yourself as a success, you will be a success; if you think of yourself as second-rate, you will always be second-rate—unless you change your self-perception. And it *can* be done.

sexual harassment Any unwelcome sexual advances or requests for sexual favors. Also, any conduct of a sexual nature when an employer makes submission to sexual advances a term or condition of employment, either initially or later; or when submission or rejection is used as a basis of working conditions, including promotion, salary adjustment, assignment of work, and termination, or has the effect of interfering with an individual's work or creating a hostile or intimidating work environment.

simulcast To bring together the audio and video so that they interact and intensify the message that's being communicated.

single-use plan   A plan developed for a specific nonrecurring situation—for example, introducing a new product, moving to a new location, or opening a new facility.

SOP (standard operating procedure)   A set of standard practices in which company plans and policies are detailed (sometimes called "the company bible").

spontaneous termination   A situation in which an employee is discharged without progressive discipline, usually precipitated by an egregious violation of company rules, such as fighting, drunkenness, or gross insubordination. *See* progressive discipline.

stress or distress   A chronic state of anxiety caused by unremitting pressures of job, personal, or societal problems.

synergy   Two or more people or units working together so that the contributions of each enhances the results by more than the individual contribution by itself. Known as "the whole is greater than the sum of its parts," or "2 + 2 may equal more than 4."

team   A group of people who collaborate and interact synergistically in working toward a common goal.

telecommuting   Technology that enables a person to perform work at home or at a location remote from a central office by receiving assignments and submitting completed work via computer.

total quality management   A management system in which the focus of an entire company is placed on producing high-quality products or services. It involves statistical processes, training in both the technical and intangible aspects of quality management, and the commitment of all levels of employees to work toward continuous improvement.

training manuals   Handbooks for teaching routine tasks. They make the training process easy for both trainer and trainees, and can always be referred to when an employee is in doubt about what to do.

trait system of performance evaluation   A system in which employees are rated on a series of traits, such as quantity and quality of work, attendance, and initiative. Ratings are usually measured on a scale from poor to superior.

upward communication   The flow of ideas, suggestions, and comments from people in lower echelons of the organization to those in decision-making positions.

WARN (Worker Adjustment and Retraining Notification Act)   A law that applies to companies that have 100 or more employees when a mass layoff or plant closing occurs. Notice must be given to those employees at least 60 days before their final day of work. There are some exceptions to this rule, so check with your legal department to determine how it affects you.

work sharing   An alternative to layoffs in which all team members share the work that remains after some jobs are eliminated. The standard work week is reduced by working fewer hours each day or fewer days each week. Another alternative is working full weeks, but fewer weeks each month. The hourly pay remains the same, but because of reduced hours, the payroll is decreased.

Appendix B

Publications Dealing with Managing People

The field of management is dynamic. Companies experiment with new approaches. New laws and new interpretations of old laws are promulgated by state and federal government agencies. The ups and downs of the economy change the ways organizations deal with their employees.

Managers, team leaders, and others who deal with people problems must keep up with what's going on. The best way to be on the cutting edge of change is to read regularly several of the magazines that cover these matters.

Nearly every industry and profession has periodicals devoted to its field—and most of these magazines have occasional articles on management techniques and inter-personal relations. Such periodicals are excellent sources of information.

Here is a list of some of the better publications that either specialize in the art of management or have significant coverage of it.

Across the Board
The Conference Board
845 Third Avenue
New York, NY 10022
Phone: 212-339-0345
Fax: 212-980-7014
website: www.conference-board.org

Business Week
1221 Avenue of the Americas
New York, NY 10020
Phone: 1-800-635-1200
Fax: 609-426-5434
website: www.businessweek.com

Forbes
60 Fifth Avenue
New York, NY 10011
Phone: 1-800-888-9896
Fax: 212-206-5118
website: www.forbes.com

Fortune
Time & Life Building
Rockefeller Center
New York, NY 10020
Phone: 1-800-621-8000
Fax: 212-522-7682
website: www.fortune.com

Harvard Business Review
60 Harvard Way
Boston, MA 02163
Phone: 1-800-274-3214
Fax: 617-475-9933
website: www.hbsp.harvard.edu

HR Magazine
Society for Human Resources Management
1800 Duke Street
Alexandria, VA 22314
Phone: 703-548-3440
Fax: 703-836-0367
website: www.shrm.org

Management Review
American Management Association
Box 319

Saranac Lake, NY 12983

Phone: 1-800-262-9699

Fax: 518-891-3653

website: www.amanet.org

Nations Business

711 Third Avenue

New York, NY 10017

Phone: 212-692-2215

E-mail: editor@nbmag.com

Training

50 S. 9th Street

Minneapolis, MN 55402

Phone: 612-333-0471

Fax: 612-333-6526

website: www.trainingsupersite.com

Training and Development

American Society for Training and Development

1640 King Street

Alexandria, VA 22314

Phone: 703-683-8100

Fax: 703-683-9203

website: www.astd.org

Workforce

245 Fischer Avenue

Costa Mesa, CA 92626

Phone: 714-751-1883

Fax: 714-751-4106

website: www.workforce.com

Working Woman

135 W. 50th Street

New York, NY 10020

Phone: 1-800-234-9765

Fax: 212-445-6186

E-mail: wwmagazine@aol.com

A simple search on the web will produce many Christian resources for Christian managers. These are just a few that you might explore:

Christian Management Association   Serves more than 3,500 CEOs, managers, pastors, and church administrators representing more than 1,500 Christian organizations and growing churches.
PO Box 4090
San Clemente, CA 92674
Tel 949.487.0900 Fax 949.487.0927
www.christianity.com/cma

CBMC   Exists to present Jesus Christ as Savior and Lord to business and professional men, and to develop Christian business and professional men to carry out the Great Commission. We are also known as the **Christian Business Men's Committee**.
CBMC
6650 East Brainerd Rd., Suite 100
Chattanooga, TN 37421
423.698.4444 / 1.800.566.CBMC
www.cbmc.com

CBMC International   Exists to present Jesus Christ as Savior and Lord to business and professional people internationally: (1) to develop Christian business and professional people to carry out the Great Commission; and (2) to serve business and professional people as followers of Jesus.
3060 Harrodsburg Road, Suite 203
Lexington, KY 40503 USA
Phone: 859-219-2440
Fax: 859-219-1566
www.cbmcint.org

CBWC (Community and Business Women for Christ)   Desires to reach women in the community, marketplace and at home with the gospel of Jesus Christ. CBWC is an organization in which Christian women can commit together to a common purpose: To present Jesus Christ as Savior and Lord to women in the community, and to develop Christian women to carry out the Great Commission. (Matt. 28:19–20)
www.cbwc.net

Many excellent leadership books also are published in the Christian market. Be sure to explore your local Christian bookstore. The titles mentioned throughout this book were all drawn from the excellent leadership series by Victor Books, a subsidiary of Cook Communications Ministries, Colorado Springs, CO, 80918. They are listed below, along with some additional resources, all of which would be excellent resources in what should be your ever-growing leadership library:

Barna, George. *A Fish Out of Water*, Integrity Publishers, 2002. Barna shares a fresh perspective of what effective leadership is–and isn't. Drawing on years of research and thousands of interviews with respected leaders, he outlines practical concepts and actions that will help you succeed as a leader.

Eims, LeRoy. *Be the Leader You Were Meant to Be*. Full of proven advice, and solidly based on biblical principles to help you become an effective leader.

Eims, LeRoy. *Be a Motivational Leader*. Valuable insight from a renowned leader for any leader who wants to help people reach their full potential.

Finzel, Hans. *The Top Ten Mistakes Leaders Make*. Explores in depth the 10 most common leadership faux pas. This well-established classic will distill down for you the essentials mistakes you need to avoid as a leader.

Jeary, Tony. *Success Acceleration*, River Oak, 2002. Fresh and practical insignts on success and personal achievement that will energize and inspire.

Mason, John. *Enemy Called Average*, River Oak, 2001. Mason weaves wisdom, scripture, and practical action steps to teach basic life issues that can combat the destructive influence of mediocrity.

Maxwell, John C. *Be All You Can Be*. Points to the possibilities within us all and provides simple game plans for transforming those possibilities into realities. "Maxwell is truly one of the inspired people-building phrase-makers of our time," says Zig Ziglar.

———. *Be a People Person*. Effective leadership through effective relationships. "Don't read this book without a stack of 3 × 5 cards in your hand," says Zig Ziglar.

Maxwell, John C. and Zig Ziglar. *The 21 Irrefutable Laws of Leadership*, Thomas Nelson, 1998. A well-crafted discussion that emphasizes the core attitudes and visions of leadership.

Rush, Myron. *God's Business.* Offers clear-cut answers to the tough questions that confront Christians in the corporate world.

———. *Management: A Biblical Approach.* Gives excellent counsel (biblically principled and biblically practical) to those who have been called by God to lead and manage others.

Appendix C

Associations Dealing with Human Resource Matters

Professional societies in your industry are excellent sources of information. Membership in one or more of these groups can give you access to the latest developments in your field, experiences of other members in dealing with problems similar to yours, opportunities at meetings and conventions to meet your peers in other organizations, and often resource material from other companies' libraries or archives.

Here is a list of associations that may be of value to you.

American Association of Industrial Management (AAIM)
293 Bridge Street
Springfield, MA 01103
Phone: 413-737-8766
Fax: 413-737-9724

An association of managers of manufacturing organizations. Provides publications and special reports.

American Management Association (AMA)
1601 Broadway
New York, NY 10019
Phone: 212-586-8100
Fax: 212-903-8168
website: www.amanet.org

Membership is by company. Provides seminars, publications, and library facilities on all aspects of management.

American Society for Training & Development (ASTD)
1640 King Street
Alexandria, VA 22313
Phone: 703-683-8100
Fax: 703-683-8103
website: www.astd.org

Dedicated to professionalism in training and development of personnel. Local chapters throughout United States. Annual national convention. Publications include a magazine, special reports, and books.

Employee Assistance Society of North America (EASNA)
P.O. Box 634
New Hope, PA 18938
Phone: 215-891-9538
Fax: 215-891-9538
E-mail: 72722.465@compuserve.com

Source to locate individuals and organizations that provide various types of employee assistance programs.

International Foundation of Employee Benefit Plans (IFEBP)
18700 West Bluemound Road
Bloomfield, WI 53008
Phone: 414-786-7100
Fax: 414-786-8670
E-mail: pr@ifebp.org

Excellent source of information on employee benefits. Accredits benefits specialists.

National Association of Personnel Services (NAPS)
3133 Mt. Vernon Avenue
Alexandria, VA 22305
Phone: 703-684-0180
Fax: 703-684-0071
E-mail: naps@dc.infi.net

Source of information about private employment agencies.

National Association of Temporary and Staffing Services (NATSS)

119 S. St. Asaph Street

Alexandria, VA 22314

Phone: 703-549-6287

Fax: 703-549-4808

E-mail: natss@natss.com

Provides information on temporary personnel agencies.

Society for Advancement of Management (SAM)

630 Ocean Drive

Corpus Christi, TX 78412

Phone: 540-342-5563

Fax: 512-994-2725

Provides publications and conferences on various aspects of management.

Society for Human Resources Management (SHRM)

1800 Duke Street

Alexandria, VA 22314

Phone: 703-548-3440

Fax: 703-836-0367

E-mail: shrm@shrm.org

Members are human resource specialists in all types of companies and organizations. Provides publications, special reports, and books. Local chapters throughout the United States conduct monthly meetings. National convention annually.

Women in Management

30 North Michigan Avenue

Chicago, IL 60602

Phone: 312-263-3636

Fax: 312-372-8738

Dedicated to special problems of women in management positions.

Index